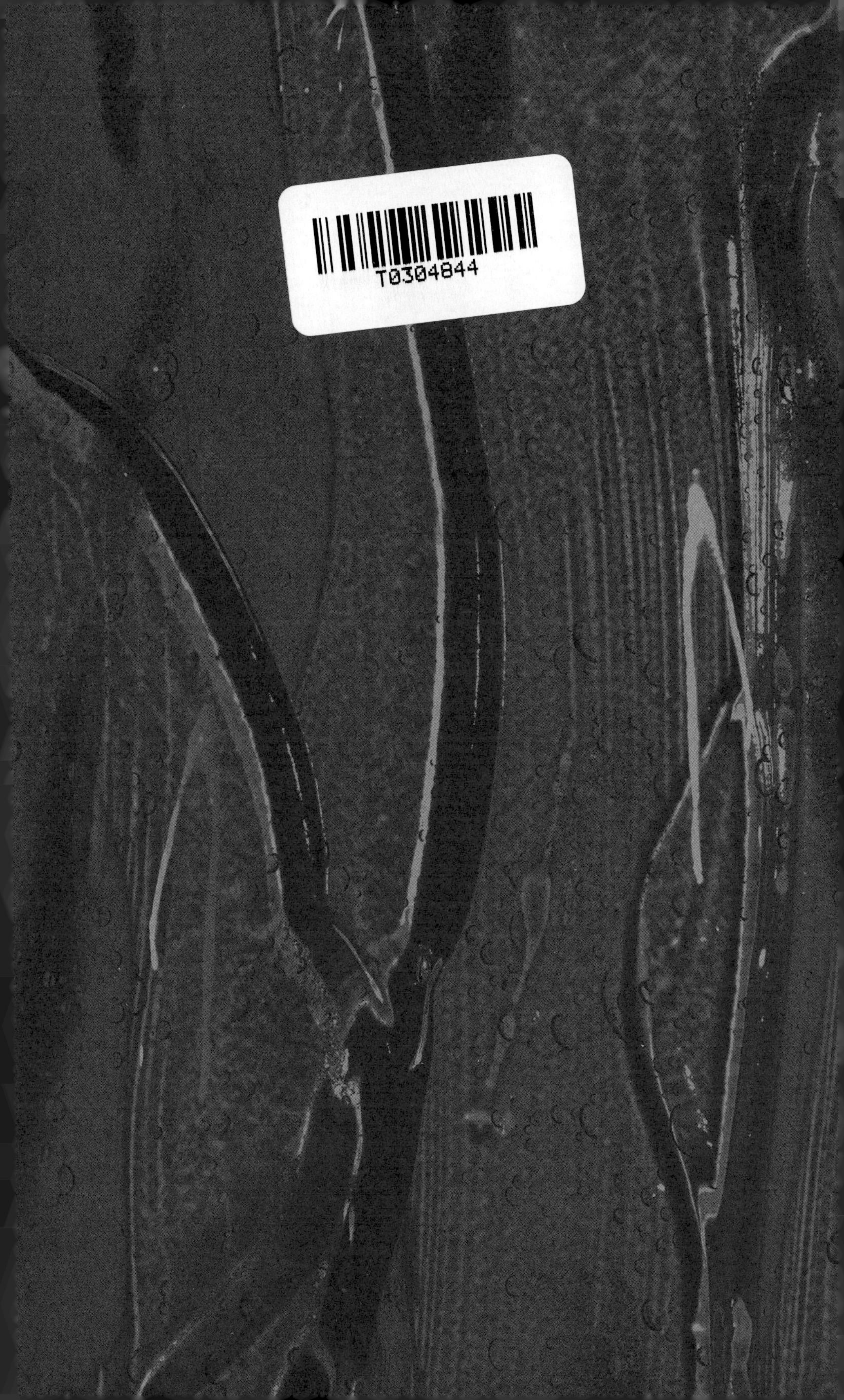
T0304844

Ellen Atlanta is a writer and brand consultant specialising in Gen-Z and millennial culture. She has worked in the beauty industry for almost a decade and was a founding editor of Dazed Beauty. With her focus on female empowerment, Ellen departed from the beauty industry in 2019 to become a founding member of both The Stack World and Communia, reimagining social media platforms and creating better digital spaces for women+. In 2021, she was headhunted to support UN Women UK on their digital campaigns, creating safer public spaces for women and marginalised genders across the country. She was awarded the RSL Giles St Aubyn Award for Non-Fiction in 2022.

Praise for *PIXEL FLESH*

'With kaleidoscopic vision, meticulously researched insights, and the narrative power of a novelist, Ellen Atlanta's *Pixel Flesh* unravels the complex tapestry of standards and perceptions that shape our identities. *Pixel Flesh* is not just a book; it's an essential mirror reflecting the profound impact of beauty culture on our lives, urging us to question and redefine our notions of allure and authenticity'

Chloé Cooper Jones
two-time finalist for the Pulitzer Prize
and author of *Easy Beauty*

'Atlanta is a whip-smart, full-hearted writer who gets to the core of beauty with expert grace that makes it look easy. Her vulnerability makes you feel seen as a reader and her expertise makes you feel protected as you navigate the chaos of the beauty industry from her perspective. It's a breezy, pleasurable read, and one I feel lucky to have on my shelf. The world is lucky to have her writing and her tenderness, too'

Arabelle Sicardi
beauty writer and author of *The House of Beauty*

'Confronting the conformity and compliance of today's beauty culture, Ellen Atlanta's revealing new book charts the course for a brave new world in which women and girls can – at long last – be comfortable in their own skin' **Victoria Bateman**
author of *Naked Feminism*

'*Pixel Flesh* cuts through the abstractions of discourse to offer a rigorously researched and deeply personal account of the modern female experience. This book is a searing and lucid appraisal of internet culture's most corrosive and diminishing aspects; from predatory algorithms, celebrity, cosmetic surgery, disordered eating and the tyranny of performing a self. Atlanta reveals the insidiousness of the patriarchy's grip on the internet and the subtle and sophisticated ways it magnifies existing inequalities and preys on women's psyches. This is a must-read guidebook on the dizzying hall of mirrors that women must navigate online and the dangerous real-world consequences that follow' **Nada Alic**
author of *Bad Thoughts*

'*Pixel Flesh* stopped me in my tracks. It took me back to my girlhood in a bold, unexpected and poetic way . . . like Grimms' Fairy Tales, but with Kylie Lip Kits. Ellen has a unique talent for helping you see through other's eyes and making you feel seen yourself. You will want to pass this on to every woman you know!'
Freya Bromley
author of *The Tidal Year*

'*Pixel Flesh* is a wise and sensitive indictment of the beauty industry – it synthesizes relatable anecdotes about living in the social media age with on-point critical theory and vigorous research. If you're struggling with the beauty industry's choke-hold, this book can be a tool in breaking free' **mj corey**
The Kardashian Kolloquium

ELLEN ATLANTA

Pixel Flesh

How Toxic Beauty Culture Harms Women

HEADLINE

First published in 2024 by
HEADLINE PUBLISHING GROUP

1

Cataloguing in Publication Data is available from the British Library.

Hardback ISBN: 978 1 4722 9877 5
Trade paperback ISBN: 978 1 0354 1163 4

Designed and typeset by EM&EN
Printed and bound in Great Britain by Clays Ltd, Elcograf S.p.A.

Headline's policy is to use papers that are natural, renewable and recyclable products and made from wood grown in well-managed forests and other controlled sources. The logging and manufacturing processes are expected to conform to the environmental regulations of the country of origin.

HEADLINE PUBLISHING GROUP
An Hachette UK Company
Carmelite House
50 Victoria Embankment
London EC4Y 0DZ

www.headline.co.uk
www.hachette.co.uk

For Livvi

Here's to looking up to you, always.

Dear reader,

This is an open conversation in which everyone is welcome. As such, there is a glossary at the back of this book in case you come across unfamiliar concepts or terms. Please don't feel shy in using it as a guide – we're all learning here.

Ellen

'Telling the truth about my own experiences as a body, I do not think I solved. I doubt that any woman has solved it yet. The obstacles against her are still immensely powerful – and yet they are very difficult to define.'

Virginia Woolf,
'Professions for Women'

'Go now and do the heart-work on the images imprisoned within you.'

Rainer Maria Rilke,
'Turning Point'

Contents

Confessional

Here are my confessions:

I am not a beautiful person. I think constantly about my body and the way I look, and when I see my reflection in the mirror I take a knife and begin to dissect my features one by one.

Sometimes I 'forget' to eat and I have taught myself to relish starvation. I am hungry. I am guilty. I will my body to consume itself.

I have logged my weight, both literally and unconsciously, since I was in high school. I have absolutely no idea how my body looks, though I look at it every day. Despite assessing its every detail, crease and fold, I am apparently blind to its appearance. I only know this because of the way people speak about my physical self and the incongruence with my own perception. I at least have the clarity of mind to realise they can't all be wrong and me the only one with working eyes. I have never been diagnosed with body dysmorphia – just as I have never been diagnosed with an eating disorder – but, like a lot of women, I exist on the periphery of categorisation. The blurred edge before intervention is needed.

I want to stop scrolling but I can't put my phone down. I know I am slipping away from reality. I delete the apps but find myself coming to, awakening from a haze of swiping through my home screens searching for something that is no longer there. My thumb moves with its own autonomy and hovers, as my brain catches up with the body I no longer seem to control.

I was sixteen when I started decapitating myself for Instagram. Cropping off my head. By then, I lived half in and half out of the world, and I was truly myself in neither. My mother could never understand why I wouldn't smile for photos. Keep in that lovely face. I never understood why she couldn't see that this was a space for slicing, for offering the best bits for the feed. This was my life in 280 characters or 1080 pixels squared. How could she ever expect to find me whole?

Sometimes I zoom into myself as far as I can go. Pinching the screen closer and closer until there is nothing left to see but a gradient of hues. I begin my sculpting, shaving down the pixels until I can zoom out and feel happy with what I see. This is how I want to be perceived. I post the picture online, to rapturous applause.

I think about getting lip filler most days. If it's not lips, it's for my cheeks, chin, jawline or the other parts of my face that I haven't realised are wrong yet. I know *something* must be wrong with my face but I can't quite pinpoint what. I have made multiple appointments to have a cosmetic doctor tell me definitively but have found myself unable to attend.

People compliment me and I do not believe them.

Before a girls' night in 2019, I bought a brand-new top because I wanted to feel sexy. I never show my boobs even though they're my favourite part of myself. I always feel shallow to admit that, but it is the truth. The top was long-sleeved and low cut. It was the right balance of flesh, I felt. (I spend a lot of time thinking about the right balance of flesh.) I took some mirror selfies and uploaded them to my stories. The verdict came in: fire emojis, heart eyes and exclamation points gave me the boost I needed to step out of the front door.

Outside, it was a warm spring night, twilight turning to dusk. Each step I took away from the door, each pair of eyes that landed on my skin tore a layer from my cells. My particles fell away with every glance up and down my body. I pulled on my coat and did the buttons up, one by one, over my chest. I wouldn't take it off for the rest of the night. I was sweating on the train to the bar and on my way back home. My brand-new top remained unrevealed and damp. I held my lapels together until my knuckles were white.

When I post online, I close the apps and throw my phone to the other side of the room. I scream. I then get back up and instantly refresh. I delete and repost, takedown and tweak. I refresh. I hide the likes. I refresh again.

A friend once uploaded a photo of me smiling to her Instagram – seventh in a carousel of others. I hated it so much that I cried for an hour.

An aesthetic doctor once told me (unprompted) that my lips were nice (and I thought that was nice) but my cheeks lacked definition (I had never considered my cheeks before). I have thought about my cheeks ever since.

I often feel there is no point existing if it's not in the right combination of things. The right lip gloss, hair style, pair of trainers, made-up but not too made-up face. When I walk into a busy room I feel the sum of my attainable attributes.

I pretend I don't want to be perceived but it is futile, and pursuing perception is its own kind of poison. It comes from a place of lacking, a void that needs to be filled. I fight to feel seen as I wish to be, to be beautiful and remarkable and luminous and perfect, no matter the cost.

I am becoming increasingly unsure of what real even means. I see the side-by-side comparisons online – what people really look like versus what they want us to see. The discrepancy is huge. I know that these images aren't real and yet they form the undercurrent of my reality. Entire bodies shifting and fluctuating, morphing into cookie-cutter moulds with razor-sharp edges. But in this digital world, everything is beautiful, and nothing hurts.

Prologue

When I had imagined buying faces, I hadn't imagined it like this. I'd pictured them made of silicon and wrapped in cellophane, lips contorted in a carton of pure expression. You'd unwrap your face and press it onto your skin like a mask until it fused, seamless and smiling. What we were discussing was more insidious than that. Sat in the middle of the Spanish desert, in a conference room surrounded by dust, we planned the future of our technology.

The app we were building was pink and peach – white screens with a gradient of flesh tones and a bold, black logo at the top. There were images: endless, endless images of women. Carousels and galleries sorted by trending part – brows, lips, cheeks – you could pick and mix and buy them all in one place. Eventually, we prophesied, you would be able to follow friends and celebrities, find out where they got their features from, and then buy the same.

Our business was beauty treatments. We allowed independent beauty professionals to upload pictures of their services to their profile, sync their calendar and take bookings from the thousands of beauty fans using our platform to document their favourite looks. We had started out with nail art, colourful braids and party makeup, but very quickly aestheticians joined the platform, and all of a sudden you could buy noses, lips, chins and a super-smooth forehead – all achieved by injectables. As a beauty lover, your profile could showcase all of your favourite treatments and styles. The nail colour you chose for that wedding, the hair you had installed for your holiday and the nose you had sculpted for graduation – all logged and linked for others to purchase. We coined trends, organised treatments for celebrities, gave free beauty treatments to influencers and became an authority on what was hot in the beauty space.

I had worked at this particular company for over a year, starting at its inception. I was twenty-three and for a while I was successful for my age. A bright and rising star. The trip to Spain came shortly after we had raised £4 million in funding. It felt like an enactment of what we imagined venture capital-backed tech companies should do, a Goop-noir parody of a Silicon Valley ideal. We slept in inflatable pods, went on self-discovery hikes and filled out prompts about our childhood trauma by the pool.

In this particular session, our head of people, a former VC scout, was leading a class on building better tech. Somehow, this meant imagining the worst possible outcomes for our company and trying to plan to avoid them. So there we sat, on high-school plastic chairs, and took it in turns to conjure a horror story of everything we could possibly do wrong. The data could leak. The software could get hacked. We could lose everyone's bank details. When it was my turn, I prophesised that eventually the algorithm would incite insecurities in girls en masse and encourage thousands to sculpt their faces and bodies into similarity, spending hundreds or even thousands in the process, before we changed the code and their features were out of fashion once more.

I realised, after announcing my beauty *Black Mirror* episode to the room, that it had already started happening. This is where my villain origin story begins.

We were doing tech differently – a female-founded beauty startup taking on the San Francisco brotopia. We marketed ourselves as a company contributing to the economic empowerment of women; we had signed up to the UN Sustainable Development Goals and our pitch centred on the advancement of women and girls towards gender equality. The beauty services workforce is 70 per cent female, many of whom use the vocational skills society has taught them to forge flexible careers, working from home or in rented studios, often around their family life and children's schedules. Once the subject of public derision, the girls who studied BTEC hair and beauty were now making thousands of pounds a month in creative careers that they loved. Beauty work, we preached, was an empowering and self-directed career for women of all ages who wanted to take control of their own economic standing and become entrepreneurs.

But it is not always that simple.

We were part of a $500 billion global beauty industry – one, according to Forbes, predicted to grow by more than 50 per cent by 2025. Across the world, the market was only getting stronger, growing and evolving in response to our increasingly digital culture. My company was one of many ventures trying to capitalise on a decade of selfie-taking and an increasing obsession with ourselves. This was a newly energised beauty industrial complex, in which body parts were designed to be easily replicated and sold to the masses.

Looking back, I can see that we were a paradigm of 'beauty-standard denialism' – a company extolling empowerment and self-love whilst profiting from the ever-higher expectations of women's bodies. We spoke about beauty treatments as if they existed in a vacuum, as though separate from the patriarchal ideal that benefits from the time, money and energy they cost women the world over. Women, we said, in pink and purple Instagram posts, could celebrate themselves (and other women) by booking beauty treatments through our app. The payment of our wages, however, came ultimately from women feeling less than and undertaking beauty treatments in order to make themselves adequately presentable to society. As feminist author Jessa Crispin states, 'Women who profit from the patriarchy will help keep it in place.'

But again, it is not always that simple.

At the train station on our way home from Spain, I pulled a small and battered notebook from my bag and started to write, to try to reconcile the questions that had taken up residence in my brain. I wrote a list of those I was struggling to answer:

- Can we promote empowerment through beauty without perpetuating sexist and capitalist beauty standards?
- Can injectables be feminist? What is true self-expression in a patriarchal society? How much choice do we even have?
- How has my life been impacted by this beauty culture? How are the women around me really feeling?
- What happens if I opt out? Can I opt out?
- How can we shift the narrative around beauty and what is beautiful?
- If everything's supposed to be getting better, why do so many of us feel worse?
- Can I ever be comfortable supporting industries that have made me feel less than my entire life?
- How can I be a part of this narrative in a positive way?
- How can we create a more beautiful future for women and girls?

I thought about the girls who had volunteered themselves for the free beauty treatments and wondered how much of it was ever voluntary. I thought about the thousands of women using beauty work to attain financial freedom. I thought about the millions more for whom beauty was the ultimate form of control. I thought about making profit *with* women without profiting *from* women. I thought about my Stockholm syndrome and wondered if I was now my own captor or if I was someone else's? I thought about feminism in a patriarchal world and realised that might be the ultimate paradox. I thought about leaving my job and then I thought about all the free beauty treatments I'd lose if I quit.

John Berger famously wrote: 'You painted a naked woman because you enjoyed looking at her, put a mirror in her hand and you called the painting "Vanity", thus morally condemning the woman whose nakedness you had depicted for your own pleasure.'

But we added another layer: You taught a girl that beauty labour was an investment essential for her worth, that braiding and preening and plucking were necessary skills for her humanity. You told her over and over again that beauty labour is only valuable when unpaid, and when she started to profit from her beauty work you reduced her efforts to frivolity. Once the feminists saw the blood money on her hands, they pushed her out and called her a traitor.

A few weeks after returning home, I quit my job. On the next few pages of that little pink notebook, I sought answers to the questions that consumed my brain. I began to write this book.

*

What started out as a personal exploration quickly expanded. In my work as a journalist, editor, marketeer and social media consultant, in my work for the beauty companies, and the startups, nonprofits and media platforms I've worked for since, I have been lucky enough to become immersed in some of the most feminist, forward-thinking institutions in the country. I work with women who are emblems of modern feminism but who admit to me in private that the hardest part of their day is getting dressed in the morning, that they edit all of their Instagram photos to appear 'worthy', that they break down regularly as a result of their appearance or that they are paying thousands for treatments because they need to look the part for their next business venture. I have been to parties where group pictures are passed around for each individual person to edit, tweak and smooth before they are uploaded to Instagram. I have consoled a young teenage family member who was caught sending nude selfies to boys in her school. I have teen girls around me who have already started injecting their faces. I have participated in a lot of this behaviour myself, and I am terrified.

I began to speak to the women closest to me and then reached out to those across the world in order to hear the truth about their experiences with beauty. In many ways, this is a book of confessions, of trying to grapple with that elusive truth – of what it feels like to exist in a woman's body today. In this book, you'll read wisdom, stories and insights from cis women, trans women, masculine-presenting women, feminine-presenting women, queer women, feminist women, gen Z women, millennial women, women with a million followers, women with none, mothers, students, sex workers, influencers, academics, celebrities and CEOs, who attempt to answer those questions, to settle the in-fighting in our brains. The more conversations I had, the more I realised the importance of our collective experience and the creation of solidarity.

I am a white, middle-class woman with a petite build, born with fair skin, blonde hair and blue eyes, and my relationship with the beauty industry has formed a cornerstone of my emotional and physical wellbeing throughout my life. Whilst it would be wrong for me to claim parity of oppression with women across the world, I think it is also harmful to disavow our shared experiences, to reject solidarity in favour of division. If my research has taught me anything, it is that I am far from unique in my day-to-day interactions with modern beauty culture. For marginalised women, these issues are only compounded further by interconnecting forces of oppression. Women of colour, working-class women, disabled, trans or masculine-presenting women only face additional adversity.

This is a book for and about young women and girls – not because men and boys don't suffer too, but because their experience is markedly different, and at this moment in time it is women and girls who are most at risk. As young girls, we learn early on that beauty matters more than anything – that it is the first dimension of the feminine gender role. From birth, we are conditioned to understand that to be beautiful is to be loved, to be special, to be good. Ugliness is inherently evil, inherently othered. And yet many of us are afraid to admit or acknowledge that beauty matters, for fear we will be mocked for attributing meaning to such trivial feminine pursuits.

In our digital age, women and girls are subjected to unprecedented levels of scrutiny. Teenage girls are the most likely of any demographic to take and post selfies, and to use filters to edit their appearance. Meta's own research concluded that Instagram was toxic for girls, making them feel worse about their bodies, whilst 83 per cent of women say that social media is negatively impacting their self-esteem. According to the Harley Medical Group, women are twice as likely as men to feel unhappy with how they look. Meanwhile, 52 per cent of eleven- to twenty-one-year-olds feel the need to look perfect, an increase of almost 10 per cent since 2016. We are currently experiencing an epidemic of perfectionism in young women, with almost half of secondary-school girls considering some form of surgical intervention to change the way they look. In the latest report by the CDC, the US national public health agency, 57 per cent of teen girls in America felt 'persistently sad or hopeless' in 2021 – almost a 60 per cent increase in the last decade. Depression rates are twice as high amongst girls as amongst boys, with social media thought to be a major contributing factor. Since the advent of these digital platforms, the incidences of eating disorders and body dysmorphia in the US and the UK have risen by around 30 per cent.

As the first generations to be exposed to digital culture en masse, gen Z and millennial women were raised in a social experiment, on stacks of images and an endless scroll of self-comparison. According to *The Atlantic*, in the early 2010s, rates of depression, anxiety and self-injury in adolescent girls surged in line with the rise of social media. Stuck in our Stockholm syndrome, we obsess over more beauty than we were ever meant to see and replicate the images that hurt us the most. Digital beauty culture is upon us and, as Claire Barnett, former executive director of UN Women UK forewarns: 'We are standing in a doorway where on one side lies healing our relationship with our bodies as a critical step in achieving equality in all areas of life, and on the other lies the destruction of women's physical and mental health. We have to choose which way we are going to walk.'

Still, many would argue that feminism has done its job – that we have the rights in law that women fought for over the past century. But the reality feels at odds with much of our supposed progress. There is a form of social gaslighting, in which women's liberation has been ticked off the list, despite many of us still feeling uneasy, unsafe or unsure of how best to act. Most of us are confused about the value we place on beauty, our relationship with our bodies, how far we should take our desire to be desired and the benefits of a quick fix over a long-term struggle.

To exist as a young woman today is to flounder in this sea of paradoxes. It's to live in a world that criticises a beauty standard whilst continuing to uphold it. It's to know that this beauty standard is unhealthy whilst being painfully aware that adherence is the best way to thrive. It's to resent the images that envelop you on social media whilst obsessively consuming and recreating the same content. It's to know that this beauty is often artificial and yet still strive for it. It's to reject the male gaze whilst profiting from it. It's being 'empowered' figuratively but not literally.

When primary-school girls are considering plastic surgery to 'fix' their faces and bodies, the work of feminism is not done. When high-school girls refuse to leave the house after school because they feel too ugly to be seen in real life, the work of feminism is not done. When eating disorder statistics are worse than they were in the 1990s, when the ultra-thin supermodel reigned supreme, the work of feminism is not done. Whilst we live in a pandemic of violence against women and girls, under a culture in which men are entitled to discuss, dissect and dominate women's bodies, the work of feminism is not done. When our bodily autonomy is increasingly being revoked, whilst hollow Instagram posts about empowerment and women's independence cloak our subordination, we know the work of feminism is not done. When trans women are being killed for failing to meet a socially acceptable level of feminine beauty, the work of feminism is not done.

I hope that in the following pages we can start to (at best) untangle this web and (at least) identify those forces and hold them up to the light. As bell hooks writes, 'Feminist ideology should not encourage (as sexism has done) women to believe they are powerless.' It should instead 'clarify for women the powers they exercise daily and show them ways these powers can be used to resist sexist domination and exploitation'.

I want us to be able to tell the truth about our experiences – to speak, to scream, to find solidarity. I want to unmask the absurdities of our current existence and confront the beauty culture we have come accustomed to with a critical lens. We may have grown up in uncharted territory, but we have the knowledge and the power to reflect on our online lives, and to create a more beautiful future for the next generation of girls.

My belief, above all, is that we need each other now more than ever – to think and act as a collective, a sisterhood, and not in the clichéd Instagram quote post kind of way but in a real, tangible, community-driven way. It is vital for our survival in this world. In a reality that fortifies our isolation and individualism, in which your community is simultaneously everyone and no one, we need to come together to fight back. We, as an assembly, need to commit to creating circles that nurture our collective wellbeing. And I mean true wellbeing, not self-loathing disguised as self-care.

This book is as close to the truth as I could get. Ultimately, *Pixel Flesh* represents a refusal to brush our struggles under the carpet. It would be impossible to contain every experience within this book – in such cases, I invite you to widen the discourse and push the parameters of the debate further. I am limited to how I think and what I know, what I have read and what I have learnt, but I hope this book inspires you to think critically about the importance of beauty culture and the chokehold it has on our world. The stories in this book are about real women, about us. I hope you find yourself reflected here, and I hope you find solidarity amongst the discomfort. I hope, even if just in some small ways, it sets you free.

1

The Cult of Kylie Jenner

I play the video again and again. Rewinding, then fast-forwarding, pausing every millisecond to see her face frozen in every facet of the movement, her famously filled lips forming the words: 'We're going for a really natural look today.'

Kylie Jenner has been trapped inside my phone for years now. Eighty-six pictures of her stacked neatly, one on top of the other like tiny Tetris blocks. Eighty-six versions of her that only I can see.

Kylie Jenner: the muse, the mother, the millionaire. Commodified by her family from the age of nine and thrust into the world of reality TV (the first ever episode of *Keeping Up with the Kardashians* shows a prepubescent Kylie spinning on a stripper pole), she reportedly started experimenting with cosmetic procedures from the age of seventeen. She founded her first company at twenty, selling beauty products to replicate her (surgically altered) look to her adoring fans, and at twenty-one she became a mother.

I spent the day with Kylie in December 2018, ten months after the birth of her daughter, Stormi. Before I worked in beauty tech, I worked in beauty magazines, and Kylie was our cover girl. As the publication's social media editor, my job was to gather as much behind-the-scenes content as possible and interview Kylie for the magazine's social channels. Six pre-approved questions, six video responses. The cover image went ahead but the rest of the content was never authorised by Kylie's team. It has been trapped in my camera roll ever since.

A few months after we met, Kylie was deified by Forbes as the youngest ever self-made billionaire (a title later revoked amid claims she forged the numbers, which Kylie denies). She is the youngest and most followed of the Kardashian clan. With over 400 million fans on Instagram, she is the second most popular woman on the entire platform. Kylie Jenner is an individual so powerful that she can shift the global stock market by more than a billion dollars with a single tweet and change the concept of beauty for an entire generation of girls.

*

It was 2020, and we had been trapped inside for three months. On this June day it was unusually hot and sticky in the communal garden, just fifteen minutes from London's Notting Hill station. My support bubble and I were sunbathing in this south-facing sanctuary. Soft bodies on artificial grass, needling our skin as we surrendered ourselves to the sun.

I hadn't seen bodies in a while. Only pixel flesh. Basking in the heat, surrounded by flora, my friends looked like Renaissance paintings: lockdown plump and beautiful, lazy and gorgeous. Their bodies were warm and velvety, dimpled in places and striped in others. There was stubble and stretch marks, rolls and razor cuts. Within the lushness of the garden, we glowed warm with a radiance you can't replicate on a screen. For a brief few moments, I escaped back to reality.

Our names – Ellen, Sienna and Eliza – aren't the only thing homonymic about us. Facially, we are the equivalent of 'yes, you can copy my homework, but don't make it too similar'. Fair-skinned, blue-eyed and blonde-haired. Our bodies are the most varying aspects of us. Sienna is small-chested and slender, Eliza is statuesque and shapely – the most womanly of us all, a veritable Botticelli. I am something in between but always feel I should be more like the others.

Sienna asked me to take photos of her and, of course, I obliged (she has over 5,000 followers on Instagram and posts every other day, like clockwork). Her face was fresh with filler she'd gotten the day before, her ripened bruises covered by concealer. It was a deal she had originally found on Groupon, a small man in the back of a hairdressers somewhere in north London. It was far to go but at £120 for one millilitre, it was worth it. Enveloped by the greenery of the garden she looked like a glitch. The hyperbole of herself. But as soon as I held the camera up and captured her within it, she was perfect. A flawless digital girl, radiating natural beauty.

Sienna has been injecting her face for six years. She is twenty-five.

We skipped lunch because we were taking Instagram photos. No one said anything but we were all acutely aware this was a conscious decision. We tried to make the most of the afternoon heat but soon retreated inside. The performance was over, and you can't see screens in the sun. As I walked to the fridge to grab water I glanced over Sienna's shoulder. She had the photo open in Facetune. A stretch of the hips, a slice at the waist, a cut of the jaw. I watched from the corner of my eye as the initial perfection I had captured moments before was tweaked even further. *It wasn't meant to be malleable*, I felt like screaming at her. Somehow in the cutting and slicing and stretching, I felt mutilated.

Forty-five minutes later, the photo made it to Instagram stories. An ephemeral post: it was visible for only twenty-four hours.

*

I knew I shouldn't stare but I couldn't help myself. This was a face I recognised, but not wholly. It looked like Kylie

Jenner was wearing the *mask* of Kylie Jenner – uncanny and unmoving. Her face didn't work in real life but I guess it didn't need to.

In every era there is a beauty ideal – from Marilyn to Twiggy, Kate Moss to Kylie – a mass dissemination of the beauty benchmark for our continual comparison. In the digital age of beauty overstimulation, in which we are constantly bombarded by attractive faces, Kylie became the poster girl for the postmodern standard, one that has been disseminated more than any other ideal in history. The mass proliferation of images online and our subsequent self-surveillance have given rise to a beauty ideal built on extremes – exaggerated features designed to appeal to the screen, to fit perfectly in pixels, to stand out when put in a box.

Jia Tolentino defined this homogeneous image of female beauty as 'Instagram Face' in 2019, describing 'a young face, of course, with poreless skin and plump, high cheekbones. It has catlike eyes and long, cartoonish lashes; it has a small, neat nose and full, lush lips.' It is the face of some of the most popular women in our digital realm, from Kylie Jenner to Kim Kardashian, Bella Hadid to Emily Ratajkowski, and has formed the foundation of a new beauty industrial complex, in which a single facial aesthetic is popularised and idealised amongst the masses – including me, Sienna and Eliza. The result is a culture of homogeneous beauty, in which women covet each other's features and strive for ideals that can only be achieved through augmentation – normalising injectable procedures, cosmetic surgery, photo editing and filter use in order to achieve the look.

To be successful in digital beauty culture is to conform to this generic sameness, to have this face. Those who are most followed online look astoundingly similar and posture themselves in nearly identical ways. In a qualitative study that analysed the faces of fifty models and influencers with the widest social reach according to Instagram follower count, it was found that 64 per cent of the women had uplifted, cat-like eyes, whilst 86 per cent had full lips. Defined, chiselled cheekbones, a strongly projected chin and a defined, chiselled jawline appeared across 100 per cent of the women. Additionally, 78 per cent displayed a straight and upturned nose, 84 per cent had high eyebrows and 98 per cent had shallow, voluminous tear troughs. As far as skin texture goes, 84 per cent of the influencers presented their faces with a complete absence of wrinkles and lines, and 100 per cent without acne. In total, almost half of the women in the sample possessed *all* of the characteristics of Instagram Face.

The beauty trends over the past two decades have not replaced one another, but have instead become cumulative in their contradictions, mutually inclusive as they compound our insecurities. Women do not only need to be thin or curvy, they must be slim in the arms, calves and stomach, with rounded curves on the hips, bum and breasts, all whilst maintaining a cinched waist, clear skin, bouncy hair and an appropriate level of muscle definition.

Despite body positivity movements online, eating disorder statistics are worse now than they were in the 1990s. Running concurrently is an explosion in the demand for aesthetic enhancements. According to the Aesthetic Plastic Surgery National Databank in the US, the number of Botox procedures increased by 54 per cent between 2019 and 2020, and fillers were up by 75 per cent. By 2022, the popularity of these non-surgical procedures had grown by a further 23 per cent. The UK is the world's fastest-growing market for facial filler, and British plastic surgeons reported a 70 per cent increase in consultation requests over 2020. A recent UK study found that 28 per cent of eighteen- to twenty-four-year-olds and 31 per cent of twenty-five- to thirty-four-year-olds have had some form of cosmetic treatment (compared with an average of just 21 per cent for the whole UK population). Over half of women aged sixteen to twenty-nine were considering cosmetic enhancements either now or in the future. As capitalism moves on to colonise another area of the female consciousness, there will no doubt be further additions to the roster of treatments and procedures women are expected to undertake in order to achieve the beauty standard.

In an interview with Kathleen Hale for *Harper's Bazaar*, Simon Ourian, the aesthetic doctor who created Kylie's lips, said that he estimates that ten years ago around 1 per cent of his patients were in 'the younger category' (eighteen- and nineteen-year-olds), whereas now that age group has grown to comprise about 10 per cent of his patient population. Although he says he doesn't treat underage clients, Kylie Jenner was seventeen when she began getting injected by him. 'I know the family,' he said, 'and I understand that she's a very mature person.'

In the reunion episode of season twenty of *Keeping Up with the Kardashians*, Jenner spoke openly about what triggered her beauty insecurities: 'I was fifteen and I was insecure about my lips. I have really small lips. And it was like one of my first kisses and a guy was like, "I didn't think you would be a good kisser because you have such small lips." I took that really hard. When a guy you like says that . . . I just didn't feel desirable or pretty.'

It all started with one teenage boy. One young man's comments – acting as a mouthpiece for misogyny – triggered a domino effect that started with Kylie and spread globally, knocking millions of young women, including myself and Sienna. Once victimised by the beauty standard, Kylie has become the standard herself, making millions from the conscious and unconscious anxieties – like those she experienced at fifteen – of young women the world over. For quite some time, Kylie refused to admit she'd had any cosmetic work done, insisting her larger lips were the result of makeup. In August 2017, Kylie launched three cosmetic 'lip kits', each consisting of a lip liner and liquid lipstick designed to replicate her enhanced pout; the products sold out in less than a minute. In the meantime, others were splitting their lips, bursting blood vessels and causing irreparable damage to their faces in the 'Kylie Jenner lip challenge', sucking their mouths into shot glasses for a cheap and temporary swell.

Dr Norman Rowe, a high-profile plastic surgeon in New York City, told *Harper's Bazaar* that he remembers about fifty underage girls pouring into his waiting room requesting lip injections – plus a dozen or so who 'needed lasers to take care of the effects [of the shot glass challenge] – burst capillaries, that sort of thing'.

When Kylie did eventually confess to having lip filler, internet searches for the term increased by 3233%, with clinics reporting a 700% increase in enquiries for the procedure overnight.

A positive view of our digital culture would lead us to believe that we have the ability to freely shape our self-presentation online, that away from the shackles of traditional media, we can create a utopia in which inclusivity, diversity and individuality are paramount. But the data suggests otherwise. Our digital worlds are creating an ever-restrictive regime of beauty ideals, predicated by a narrow set of desirable features and facial characteristics that can be obtained by any woman if she makes the 'right' consumer choices.

*

In my delicate attempts to discuss the topic with Sienna, I had posed myself as an admirer, asking about the cost and how much she'd had done, taking notes for my future foray into face enhancing. She answered candidly: 'I had never been insecure before, but I saw the pictures of Kylie Jenner and I just wanted to look like that.'

If Kylie is the Aphrodite, then we are the Graces, faithful servants tending from a distance, dedicated disciples in the labour of vanity, who feed from an artificial dosage of authenticity and anatomical perfection. Instead of braiding her hair and kissing her feet, we buy her palettes and like her posts, practising her teachings and spreading the word. Sometimes we volunteer ourselves for this role, other times we are coerced against our will.

Research shows that as celebrity worship increases, self-esteem decreases. Studies show the correlation between viewing idealistic images online, feeling insecure about your own appearance and then fantasising about changing your looks. As humans, we were only ever meant to exist in small communities – anthropologist Robin Dunbar theorises that we can only maintain networks of 150 connections. Our content-saturated landscape allows greater opportunity than ever for these comparisons: you can see over 150 images of other humans in just a few hours of scrolling your feed. We were never meant to see this many beautiful people; our brains were never built to experience humankind like this, let alone via an algorithm by which those who adhere to the standard are pushed up and out, to increased visibility.

The phenomena of self-scrutiny against a beauty standard is, of course, not new; it predates our access to the internet and social media. It is not Kylie's fault, nor is it Instagram's, that this problem exists, but both have a role in perpetuating and exacerbating the issue, just as we do as individuals. Some argue that beauty influencers have transgressed the traditional trappings of beauty culture to create empowering feminist spaces separate from the control of the ideal. Beauty, both as an industry and a concept, is now far more diverse, intersectional and accepting. However, most fail to interrogate the social order that makes it difficult for women to opt out of beauty culture all together.

*

'If I can afford it, why should I not look like the best version of myself?' Sienna shrugs and turns to face me.

The majority of us can't afford to live like Kylie Jenner but, with the increasing accessibility of these treatments, we can try to look like her. Ranging from £100–400 or US$400–800 per session depending on the procedure, and taking only a matter of minutes, facial fillers have become a normal activity for people with expendable income, and a type of status symbol for aspirational women, equivalent to that of a designer bag. In a trend largely led by celebrities, young women and girls are showing their folders of edited faces to doctors and non-doctors, the trained and untrained, and asking to be made the same, the fragments of their idols coveted and consumed.

Sienna tells me she feels empowered. She earns good money, why shouldn't she invest in her image? Look after herself and boost her confidence? But she also tells me she can't stop dissecting her face to find her next fix. It's the perfect patch-up to push her pain to the side; her autonomy allows her to take the situation into her own hands and 'improve' herself.

The language of empowerment was co-opted in the 1970s with L'Oreal's 'Because you're worth it' campaign, designed to sell more hair and beauty products than their competitor Clairol. Our current state of beauty and feminism is simply the logical extension of this capitalist colonisation of the female consciousness. Pharmaceutical giant Allergan even started tailoring its advertisements of Juvéderm, one of the most popular global brands of dermal filler, to millennial women. Their 2018 commercial lists the treatment's potential side effects (swelling, pain, lumps, bruising, vision abnormalities, stroke and blindness) before pink and purple text fills the screen, telling consumers to 'Live it, work it, pose it, command it, boss it'. Every part of your physical self can now be improved, tweaked and changed to fit the societal ideal, and it has become your responsibility to do so. Regardless of the systemic powers in place that drive you to detest your features, the onus for 'success' lies with you, as an individual.

It was a word that came up over and over again in the research for this book: everything from injectables to cosmetic surgery, editing apps and selfies were described as 'empowering'. I'd once said the same but it started to feel meaningless, a blanket term for 'it makes me feel better for a bit', whilst the undercurrent of anxiety and inadequacy still swirled beneath. The word started to feel more ominous as time went on. It became a deflection, an act of concealment, and a way to end the conversation on beauty standards entirely.

Despite us all driving towards this idealised aesthetic, it seems we can't admit that we are doing it for anyone except ourselves. Most of us can't admit to doing it at all. Running parallel to the discourse of empowerment is an undercurrent of shame. Claiming you've never undergone cosmetic surgery – that you simply woke up more attractive – forms an insidious undercurrent in our beauty culture. Kylie, for one, has never confessed to any augmentations other than her lips and, in 2023, a breast augmentation, despite claims that she'd spent hundreds of thousands of dollars on multiple surgeries before turning 25. The best plastic surgery is inconspicuous and, despite the rising treatment statistics, the illusion of natural, effortless beauty continues to be upheld. Paradoxically, none of us want to take responsibility for our choices even if we all claim to be empowered by them. And, if we are truly making these decisions for ourselves, as a tool of self-expression and empowerment independent from patriarchal control, why is one form of beauty (and femininity) – such as Instagram Face – so prevalent?

An aesthetic of homogeneity, to me, is a reductive tactic. Not only is it a genius marketing tool, as a globalised beauty standard creates an incredibly exclusive set of ideals that *everybody* must augment themselves in order to achieve, but it is also a tool of our collective oppression, a way to keep us in line. Uniformity has been used historically as a form of control and subordination: by conforming to copy/paste versions of one another, by assimilating into an assembly line of identical faces, we lose a sense of our individuality and of our humanity. It goes beyond aesthetics; it's a political act that hinders our self-definition and ultimately strips us of agency.

Conversations around bodily autonomy and our right to choose have become focused on beautification and cosmetic procedures, whilst women's rights to abortion, safety from violence and access to contraception are being revoked across the world. We are 'empowered' in our preoccupation with physical perfection whilst governing structures take power over our bodies. We absorb the pastel posts about girl power whilst our actual powers are being stripped away.

Feminist writer Andrea Dworkin wrote that beauty standards 'define precisely the dimensions of [women's] physical freedom' – their narrow constraints on our bodies creating straitjackets, inhibiting our ability to move through the world with ease. We are trapped – physically, psychologically and financially. Not even billionaire status can set a woman free. The rhetoric of empowerment and choice is simply covering up the continuous objectification and subjugation of women under modern beauty culture. Cosmetic enhancements may be sold to us as empowerment tools but these ever-intensifying beauty standards continue to reinforce gender inequality. What's worse, we have been made to think we're winning.

We cut ourselves up, stick needles into our faces, invest our precious time, part with our hard-earned money and even put our lives at risk under the guise of liberation. Where this heightened level of self-scrutiny becomes a marker for our new-found freedom, our increased body surveillance is reframed as a tool for a better life, rather than a side effect of a harmful beauty culture.

Of course, beauty practices are also used by individuals across the globe to express genuine creativity and passion. If there's one constant in human history, it's that we've always embellished our bodies – from scarification to kohl eyeliner. There is huge power in the artform of self-expression but much of this beauty work is the antithesis of creative freedom. Our digital culture creates opportunity for competition and comparison on a scale never seen before. Combined with the advancements in beauty technology, we are left with a culture in which the small 'imperfections' that make us unique can easily be erased, 'corrected' and replaced with trending catalogue parts. The illusion of beauty as self-care allows us, for a moment, to believe that we have some freedom in the creation of our own aesthetic, whilst an omnipotent beast continues to control and shape it.

*

Eliza was fed up. We were on a day trip together a few months after our sunbathing session – Sienna, Eliza and I, with a few other girls we knew and loved. No one else in the group had really noticed the shift in Eliza's psyche, but she's one of my oldest friends and her mood swings are more familiar to me than my own. A fellow northerner, another outsider, we ground each other in familiarity. We often catch eyes as the others talk, sharing a mutual feeling that, despite the ridiculousness, we are both in this together. We aren't like them. We are something else. Today, she'd become quiet, drawn into herself. Sienna and the other girls were behind us, quite a few paces back. Eliza and I had walked ahead, intentionally speeding up for those precious few moments of alone time. I knew she was on the precipice of an eruption and if I could get her alone I could minimise the devastation.

'I just can't do this anymore,' she said. The lava began to flow.

'I can't cope with the constant fucking chat about Instagram girls and nose jobs and what we all look like. I just can't do it. Yeah, I've gained a bit of weight, but you know what? I actually don't care. I'm never going to look like those girls and that's fine, I've accepted that. I just want a day where I don't have to think for a single second about my appearance, or if I'm going to get the right photo, or if I can eat a croissant for breakfast, or if my bum will look good in my outfit. I don't fucking care. There's more to life! Every single day we have to talk about Kylie Jenner or Bella Hadid or Hailey Bieber, or what this person is wearing or what this person has had done. I'm just so bored of it, Ellen. Not everyone wants to look like Kylie fucking Jenner. I'm trying so hard to be confident and I just can't keep talking about every inch of my face and body like I'm some kind of DIY project someone forgot to finish.'

Experiencing girlhood in the early 2000s, our generation grew up with the makeover as a cornerstone of pop culture – from the iconic *Princess Diaries* scene to the countless episodes of *Extreme Makeover*, *10 Years Younger in 10 Days* and *The Swan* that we binged throughout our formative years. The term 'glow up' became rooted in our everyday vocabulary and we yearned, secretly, to one day be transformed.

Viewing bodies as objects awaiting improvement has been dubbed the 'cosmetic gaze'. The body we are born with becomes the prototype, in need of adjustments and tweaking in response to feedback. The ideal body can then be envisioned as an 'after' picture or final product transformed by experts –

in this case, aestheticians, beauty therapists, makeup artists, influencers and personal trainers. We internalise the cosmetic gaze, encouraged to view ourselves as a 'before' image awaiting transformation. We want to be seen to be improving, to be eternally optimising.

Noticing the rising trend for Instagram Face, aestheticians began selling dermal filler packages named after Kylie Jenner, inaugurating her as the archetype for the 'it girl' look. In exchange for your monthly salary, you were promised an instant transformation to the internet's ideals. You could buy Kylie Jenner's face and mould it onto your own. The Advertising Standards Authority banned a number of so-called 'Kylie Package' ads from Instagram in 2019 for misleading consumers, though the treatment combinations themselves, of course, still exist. Women are incentivised financially and aesthetically to market these procedures to other women – influencers are given free or discounted treatments in exchange for promotion – fuelling anxiety about flaws we never realised we had, making us all into the image of each other.

Any features that don't align with the ideal then become problems waiting to be 'fixed' by the aesthetics industry. Online, images of women's faces marked by arrows and dotted lines demonstrate how noses, chins, lips, cheeks and jaws can be rectified in order to be made beautiful, how they may be 'improved' in order to maximise a woman's potential. As Tolentino writes, women are encouraged to analyse their faces 'the way that a McKinsey consultant would think about a corporation: identify underperforming sectors and remake them, discard whatever doesn't increase profits and reorient the business toward whatever does', the 'profits' being the currency of beauty. Through likes and follows, we are given a daily measure of how our faces and bodies are performing, with instant validation or ostracisation. In one study of interviews with young women, many said they would delete their photographs if they didn't receive an 'acceptable' amount of likes – something Kylie also admits to. Eighty-one per cent of women surveyed said they set a benchmark for how many likes they should receive to be performing well amongst their peers. If they didn't receive them then they viewed themselves negatively in comparison with other women.

Self-surveillance acts as an extension of French philosopher Michel Foucault's notion of the panopticon effect: in an open, circular prison structure, prisoners self-monitor under the assumption that they are always being watched. The way in which we, as women, have come to internalise the beauty ideals and monitor ourselves accordingly is a similar form of entrapment. Our now omnipresent beauty culture and self-commodification under social media have led women to continually survey and objectify themselves, internalising this 'panoptic gaze', monitoring our faces and bodies for any deviations from the ideal.

There are millions of photos charting Kylie's before and after pictures and entire accounts dedicated to comparing images of celebrities before and after beauty work. Whilst these can be praised for their attempts to create transparency around cosmetic enhancements, they also function in the same way as bikini body analyses in gossip magazines throughout the 1990s and 2000s. Rife with judgmental comments about both the unaltered 'before' picture and the edited, augmented or surgically enhanced 'after' image, these accounts serve as a reminder that women will never win in a world designed to scrutinise their physical appearance for profit.

In digital beauty culture, our bodies are surveilled and dissected in ever more intense, ever more extensive ways. The more I immersed myself in the digital beauty world, the more I felt the pressures mount. All of a sudden, I knew terms like buccal fat, hip dips and naso-labial folds, names for things that I hadn't even noticed just months prior. If you don't know what these mean, don't worry about it, things are better that way. I was analysing my face for its failures – noticing every opportunity for optimisation. Every time I thought I knew where I stood, I was served something else to scrutinise.

This is all indicative of the self-surveillance demanded by these hyper-visual platforms – of our monitoring and performing an idealised self for a public audience. Every girl has access to digital worlds and every girl engages in discourse that reinforces our standards of beauty. With the ability to like, comment and follow, we all have the power to cast our judgement on others' physical appearance. The judgement that each woman receives is public and permanent, and becomes a marker for social status in the digital age.

Those pressures to attain and retain the perfect face and body are then compounded by a need to present this perfect image across multiple media channels, and then to exist in constant comparison to your curated feeds and the version of your life that you present online.

*

Kylie's hair and makeup took almost two hours. Wearing a white robe, she held the centre of gravity in the room. I had expected Kylie Jenner to be the epitome of abundance itself but in front of me on set she looked like anxiety. She seemed smaller in real life – more fragile. Her eyes were big and brown, Bambi-esque in the way they darted around the room. She was skittish and scared, desperately searching for security in her staff or seeking solace in the screen of her phone. Sat in a collapsible fabric chair, surrounded by mirrors, Kylie was waiting to be shot.

I orbited her slowly, taking pictures with my phone, documenting the process. It felt wrong. For someone whose entire life revolves around being observed, Kylie didn't seem to like being looked at, to be captured by anyone but herself.

I stared at her on my screen, then in real life, then back to my screen. I wondered what it was like to have a whole room operating on your terms. To be in the public eye for the majority of your life. To know that anyone in the room would bend over backwards at your beck and call. To have two security staff watching you at all times. To skip lunch and spend your break sitting alone. To flinch every time the blinds opened. To run and hide when someone opened the door. To be in business with your entire family. To plan your exit from a building four hours in advance to ensure your safety. To have to keep your pregnancy a secret in order to protect your unborn child from the media. To have your mother take 10 per cent of everything you earn. To have the money and influence to make a real impact in the world. To sell beauty products instead.

In a 2017 interview with *Glamour* magazine, Kylie described herself as a 'feminist': 'I'm a young woman, for one thing, and I don't depend on a man or anybody else. I make my own money and start my own businesses, and I feel like I'm an inspiration for a lot of young girls who want to stand on their own.'

To me, Kylie Jenner personifies the biggest contradiction of modern feminism. If economic empowerment and freedom from marriage was the goal, she has won. Online, a new female archetype has emerged in response to the traditional domestic roles assigned to women historically. The 'girl boss', as it is often coined in digital spaces, is career-driven and ambitious, but is still required to be attractive and to ascribe to conventional standards of femininity. Kylie is the archetype for how to be a mother and an entrepreneur: sexy and successful, self-directed and surrounded by other women. Theoretically, she has achieved freedom from the structures we all fight daily. However, she doesn't make me *feel* like we have won. Kylie's feminism does not challenge or critique the patriarchy, but rather aspires to have it all.

If feminism is ultimately about the liberation of women, what Kylie has achieved is liberation for herself. Kylie's success has come at a cost to the collective, upholding and profiting from a beauty standard that ultimately harms us all, and creates a heightened level of beauty that holds all of us hostage. This form of feminism feels like a distraction, one that keeps us in line whilst presenting the illusion of choice and success. Beauty, when defined exclusively, becomes a weapon and can bolster the structures from which we are trying to break free. As young women become increasingly autonomous, wealthy and averse to the domestic, the beauty standard functions as an alternative form of control. Both my friend Sienna and Kylie out-earn their peers (and every previous generation of women before them), but the more they earn, the more this 'self-imposed' beauty tax increases and the more self-scrutiny wins. If a master's tools cannot dismantle the master's chains then this feminism is a false promise. One that makes you feel in control of your own oppression whilst continuing to profit from your suffering.

The patriarchy preyed on Kylie's vein of self-hatred and physical obsession and got us addicted to the IV. Emerging now is a more covert colonisation of the female consciousness, one that continues to carve out competition and isolate its victims. It turns us into both the oppressor and the oppressed, and keeps us trapped in a cycle of self-flagellation until it has eroded the ground we have spent decades gaining. Instagram Face, and the ever-narrower beauty standard it stems from, reinforce patriarchal power under an illusion of women's empowerment. For the first time in history, we, as consumers and captives, are also part of the mass perpetration of the images that harm us.

As I stared at Kylie, I hated her. I resented her. I wanted to snatch her phone and fix things – for herself, for Sienna, for Eliza, for me. The day after we met, Kylie posted a selfie. Sat in another collapsible makeup chair in another white bathrobe, this time with a platinum blonde wig and an overlined red lip. The caption read 'no days off'.

*

A few weeks after I'd last seen her, Eliza came to my apartment to work and I felt my body lighten as we hugged. Of all my friends in the city, she is my safety blanket. She'd gotten three new tattoos since I'd last seen her – the first beauty bookings of the season. A snake curled around a rose on her left shoulder and a dagger sliced through the fauna beneath.

We talked endlessly, the clicking of laptop keys punctuating our sentences. We typed. We talked. We typed. Falling comfortably into the silent spaces between. I told her about the new man I'd been dating, the guy from six months before who wouldn't leave me alone, the new business idea I'd had, the outfit I wanted to wear on Saturday night. I told her I was struggling with myself, that I had been eating three meals a day recently and had gained weight. It was the heaviest I'd ever been, the most space my body had ever taken up. I told her I was fighting every urge to restrict myself, to start logging calories or skipping meals, but that it felt like an uphill battle. I told her that I was sick of hearing colleagues, friends and mentors discuss food groups they needed to cut out, the latest diet trend or detox they needed to finish. I told her that I had felt a sense of pride seeing myself in the images I saw online, but that now I didn't recognise where I fit in. She told me about her freelance career, late invoices and the filler appointment she'd booked for the next week: 'Well, I'm just getting a bit, just on my top lip to even things out, and it's with a trainee so it's not expensive at all. The instructor watches the whole time so it's safe, but the price is super-reduced. I might get my nose done too. I always thought about getting a proper nose job but they're so expensive, so I might just get some filler to fix it instead.'

In an instant, the comfortable silence was sucked from the room, taking my breath with it. I looked up at the face I loved with all my heart and I felt betrayed. I felt resentful. I felt jealous.

The cruelty of modern beauty culture is that though we may be acutely aware of the spell we're under, none of us can figure out the undoing. Instead, we pretend we're one of the lucky ones who escaped the hex, whilst continuing to suffer in silence.

I am not allowed to be angry at Eliza because Eliza is a woman and I am also a woman. To criticise Eliza's choices would be the ultimate 'fuck you' to girl power. I might as well shoot one of the Spice Girls. Much of feminism today insists that women's choices automatically constitute acts of empowerment in and of themselves, irrespective of the consequences of those choices. Girl power has come to mean a woman's consumer power – her lifetime customer value in a capitalist cycle of beauty trends designed to keep her invested in the idea of self-improvement.

It is difficult to differentiate the views you genuinely hold from those enforced on you by wider cultural forces, almost impossible. But we have to be able to hold two notions in our mind at once: that women can simultaneously have agency, autonomy and ability whilst also being subjected to a ubiquitous patriarchal agenda that profits from our self-loathing, self-surveillance and subsequent self-sabotage. To admit that we are not cured of cultural conditioning isn't a fundamental flaw in our womanhood but a necessary step in assigning accountability to the right structures. To feign ignorance of the forces that oppress us and to take it upon ourselves to 'fix' the 'flaws' they highlight and conform to conditioning is only playing into the hands of the patriarchy. Our consumer power and newfound economic emancipation does not negate our oppression under capitalism.

I don't believe that altering your appearance to appease the beauty standard can be a choice made from a position of empowerment, nor do I believe it is an inherently feminist choice, even if it is glossed in a narrative of agency and progress. I would argue that in undertaking this beauty work we are contributing to the oppression of other women, especially those further removed from the ideal because of race, class, disability or proximity to the desired traits. The beauty ideal is more attainable for women who already closely resemble it. But the more beautiful you are, the more beautiful you must become, the more the standard intensifies.

There is a conflict between the individual experience of the self and the collective experience of womanhood. The individualism of contemporary celebrity and the hyper-individualising of neo-liberal feminism mean that 'feminism' today translates to supporting my sisters at all costs, regardless of the impact of their actions on the sisterhood as a whole. Social media platforms, editing apps and aesthetic procedures have become tools that fortify our isolation. The 'I' in Instagram, in the Internet, has come to stand for the individual, at the expense of all else. We can choose to look out for ourselves – to share our perfect images whilst censoring our real faces and real experiences. We can do the things that make us feel better to the detriment of ourselves as a society. But feminism, ultimately, is not about our individual choices at all; it is about freedom from the patriarchal oppression from which we all suffer.

I can't help but feel like Naomi Wolf's vision for the future is coming true: 'As each woman responds to the pressure, it will grow so intense that it will become obligatory, until no self-respecting woman will venture outdoors with a surgically unaltered face.' What she couldn't have predicted was that no self-respecting woman would post a selfie without any edits. That it would not be as simple as indoors or outdoors, but that the boundaries between private and public, between real and the digital, would render the performance of a perfect self never-ending.

As popular discourse lauds the unprecedented opportunities available for women and girls, there is an implication, defined as 'post-feminism', that young women are unaffected by gender constraints. Post-feminism refers to the belief that gender inequality has been solved and women are now on equal terms with men. This, combined with self-optimisation and the glory of entrepreneurship highlighted by girlboss culture, creates an intoxicating atmosphere filled with irresistible messaging about liberation, independence and opportunity that assumes we are all out here having a great time. As we have seen, however, the data shows otherwise. The result is a form of symbolic violence, in which our suffering is largely disavowed, only acknowledged momentarily to tell us how we should work on ourselves to overcome it. Contemporary feminism fails to challenge deep-rooted inequities and instead focuses on individual and commercial gain.

But the cruellest twist of all is that beauty, ultimately, is defined by rarity. The ideal is always that which is most difficult to achieve in any given period, one reserved for the privileged in power. If too many women can attain the beauty standard, it will inevitably change in order to maintain its exceptional nature. As soon as we have caught up, shifted into similarity, the goalposts will move and the intensity will increase. Those who can afford it will keep up, those who can't will be swept to the side. For many of us, failure and disappointment are inevitable.

The next time I see Eliza, her lips are plump and her face taut. During her filler appointment, she had been advised to get Botox as well. It was better to start young, they said.

In season three of *The Kardashians*, which aired in 2023, Kylie expressed her regret over the work she'd done on her face and body, adding that she would be 'heartbroken' if her daughter wanted to do the same. 'I wish I could be her and do it all differently because I wouldn't touch anything,' she said.

The trailer for the season ended with Kylie announcing to her sisters: 'All of us just need to have a bigger conversation about the beauty standards that we're setting.' We waited with bated breath for this conversation, for the tide to change, for the beauty mogul to do something differently, to challenge the standards she'd helped to cement in our psyches. But it never came. Once again, they had drawn us in, caught our attention and left us longing.

How can we create a more beautiful future for women and girls?

'By not trying to constantly slant everything with the positive. To actually look hardship in the face – talk about it, analyse it, and figure out action from that discourse. We can't gloss over the depressing parts, we have to sit in that, be honest about it, and try to acknowledge it and to take accountability for it, to create something from that difficulty. We need to look at the ugly side of things and we need to do it together.'

Gina Martin,
activist and author

2

Venus and the Voyeur

As I enter the room, I see her against the far wall, reclining on her side, facing away from me. She is looking into a small mirror but her features are obscured, blurry even. The pearlescent skin of her back glows smooth and unblemished against silk sheets, her impossibly small waist and rising hip curved against ripples of white. Surrounded by noblemen, hers is the only naked body in the room.

I had looked for her in this cavernous place – entered the sandstone building through immense wooden doors guarded by twelve pillars, slipped up the shallow stairs flanked with gold and marble, and headed straight to room 30. She has been lying on these sheets since 1651, in this room since 1906. The *Rokeby Venus* is one of the National Gallery's most prized portraits, one of the most prized nudes in the country.

Venus – the Roman goddess of beauty, also known as Aphrodite in Greek mythology – is the archetype of ideal femininity and one of the most canonical figures of perfection in art history. Countless images of Venus have been created across millennia. From the famous Greek statue the *Venus de Milo*, sculpted in 130–100 BCE, depicting a topless goddess with pert breasts and a contoured stomach, to the Roman *Lely Venus*, dating back to the second century CE, a nude marble goddess crouching with her torso bent over, stomach slightly rolled and her arm covering her chest. Nearly 1,500 years later, Botticelli's *The Birth of Venus* (1482–1485) entered the Western art canon – an image of ideal female beauty that is still replicated and celebrated today. The painting depicts Venus emerging from a shell, her fair hair flowing over her shoulder, her body leaning to the left to emphasise her soft curves. Venus as depicted by Botticelli was lusted after and idolised: beautiful, pure and divine. It reinforced an unrealistic beauty standard for women and depicted them as objects to be exhibited for male pleasure. Cemented in our visual culture, the painting has utterly informed the way we perceive the female body today.

Artists continued to portray feminine beauty in much the same way all the way through the seventeenth and eighteenth centuries. There's *The Birth of Venus* by Alexandre Cabanel, painted in 1863, and *The Birth of Venus* by Ettore Tito, created in 1903. To craft an image of Venus is to craft an image of ideal beauty, and a few things are abundantly clear. Beauty is alabaster white, with defined curves, hairless and poreless. It is unblemished skin, smooth and soft. It is female, in the most binary sense. It is to appear nude but modest, often caught unaware. It is the promise of fulfilled sexual duty. It is to wait patiently and decoratively. It is decided by a man and designed for male spectatorship. It is a framework dictated over centuries by the men with the tools to craft our expectations of how women's bodies should look and behave. It is about who gets to make an object out of whom.

Our frustration with an ideal beauty goes back centuries, an inherent rage of womanhood that comes with having your body dictated to and controlled by those who believe they own it. Jean Liebault, a sixteenth-century Parisian doctor, professed that a woman's face should be pale with soft dimpled cheeks, rosy and flushed like a child's. Her eyes should be big, with small ears and good teeth. In what might be the original subtweet, his wife countered with her own book titled *The Miseries of the Married Women*.

In *Communion*, bell hooks writes that 'as females in patriarchal culture, we cannot determine our self-worth. Our value, our worth, and whether or not we can be loved are always determined by someone else.' The same can be said for beauty. The script has been set by a history dominated by white, wealthy men, and we are taught it from the moment we are born (if not by our parents then by society at large). Over time, the off-the-cuff comments about smiling more, or taking up less space, or subjugating, sink deeper and deeper into our bones until they form the exoskeleton of our psyche. To be beautiful is to be perfect, and to be perfect always requires effort. Whether it's tanning or lightening your skin, buying more products, investing in risky procedures, concealing some features and emphasising others. Something must always be changed or maintained or sustained in order for us to uphold the most vital of virtues.

Whilst there is a widely held belief that beauty standards are constantly changing – that women's bodies, although chastised at times, will have their moment in the limelight, no matter their shape or size – it is a myth. For at least 2,000 years, women's bodies in the West have been held up to a largely unchanged ideal. Whilst micro trends give us the illusion of control in this largely static system, they are often in service of the wealthy or ruling classes. Whether it be plucking your hairline to achieve the same look as Elizabeth I in the 1500s or getting lip filler à la Kylie Jenner, these slight deviations of the beauty standard work to deify those in power and keep us stuck in a cycle of self-development in pursuit of an ideal. Easily disseminated and commodified, these trends make us feel as if we can strive for the standard, even if we can only get one step closer. The devil finds work for idle hands and the ruling structures would rather keep us busy with beauty work by adding an inclusive layer to a largely exclusionary system.

Throughout the past century, although there have been iterations on the ideal, the poster girl body hasn't exceeded a UK size 12/US size 8. We herald Marilyn Monroe as a plus-size icon but our contemporary 'curvy' starlet Kim Kardashian had to lose a significant amount of weight in order to fit into her famous dress for the 2022 Met Gala. We are told to look at the changing face of beauty, from Marilyn to Twiggy, Kate Moss to Kylie, and laud a huge shift in beauty ideals because their dresses may have increased by one or two sizes, their curves varying by degrees. But whilst we're encouraged to note their differences, we lose sight of their similarities. All visions of ideal beauty – from ancient Greece to cyberspace – are young, fair-skinned, hairless and poreless, with smooth skin, a symmetrical face, sensual yet pure. The spectrum for beauty has always excluded more than it has included. There is no room in the ideal for ageing or maturity, cellulite, sagging flesh, veined, pitted or wrinkled skin, uneven breasts, acne, body hair, stretch marks, dark skin, uneven skin, short hair, disability or strong facial features. The ideal ignores the fact that there is often more natural physical variation within a gender than between genders – not every woman is petite with large breasts, wide hips and a soft voice, just as not every man is over six foot tall with chest hair.

We are accustomed to an image of beauty that is polished and perfected, glossy and gleaming. We learn, from a young age, to feel disgust at any deviations. Any 'defects' are deemed repulsive, even when natural to our own bodies. To look like a human woman is to be ugly. By and large, the female body has been shamed throughout history for its inherent functions; we learn from art, media, advertising and social platforms that it is to be fixed, edited, concealed or reduced in order for us to be 'acceptable' women in society, the cutting room floor covered with necessary flesh. That we have any autonomy in our ability to love ourselves is a lie and yet our current beauty climate continues to put the onus on women to fix the problems inflicted on them by a culture that refuses to acknowledge it is sick. Our bodies have always been held within a narrow ideal that is near-impossible to fit ourselves into and social media is only tightening the squeeze.

A portrait was at one time a status symbol – a luxury previously reserved for the wealthy and powerful. Plato wrote that 'those who tell the stories rule the society', and historically, we hadn't been able to tell ours. With the rise of social platforms, phone cameras and editing apps, we could document ourselves in ways previously forbidden. Women post the majority of selfies in every country in the world, and 84 per cent of online influencers are women. We rule the content creation domain by a significant margin.

Much like Sylvia's Plath's famous line in *The Bell Jar*, as Esther tries to reassure herself of her place in the world – 'I took a deep breath and listened to the old brag of my heart. I am, I am, I am' – the fervour with which we create content, capture ourselves, our rooms, our outfits, our possessions, and the ardour with which we turn ourselves inside out in the digital realm feels like a repeated reassurance: I was here, I was here, I was here.

But of course, that liberation has not come without loss. How much of a say do we have in our self-image? Are we proprietors or producers? Within a narrow spectrum, over centuries, beauty standards have shapeshifted in response to women's wider autonomy; as Naomi Wolf argues in *The Beauty Myth*, each emancipatory win for women has been accompanied by an intensification of the attempt to control our bodies:

> *The more legal and material hindrances women have broken through, the more strictly and heavily and cruelly images of female beauty have come to weigh upon us . . . More women have more money and power and scope and legal recognition than we have ever had before; but in terms of how we feel about ourselves physically, we may actually be worse off than our unliberated grandmothers.*

As soon as women make gains in political, economic or sexual autonomy, the ideal tightens its grip. Corsets and restrictive shapewear garments were replaced by diet and exercise. In today's digital age, in which women have more autonomy and rights than ever before, the two have combined, with a focus on wellness, shapewear and eating clean compounded by an ideal that requires surgical and cosmetic intervention to be achieved. What remains unchanged, however, is the idea that in order to achieve beauty you must change yourself in some way, and you must invest effort into maintaining the ideal.

For those who are willing to physically alter their bodies in the name of beauty, the long-standing rhetoric that 'beauty is pain' persists. Painful historical practices of female bodily manipulation to achieve the beauty standard – from ancient Chinese foot binding to Victorian corseted waists – prevail in our current beauty culture in the form of invasive surgical procedures, vampire facials, laser treatments, injectables and extreme diets. In a 2020 post uploaded by Kourtney Kardashian, in which she undergoes a plasma treatment by Dr Jason Diamond, she writes 'torture day' over videos of her face being injected. In 2022, her sister Kim posted an image laying on a medical bed, her stomach red raw as a microneedling laser gun points at her abdomen. 'This is my fave laser but it's painful,' she wrote. In an age where our beauty standard is ever-reliant on physical manipulation, surgical intervention and high-end treatments, the notion that women must suffer for their beauty is perhaps as prevalent as ever.

John Berger's seminal 1970s work *Ways of Seeing* described how women are subjugated in cultural representations throughout both high and low culture. As Berger put it, 'Men act and women appear. Men look at women. Women watch themselves being looked at.' This concept was then further articulated by film theorist Laura Mulvey's canonical 1975 essay 'Visual Pleasure and Narrative Cinema', which coined the term the 'male gaze' – a theoretical framework that argued that the lens of classical Hollywood cinema represents an inherent male perspective and a subsequent voyeurism of female characters. Through the male gaze, the female body becomes territory without agency, a valuable resource to be consumed and acquired.

Margaret Atwood describes the male gaze in her 1993 novel *The Robber Bride*:

> *Even pretending you aren't catering to male fantasies is a male fantasy: pretending you're unseen, pretending you have a life of your own, that you can wash your feet and comb your hair unconscious of the ever-present watcher peering through the keyhole, peering through the keyhole in your own head, if nowhere else. You are a woman with a man inside watching a woman. You are your own voyeur.*

The objectification of our bodies and faces is one of the cornerstones of our oppression in the modern age, as it has been for centuries. Growing up with these images and archetypes – from advertisements to music videos, fairy tales to Barbie dolls – we are exposed to a feminine beauty ideal that becomes central to our ideas of self and success. It becomes impossible not to internalise the narrative that we exist solely for the pleasure and appeasement of a patriarchal gaze. The feminine beauty ideal roots itself in all of our consciences, affecting how we feel about ourselves and how we judge others. To wage this war upon women across the world, there has been no need for arms or physical violence, as Foucault points out – only a gaze. A gaze that becomes so intense that it is impossible not to internalise it. We become our own overseers, exercising surveillance over ourselves.

Inadvertently, we create a self-fulfilling prophecy – we are pressured into adhering to the ideal in order to step out into the worlds, both physical and digital, and thus force our bodies to conform, investing time, money and energy into performing femininity the best we can. Now, images of Venus sell us tools for this job – from razors to cleansers. Young girls then look to us, ideal women, to discover that their pursuit of beauty means lifting, shaping, dieting, dyeing, injecting, slicing, scarring, painting, curling, padding, cutting, starving, concealing and revealing. When women are already socially conditioned to compete with one another, narrowing the ideal only makes the competition more fierce. Girls are imitating and even exaggerating images they see online, creating an echo chamber that amplifies our already narrow ideal. In one study, 80 per cent of women interviewed said that they competed with other women over physical appearance.

Digital beauty culture, with its continuous surveillance and feedback loops, further trains women to discipline each other's bodies as well as their own. When our increasingly visual culture defines adherence to the beauty ideal as a divine feminine virtue necessary for success, but something that can only be achieved by a chosen few, it's easy to see how social media creates a hotbed for individualism and competition amongst women specifically. What's more, when you're constantly giving and receiving feedback on physical appearance via post engagement, judging others whilst they judge you, it is bound to lead to dissatisfaction, comparison and disappointment.

When you're exposed to millions of people, there will always be someone who fits the ideal more, someone who has more likes, comments and followers. Social media creates the ideal space for subjugation – reducing us, once again, to a visual. We are encouraged to police each other and we have to acknowledge that we are all complicit. We all enforce the standards that keep us oppressed.

We are all performing femininity in one way or another. The majority of us perform every day, by applying makeup, wearing high heels or apologising! profusely! as a form of subservience. The performance exists on a sliding scale – from applying lipstick to injecting your lips, from dieting to achieve a smaller waist to undergoing intense plastic surgery to create an hourglass shape. We monitor and discipline our bodies in ways that reproduce the social order and contribute to a homogeneous ideal, reinforcing gender hierarchies and alienating ourselves from our own bodies in their natural state. In our recital of the ideal, we are complicit in our own oppression. Forced to view our bodies constantly through an external lens, we become detached from our corporeal reality and our sense of self in favour of public viewing. We are often more focused on how we appear than how we feel, putting the visual pleasure of others above our own comfort and basic bodily functions. Our agency and individuality are suppressed in order to conform. All of these elements of incessant feminine performance cost us dearly in time, money and brain space. We must look like art, all of the time, especially now in the digital age of mass self-surveillance where we can be captured and immortalised at any moment.

It's an issue that transcends fame, fortune and follower count, a state of being that envelops and embalms. At dinner one day, I sat across from a twenty-one-year-old former viral sensation who told me that every living moment is an out-of-body experience, a never-ending Big Brother experiment:

'Even when I'm crying I'm wondering if my tears are falling beautifully or if my mascara is running in an aesthetic way,' she says. 'Just talking to you right now, I'm holding my stomach in and arching my back, I'm thinking about how I would look if someone were to capture me. If they were to take a photo of this moment, would I be beautiful enough?'

According to research by Dr Claire Pescott, girls as young as ten are conscious of this voyeur, this omnipresent dictator that looms over them. Their male peers are entirely unaware of its presence – focused instead on their skills and hobbies, growing and having fun as children should. Meanwhile, the girls spoke of surveillance, of being watched, of needing to be 'perfect' and 'flawless' at all times, stepping outside of themselves to focus more on how they will be perceived and less on their own wants and desires. The male gaze is internalised as we try to procure this ideal feminine image in the digital world, and the real one.

Mulvey notes that in film, women as objects are created, framed, controlled and subsequently displayed, much as they are in static art forms and online. From the miniatures of Marie Antoinette's portrait that were circulated for mass consumption, judgement and mockery when she was just a teen to the intimate images shared today without consent, there is a violent history of capturing and owning women's bodies. This desire to possess the female body is made ever more possible with digital technology and social media. You can now hold thousands of images of Kylie Jenner, Marilyn Monroe or Botticelli's *Venus* in your hand and manipulate them at your will.

The idea that we have control over our own image now, with the rise of digital culture, is a fantasy. From the 'masters of the arts' who sculpted and painted women, and thus decided how beauty was crafted, to the media moguls who have dominated our press and its advertisements, to the majority male-run tech monopolies that rule today, we are still subjected to a wealthy white man's ideal. Whilst historically, women have been sculpted and painted into an image outside of their control, women's faces and bodies today are assessed and dissected by male surgeons and sold products by largely male-owned capitalist beauty conglomerates.

When our beauty standard is dependent on surgical intervention and 90 per cent of plastic surgeons are male with a 90 per cent female consumer base, the historical power of men to dictate ideal femininity is upheld. The Kardashian/Jenner plastic surgeon Dr Ourian has been dubbed 'the da Vinci of our time' with Kim Kardashian herself referring to him as 'the artiste'. Much like the ancient Greeks, Ourian grounds his theory in symmetry, as well as the Fibonacci sequence. Central to the makeover paradigm, these modern-day artists and sculptors become the authority that we deify and accept. Cosmetic procedures reflect the surgeon's style, not the patient's, with many stories circulating of doctors taking liberties with women's bodies – inserting larger breast implants, guiding patients towards a specific aesthetic, or adding more filler than agreed. The surgeon's overinvestment in his own aesthetic has been called the 'Pygmalion effect', derived from Roman poet Ovid's *Metamorphoses*, in which a sculptor falls in love with his own statue of Venus.

In one of Ourian's posts, he shows before and after pictures of a woman's jaw treatment. The caption describes the 'ideal Gonial (jawline) angle'. He goes on to explain: 'If the angle is too narrow, the face could look too masculine . . . For women I try to achieve 120–130°.' Femininity, as an ideal, is now so narrow that it must fit within a 10-degree range of acceptability, a few millimetres of eligibility. In order to practise 'good femininity', women must now also measure their jawline with a protractor, surveilling every angle of their face to ensure they adhere to the ideal.

*

In 2015, poet Rupi Kaur posted an image of herself on Instagram, her pose mimicking that of the *Rokeby Venus*. Fully clothed, lying on floral bedsheets, the artist is turned away from us, her hair in the same loose bun. Much like the *Rokeby Venus*, our attention is drawn to the curve of her hips at the centre of the image. Except, in Kaur's photograph, a dark spot of blood marks her tracksuit bottoms, the red stain mirrored on the sheets below. Unlike the *Rokeby Venus*, however, this artwork barely stood for twenty-four hours. It was removed by Instagram twice for breach of community guidelines.

In 2020, plus-size model Nyome Nicholas-Williams posted a portrait she'd had taken by female photographer Alex Cameron. The image showed Nyome, who is Black, sitting on a stool in front of floral wallpaper, wearing long black cycling shorts and holding her bare breasts with one arm. The image is soft and powerful; Nyome's head is shaved and her unapologetic gaze holds the viewer captive. It was removed from Instagram after only a few minutes. When photographer Alex posted the image to her own account, the same issue persisted, despite Alex (who is white and blonde) having posted similar semi-nude shoots of herself that had been allowed to stand for years.

In 2022, body positivity activist Joanna Kenny posted an image she'd taken to her account. A self-portrait, the photograph shows Joanna crouched forward with her stomach rolls relaxed and exposed, much like the *Lely Venus*. Posted with the goal of resisting the male gaze, Joanna shows herself intentionally from an 'unflattering' angle and demonstrates a refusal to pose seductively or suck her stomach in. Her post was removed instantly by Instagram's algorithm for displaying 'offensive' content.

Every era has its Rome and ours is Silicon Valley. Now, those who can dictate the ideals are building algorithms and digital platforms designed to host millions of images of beauty a day. The curators of old have simply been replaced by tech bros who decide who gets to be on display and who gets ostracised. Despite being lauded as a promised land for equality, digital culture subjects women's bodies to the patriarchal gaze as much as ever. But this tech wasn't built in a vacuum, nor was it built from a place of equality and unbiased views on bodies.

Our online spaces are both a reflection and a reinforcer of the issues that plague our physical world. The patriarchal gaze, sexism, misogyny, ableism and racism are alive and well, and our digital landscape is symptomatic of these existing structures. The tech industry is 75 per cent men and they're building platforms with their inherent biases built in. Although inadvertent, the result is a censorship of women's bodies, but notably bodies of women of colour, fat women and queer women, anyone who deviates from our narrow spectrum of beauty and the feminine ideal.

'It's a dictatorship,' Joanna tells me when we speak one afternoon. 'My images are censored when I'm just existing in my body as a bigger woman. I was always taught my body was for my husband. For me, this is about reclaiming the female form, to not be penalised for showing up as myself. I rebel out of pure exhaustion. I just couldn't live up to the ideal anymore and I knew I would break in a disastrous way if I didn't change how I viewed myself and the way I behaved. I like to feel pretty and it's okay if you want to feel it, but you don't owe it to family, friends, men or these platforms.'

Survey data released in 2020 by Salty, an online platform for women, trans and non-binary people, highlighted the fact that plus-size profiles, queer people and women of colour have been experiencing shadowbanning at a disproportionate rate to those within mainstream communities. They heard from businesses unable to advertise breast pumps for new mothers (whilst penis pumps were allowed), plus-size women unable to post in swimwear, charities unable to demonstrate a breast exam on a real body and body positive profiles flagged for inappropriate content.

Frequently framed as a democratising tool supporting the creation of a more equal world, our digital realm is currently suppressing communities who are most marginalised offline. When plus-size bodies and body positive profiles are flagged for being offensive or inappropriate, our ability to create a more diverse, human image of female beauty is hindered. Perhaps if we had seen more of those images growing up, we'd feel more accepting of our bodies as they are – without the need for manipulation, slicing and dieting. Very few of us subscribe to every gender stereotype assigned to us and we need those who are pushing the boundaries of the binary in order to create a more accepting space for all of us. There can be huge freedom in platforms that truly allow us to explore images of women, created by women, in all of their glory. Existing as we wish to exist without external forces. For now, however, that sense of freedom is at the whim of largely white, male tech companies. It seems that these tech monopolies are giving us the illusion of protection whilst continuing to replicate the structures that safeguard their interests.

'No one told me at eleven or twelve when I first started shaving that I actually had a choice,' says Joanna. 'No one said, "Oh, you don't actually have to do that if you don't want to." When I worked as a beauty therapist, women would constantly apologise for not shaving their legs, for not having makeup on, for not having freshly washed hair. The guilt attached to beauty and womanhood is so debilitating at times. Even when I was sexually assaulted, I didn't want to offend the man who attacked me. I'm trying to show women that there's another way to be but I'm having to dilute my content to stop it from being taken down.'

The total representation of women in big tech jobs decreased by 2.1 per cent between 2020 and 2022 and despite Meta's promises to achieve gender parity by 2023, only 37.1 per cent of their employees were women in June 2022, showing a 1 per cent increase since 2018. What we're left with is technology built by men, embedded in systems of oppression and the male gaze. Many of our largest social platforms were in fact created to feed a culture that objectifies and violates women and girls, originating from the very voyeuristic desire that has kept women captured within frames for centuries. Mark Zuckerberg notoriously built the original Facebook platform as a way to rank and rate women's bodies, posting photos of girls to denigrate and assess. Whilst at college in Stanford, Snapchat founder Evan Spiegel sent messages referring to women as 'bitches', 'sororisluts', to be 'peed on', and discussed getting girls drunk to have sex with them. Snapchat, his creation, is built on a model of disappearing photographs and messages, allowing men to comment on women's bodies and send unsolicited images without consequence or recorded proof. Both founders of Tinder, Sean Rad and Justin Mateen, have been involved in sexual harassment suits filed by Whitney Wolfe Herd, former VP of marketing at Tinder and now founder of feminist dating app Bumble. Mateen was accused of messaging Wolfe Herd, calling her a 'slut' and a 'whore'.

Whilst women only make up a quarter of the tech workforce (at best), 25 per cent of *all* internet search requests are related to pornography and a significant portion of the internet is devoted to the distribution of images of women. Images that are apparently only viable online if they adhere to a narrow beauty ideal, fit the fantasy of the male gaze or are part of an historical art canon created over centuries by privileged men. When women take control of their own image, they face retribution.

As Nyome points out, there are countless images of slim, white women wearing very little clothing posted to social platforms every day. The Kardashian-Jenners frequently pose semi-nude without facing any consequences. If anything, their sexuality and the exposure of their bodies only increases their success on the platform. In 2023, Kylie Jenner posed as Botticelli's *Venus* emerging from a pool. In a series of posts wearing a pink string bikini from her sister's brand Skims, the carousel of images shows Kylie arching her back as the camera crops in on her sculpted body, glistening and wet. The posts have over 12.5 million likes and almost 36,000 comments. 'If you are white, rich, and conventionally sexually attractive, it seems you can post as you wish and what you wish,' said Nyome in an open letter to Instagram. White men, it seems, have a free pass to post whatever they want, even if that involves harassment.

In what Foucault considers a paradox of contemporary culture, women are often rendered inaudible and invisible across power structures in culture, society, politics and now tech, whilst our bodies are hypervisible, over-exposed as material objects and commodifiable beings that can be used for pleasure and profit. Even the most attractive women in the world are belittled based on aesthetics, but to refuse to conform, or to fail to conform, is to risk total disappearance.

We're far from a postfeminist phase in which women truly have power and control over their bodies in digital spaces; we will never have true freedom as long as algorithms created by men continue to reward conforming bodies and censor those that are not.

Beauty, of course, can be subjective, but Beauty with a capital B – Beauty as power, as privilege, as capital – remains anything but. I was reminded of this during a conversation I had whilst writing for *Dazed* magazine with author and academic Chloé Cooper Jones, whose book on defining her place in the beauty conversation as a disabled woman deals with the ideas of objective and subjective beauty. 'People say things like "beauty is in the eye of the beholder", which I hate,' she told me. 'Why do we deflate this really important and weighty concept?'

To claim that beauty standards are something we can just think our way out of, that the hierarchy they create can be ushered aside with some positive thinking, is incredibly naive. To say that 'beauty is in the eye of the beholder' as a retort to the experiences of those on the edge of visibility is to deny the very real consequences and tangible structural inequality people face based on their appearance and proximity to the beauty ideal. In 2019, TikTok took measures to prevent visibly disabled creators from gaining widespread attention on the app due to concerns about bullying, essentially marginalising them based on how they look. Despite being designed to reduce online violence, it largely worked only to censor victims.

'While outwardly it may appear as though we have progressed forward with a widely accepted more liberal mindset when it comes to body image, self-love is little more than smoke and mirrors,' writes Ione Gamble in her book *Poor Little Sick Girls*.

> *Cloaked in the language of progressive politics but still peddling the same damaging ideologies, our attitudes to what is or is not beautiful have in fact become more conservative. A marginal amount of acceptance for diverse bodies has been incorporated into our everyday lives, but only as long as you adhere to the specific set of acceptable flaws outlined by the same authorities that taught us to resent ourselves in the first place.*

What we see online has huge implications for how we see gender and beauty in society, especially when we consider how much time is spent looking at images in the digital space. Women face a vicious cycle: the centuries-long focus on female appearance draws us to highly visual platforms that then encourage us to hyper-focus on our appearance in the name of content creation. Studies have shown that the more friends and followers a woman has online, the more pressure she feels to monitor her appearance and adhere to the beauty norm. The same is not true for men, who generally experience no increase in appearance-related pressure with online success.

'I'm worried that we're entering into a territory with social media, immaculate beauty routines and secrecy around cosmetic treatments, where we forget what we look like naturally. If you don't wake up looking perfect, it's as if there's something wrong with you,' says Joanna.

Without these highly prescriptive beauty standards, gender expression, self-acceptance and access to opportunity would be far easier for us all. This narrowing of our beauty ideal and the obsession with a binary approach to beauty has impacts for all women, regardless of gender presentation or gender assigned at birth. Our beauty ideals are so tied to our idea of binary gender – of an ideal man and an ideal woman – that gender-affirming surgeries are something we see across the board. Not all women have large, pert breasts or a perfectly round bum, and yet we see countless procedures undertaken by cis and trans women each year in order to feel more at home in their bodies. Dysphoria, body dysmorphia and identity struggles are only fuelled by a very rigid beauty ideal, prescribed in accordance with rigid gender roles.

There is a pressure for all women to attain the feminine ideal and that pressure is only amplified for trans women – to be taken seriously as a woman, to be called by the correct pronouns and to avoid the shame and humiliation that comes with public mockery. The benchmark for being perceived as a woman is already so high. Being trans, to much of the general public, is about the 'transition' – your worthiness is often gleaned from how well you manage to adhere to the beauty standard of the gender you are inside. How trans women are treated in the world is dictated by their proximity to the concept of femininity and, often, how well trans women 'pass' as feminine is directly correlated to their safety in public spaces.

'People don't come up to me and say, "Oh, you're a lovely person. I loved your book,"' says trans activist and author Charlie Craggs. 'They say, "Wow, I'd never guess you're trans. Oh, you look amazing."'

'You fuse these ideas in your head – being beautiful and attractive is tied to being worthy and socially desirable; if you're trans that also gets fused with passing,' agrees trans author Shon Faye. 'Passing is the idea that people wouldn't necessarily know you were trans. If you transition as an adult trans woman, it's unlikely you're going to move immediately to passing, so what starts to happen is you associate looking trans with looking bad, looking in any way androgynous is bad, but passing is beautiful and passing is safe. Beauty, passing and safety all become fused in your mind, and you start to move towards that as a goal. It's only in recent years that I've started to try to disentangle that nexus in my head.'

Including laser hair removal, facial feminisation surgery, a breast augmentation, a Brazilian Butt Lift (BBL), hairline-lowering surgeries and two hair transplants, Charlie has spent over £50,000 on her transition thus far. She tells me she almost feels 'complete' but admits it's difficult to know when to stop, especially as she's now so unfazed by the idea of going under the knife and has experienced the buzz that comes with waking up altered, more beautiful than before – 'You just think it's going to improve your quality of life, but when everyone else is raising the bar, you feel like you have to raise the bar even higher. I had my facial surgery quite early on and I remember seeing other trans girls having it done after mine and I felt like I almost had to have it done again. I remember being so jealous. When people raise the bar, this is what cis women, trans women, everyone else has to keep up with, that's what people expect, we expect, men expect from us as well.'

I wonder where the line is – when any of us will feel complete as women, when any of us will stop tearing ourselves apart, fragmenting ourselves into tiny pieces, and feel like we're enough. We now see ourselves not as passive objects of the male gaze but as actively engaged in our self-presentation strategies as freely choosing subjects. Our social media landscape is full of messages, posts and captions that preach a celebration of unique beauty, whilst reinforcing a homogeneous image and rewarding a narrow feminine ideal. We are expected to be both Venus and her voyeur, and we're supposed to enjoy the voyeurism of our bodies. In our culture of individualism, this is painted as a direct result of individual choices and desire rather than the fault of wider structural powers.

'Saying you can be emancipated through beauty culture is almost like saying it feels good to take a corset off,' Shon tells me. 'Yes, it feels good but it feels good because you've been constrained. What we're trying to do is find a liveable, breathable way to exist in a system that is constraining us. We can't punish someone for feeling good when they take the corset off because they weren't responsible for putting it on in the first place, they didn't create the culture they exist in. At the same time, I think it's very dangerous to say that all cosmetic modification of the body is an inherently positive and desirable thing because the conditions they were created in then go unexamined.'

During Charlie's transition, she would stick before and after pictures of other well-known trans women into a book, to keep as a reminder not to keep comparing herself to the perfect pictures she was seeing online. It's something she describes as necessary to keep her sane during her surgeries. She also confesses to me that even now, despite feeling 'complete' in her womanhood, she has many trans women, and many of her cis female friends, muted on Instagram for fear of spiralling into self-comparison.

'They're my friends, but it makes me feel absolutely shit seeing how good they look. I'm jealous. I'm just gonna be real. I wish I looked like that and I could, if I pay for loads more surgery. I've chosen the body that's housing my soul over a house that would be increasing in value. It's just not healthy for me to be following people and seeing those images when I know it'll make me feel worse.'

Charlie tells me that she loves beauty culture, that makeup saved her life in the early years of her transition and that surgery has given her a reason to live now. But she also tells me that she doesn't feel beautiful; despite the £50,000 of investment, she is still insecure.

'I paid to look this way so I know it isn't bad, but, at the same time, I'm so insecure of my skin, my weight, my pores, my acne scarring, my lips, my wrinkles. I'm always comparing myself to other women (cis and trans) online. It really is the thief of joy.'

'Failing' at femininity isn't just an experience of trans women but any woman who deviates from the archetypal ideal.

'I know there are trans women who will say, "I'd still need my FFS [facial feminisation surgery] or my hormones even if we lived in a society without any transphobia or misogyny," and I believe they emphatically mean that, but we don't know,' Shon tells me. 'I have no idea what it would be like to not have to live with a degree of hypervigilance. I don't know what it's like to not exist under a patriarchal gaze, to not be targeted for being visibly different. No woman does – cis or trans.'

Despite our increase in autonomy, awareness of the patriarchy and access to the public sphere, we are yet to produce a powerful enough rejection of the feminine beauty ideal. Whilst we understand how harmful these ideals are, it is incredibly difficult to push back on the norm and deviate from desirability. Whilst some are trying and facing ostracisation, it will require all of us, working together, especially those of us with privilege, to support those who are rendered invisible on such platforms. The best form of resistance is unrelenting conviction and commitment to rejecting the conditions that contain us. As clichéd as it may sound, our differences are our strengths, and embracing marginalised genders and communities in their expression helps us to disband the binary ideals of beauty to which we are all held.

*

In March 1914, not long after 10am, Mary Richardson entered the sandstone building of the National Portrait Gallery, slipped up the shallow stairs flanked with gold and marble, and began slashing at the *Rokeby Venus* with a meat cleaver. She cut the canvas body five times, from the nape of the neck to the curve of the hips. Gaping wounds in painted flesh. Mary, a suffragette, attacked the picture to protest the arrest of leading feminist activist Emmeline Pankhurst.

'I have tried to destroy the picture of the most beautiful woman in mythological history as a protest against the government destroying Mrs Pankhurst, who is the most beautiful character in modern history. Justice is an element of beauty as much as colour and outline on canvas,' she said at the time. Years later, she clarified that it wasn't the painting's value that had made it a target but the way 'men visitors to the gallery gaped at it all day'.

How can we create a more beautiful future for women and girls?

'A beautiful future for women begins when we start teaching our girls not to care what men think of them.'

Allie Rowbottom,
author of *Aesthetica*

3

Algorithms of Desire

There was a time when our bedrooms were our sacred spaces, the shrines of our evolving selves. Girlhood was an in-between state and this was our incubator. Beneath a canopy of glow-in-the-dark stars lay lotions and potions and bottles of glitter left to congeal; nightstands and dressers decorated with pastel eyeshadows; satin ribbons and music boxes; walls pocked with tack marks and peeled posters; mirrors splattered with spray and spit and serum; tables sticky and our beds musky with sweat and bloodied sheets. There were dishes filled with trinkets, tiny precious things, all sparkling under a thin layer of dust, the air saturated with the sweet, synthetic smell of plastic. Before Pinterest boards and Tumblr feeds and saved folders, we had our bedroom walls, an ever-evolving glimpse into our inner worlds. If girlhood was a period of 'acting something out', then this was simultaneously our studio and our sanctity, a space of safety and self-expression, of curation and contemplation for our hatching hearts. We smeared lilac eyeshadow over our lids, dragged mascara over our cheeks, drew lipstick outside of the lines and whispered to ourselves that we might actually be quite beautiful. It was here that we became ourselves, allowed ourselves, gave ourselves permission – safe from the eyes of others. A room of one's own, to hold our daydreams and nightmares, dark and light, and all that we were.

We invited each other into our spaces when parents would allow – girls only in these altars of beauty. We were christened into girlhood not by holy water or the consumption of Christ's body and blood but with these rituals – painting each other's faces, playing with each other's hair, making each other over, doing our worst because we were allowed and laughing until we lost all control of our limbs, collapsing in a heavy pile of happy tears. There was an intimacy that was so pure, as deep as if we were real sisters. Our lips frosted with sugar, giggling under duvets, talking about kisses and crushes and trying our hardest not to fall asleep – fighting to keep the night alive.

That was a time when public and private were two distinct things, two different realms, before contexts collapsed and our spaces were invaded. Now, guided by the algorithm, we learnt a new gospel. Now, there was nowhere you could hide.

We had been taking it in turns to pose in the grainy square of the webcam photobooth, playing with the distorting filters and pulling silly faces to make each other laugh, before someone had suggested playing on Omegle or Chatroulette – sites that would allow you to talk to anybody, anywhere in the world, video cameras on, entirely at random. We sat there in a huddle on the carpeted floor in front of a laptop and giggled as people would chat to us, screaming with thrill and horror each time we refreshed the page to see trousers around ankles, a man's hand jerking rhythmically at our faces, aghast and enthralled. The first time I saw a penis in a sexualised context was in one of these chatrooms – at a sleepover one night at the age of thirteen. I couldn't tell you how many videos and pictures of penises I saw before I turned sixteen. I didn't ask to see them. I didn't want to see them, but once I saw one they were everywhere – waiting in the screens ready to pop out at me at any point.

The idea that an older man would masturbate to strangers online in a chatroom full of teenagers felt like a fun prank, in much the same way that '2 Girls 1 Cup' became standard viewing at parties or in the playground, and most girls in my year had received a dick pic by the time they were legally able to consent. Porn was everywhere, penises were everywhere, men and their desire for us was explicit and omnipresent. Girls have told me about jokes they would make amongst their friends as young teenage girls as to how many men would send dick pics to their open Snapchat messages in one night. Sometimes the numbers would be in the double digits.

It was a morbid fascination that quickly felt violent. We had felt a semblance of safety in numbers – in groups at sleepovers being salacious and silly felt worlds apart from the discomfort that started to burrow itself into our skin, down to the pit of our stomach, once we were alone. Every girl knows the feeling of wanting to be seen so badly and then wanting to shower off the gaze. Every girl knows the feeling of being looked up and down, dissected with his eyes. Every girl knows the feeling of getting everything you've been taught to desire, only to realise it is everything you dread.

*

It was instilled in us from a young age that we were to be sexual objects, decorative fantasies that exist to please men. To make them happy and horny was our power. We were algorithms of desire – forbidden flesh to be captured and consumed – and that felt totally normal, encouraged and competitive even. At sleepovers, sexy photoshoots soon became the norm. I was obsessed with music videos, glued to clips of countless fully clothed men surrounded by half-naked women. I knew all the words to Britney's 'Born to Make You Happy' and I knew the dance routine to 'Dirrty'. I was annoyed that my mum never let me wear tight clothes to school like all the popular girls did. I begged her to let me wear a slutty Halloween costume year after year – and when she finally relented when

I was sixteen, I went as a maid. She's sexy *and* domesticated – the dream!

'Women and girls are socialised to believe that the most important thing about themselves is how they look and their sexual appeal,' says psychologist Dr Sophia Choukas-Bradley. 'For girls, how they look is the number one predictor of how popular they are. We live in a culture that says the most important thing teen girls and young women can be is sexy.'

We traded on the currency of popularity, the longing to showcase our desirability like a desperate thirst. I didn't have the language for it at the time but I knew what it felt like to be desired and then discarded, to be a possession prized for nothing other than what I looked like, to not be listened to, to not be taken seriously, to feel reduced to my body, to feel eviscerated of any sense of self, to be told to smile more, to stay pretty and quiet and small. What I was feeling was coined in 1997 by academics Barbara Fredrickson and Tomi-Ann Roberts as 'objectification theory', which describes the treatment and perception of women as mere objects. When women are objectified they are treated as instruments for the use and pleasure of others, they are deprived of their personhood and considered as mindless entities, unable to experience human mental states.

Later, in 2009, self-objectification theory was developed during the nascent years of social media. When we are exposed, as we have been, to sexually objectifying messages and portrayals of women, we are socialised into adopting an external view of our bodies and begin to perceive ourselves merely as objects designed to satisfy the male gaze. It often manifests in giving more attention to our physical appearance rather than to ourselves as a whole person, fixating on an observer's perspective of our bodies and learning to treat ourselves as objects to be looked at and evaluated for their appearance alone. When we self-objectify in a culture that rewards the objectification of women there are status gains that can be cashed in on, but there are also psychic, cognitive, emotional, physical and economic costs to be paid. As a body project, it can drain us of a significant amount of time and energy. What follows is often a long-term degradation of self, diminishing our presence and quieting our voice. The prophecy becomes self-fulfilling – as a result of being treated like objects, we quite literally reduce ourselves in order to be desirable.

When I was a little older, I started dating a boy I met in university. On a walk around south London one afternoon, he turned to me and asked: 'If you were in a movie, what character would you play?' I didn't need to think it over because it was something I had considered before. I'd imagined myself on the screen countless times, romanticised my life through every possible lens. I didn't hesitate when I told him that I would be the love interest. The sexy, seductive girl with a mysterious edge who moves like liquid gold and blinds men with her beauty. The woman the protagonist spends his two-hour onscreen lifespan trying to demystify and decode, until he eventually falls unequivocally in love with her. I was confident in my answer. In my desire to be desired. But he looked at me confused.

'You wouldn't even be the main character in your own movie?'

I was floored. Even in my wildest fantasies, I was a fantasy. An attainable object. A submissive and predictable ideal. An archetype in a story that happens to someone else. In trying to shave and slice and submit every aspect of myself for a story boys had grown up expecting, I had no idea who this film was really for.

'Positive sexuality is very different from sexualisation and self-sexualisation in a beauty-sick culture,' says Dr Choukas-

Bradley. 'What we see when adolescent girls feel empowered by displaying themselves in sexualised ways online is a perfectly understandable response to a culture that objectifies and sexualises young girls and rewards them for that behaviour.'

And there are rewards – especially online.

The mid-2010s saw the rise of the naked selfie as a form of feminist protest, with a 2016 *Vogue Australia* article declaring: 'Naked selfies are the new feminism.' The piece details how celebrities from Emily Ratajkowski to Kim Kardashian have posted sexy body shots unashamedly as a form of empowerment. In an interview with *Women's Wear Daily*, Emily said: 'My response to people saying I post oversexualised images is that it's my choice and there's an ownership and empowerment through them. When I take nude photographs, I'm not there for the boys. It's about owning my sexuality and celebrating it.'

After her viral nude selfie-gate, in which she posed naked in front of a mirror and edited thin black bars to cover her nipples and crotch, Kim Kardashian penned an essay on her sexuality: 'I am empowered by my body. I am empowered by my sexuality . . . And I hope that through this platform I have been given, I can encourage the same empowerment for girls and women all over the world . . . I will not live my life dictated by the issues you have with my sexuality. You be you and let me be me. I am a mother. I am a wife, a sister, a daughter, an entrepreneur and I am allowed to be sexy.'

What Kim and Emily were protesting was a digital extension of the virgin/whore dichotomy – a term coined by psychologist Sigmund Freud in the early 1900s that describes a phenomenon in which men cast women into one of two categories: the virgin, women he admires and respects, and the whore, women he is attracted to and therefore disrespects. To resist either stereotype, we must toe the line of the in-between, concocting the right balance of desire and desirability, of virgin and whore – to perfect this performance of womanhood is to gain respect in a patriarchal world.

It comes in many forms: a message from a man on a dating app that reads 'I can't tell if you're innocent or an absolute baddie'; being the 'good girl'; castigation for being either a diva or a doormat; feeling a need to choose between a state of docility and domesticity or being smart and strong; needing to be sexy but not too sexy, smart but not too smart, beautiful whilst simultaneously unaware that you are. We see it manifest online in men's obsession with making podcasts to discuss 'acceptable body counts', the horrified response to women making money from their sexuality and discussions around what behaviour makes a woman 'wifey material'. As Melissa Febos writes in *Girlhood*, 'sex is a moral duty but to enjoy too much sex is a crime'. It is yet another paradox of womanhood – yet another fine line we were expected to walk. As a strategy, it transcends race and class, its nuances ensuring that every woman from every background finds herself marked as one of the two in different contexts, the subtle distinctions controlled only by the beneficiaries: men. Febos continues: 'This way you can punish her for anything. You can make her humanity monstrous. Now you can do anything you want to her.'

Some marginalised groups are often assigned default status – hypersexualised or desexualised because of their bodies and relation to the beauty standard. Trans and Black women are often instantly fetishised and placed in category 'whore' in opposition to white cis women, whilst disabled women are stripped of all sexuality. Both can lead to an increase in violence or dehumanisation.

With many of these sites of struggle, it can feel like we cannot win. That we're walking a tightrope with eternal damnation at either side. We are both empowered and powerless, oppressed and oppressors. We are given so many shaming antisexual messages whilst simultaneously being valued for our youth, attractiveness and overall sexual prestige by society. Why can't we be both respected and desired? Sexual and safe?

What we wanted was to resist this flattening, to resist the reduction that objectification brought. To be 'allowed' our sexuality, to 'own' it, to take it back. Both Kim and Emily's success had been catalysed by their sexuality, but now they were asking to be valued for more than that – to be sexy, yes, and to do so on their own terms, without shame or scandal. The message became pervasive. That by taking a sexy nude selfie, women were reclaiming their sexuality from the male gaze. The main point of contention was that the majority of the images came from women who very much met the requirements of the beauty standard – who fit the desirable archetype of femininity that the male gaze rewarded, and who spent huge amounts of time, money and energy to construct their physical appearance as such. The word 'empowered' was everywhere once more and it started to lose all meaning as it was co-opted and sold to those who needed it least. The celebrities who profited from 'empowering' naked selfies were actually already in possession of a great deal of power – including pretty privilege.

Sociologist Ben Agger described sexy selfies as 'the male gaze gone viral'. For me, posting this kind of imagery became a loophole, a way for me to receive validation, to feel better about my body and to gain social status, all under the guise of pseudo social justice. The reality was that I experienced a short-term thrill from posting and receiving instant positive feedback, but (I imagine) my followers instantly felt worse about themselves. I had shaved, tanned and moisturised my body until completely smooth; I had put on my most flattering bikini and lay in the most flattering position; I had sucked in my stomach and pushed out my hips; I had contorted myself into a pose I couldn't maintain for more than a minute without pain. I then selected one image from hundreds I had taken, perfected the angle, cropped out my face, added a filter and posted with a caption about self-love. Really, I only wanted to feel good about myself, and for the guy I was talking to to text me back and fall in love with me. Men would send the image to me to tell me how much they wanted me, but I soon realised none of them cared about my work, my writing, my degree or my hobbies. They didn't care about my face, or my smile, or the colour of my eyes. The image is now archived on my feed but it remains one of the most liked images I've ever posted. When I started dating again, it took everything in me not to pin it to the top of my profile.

*

Emma Breschi and I sit with our hands laced around warm lemon and ginger tea in her east London bedroom, her French bulldog LeBron sprawled out on the floor by the bed, our feet tucked under our knees as we nestle in. Emma's bedroom reflects her vivacity – it's sensorial and evocative, with patterned sheets, portraits and incense sticks filling the room with comfort and charm.

Emma broke onto the modelling scene in 2017 as a muse for Vivienne Westwood and soon found herself sought after by some of the world's biggest brands. Considered 'plus size', Emma made waves in the industry as a disruptor. I had come over to talk about body image and beauty standards, but our conversation quickly takes another turn. In the safety of her bedroom, Emma begins to tell me about her relationship to her body via sex.

'There's so much shame wrapped up in beauty,' she tells me. 'And so much shame wrapped up in sex. From the age of twelve, I was sexualised for having boobs. I wasn't allowed to wear certain clothes because I developed so much earlier than my peers. I was totally isolated because other women resented me; I was called a slut just because of my body and how it was developing, so when I ended up getting raped at thirteen by an older boy, I couldn't talk about it for so long. I thought it was my fault because I thought I had chosen him, I had agreed to date him. I didn't date or have sex again until I was nineteen. It's funny how at thirteen I was being called the slut and then at nineteen I was being called the nun. I didn't start masturbating until I was twenty-three and even to this day I can't orgasm. When I have sex, I think my body goes into survival mode because I had to as a teenager for so long. I was put in situations where I just gave myself to this older boy and let him do what he wanted because I thought that was love. He had chosen me, made me feel beautiful, and so I became what he wanted me to be – this submissive girl. My idea of love or sex or intimacy became this Stockholm syndrome.'

One of the rarely discussed responses to sexual trauma is hypersexuality, which often comes from internalising the sexual objectification thrust upon you and can have a huge impact on self-worth. According to an investigation by UN Women, 97 per cent of women in the UK have been sexually harassed. Globally, one in three women have experienced violence and/or sexual violence. In this way, male aggression fuels sexualisation in girls and misogyny then denigrates that sexuality. We are traumatised by men and then punished by a patriarchal society for our response.

'Modelling really helped me feel like I was taking back my power. I know a lot of people think that posing nude is such a narcissistic thing, or you just want attention, or you are thirst trapping or whatever, but for me, it was a very liberating form of self-expression, a way of taking back that sexuality that was taken from me at such a young age,' Emma says, pausing to take a sip of her tea. 'If you read interviews from when I first started modelling, I am like, "Yeah, I don't give a fuck, I will be naked." Because that's how I felt at the time. Sex isn't for women. And there was a time when I thought being super "sexy" of my own choice was the solution. But it's so nuanced because I don't really feel like getting naked anymore. It's deeper now. I want to orgasm now. I don't want to get naked and show you that I can be sexy. I want to find pleasure and reconnect with myself and my desires.'

Wanting to appear sexy and desirable is not an inherently oppressive or patriarchal imperative. Misogyny isn't about the amount of clothes you wear or your adherence to the beauty standard, it's about the impact that adhering to these expectations has on your quality of life. If being seen wearing a bikini or lingerie is one of the only ways you feel you can gain social status, economic power or likes online, that is just as problematic as it would be if covering your body from head to toe were the only way to attain respect and status. If we feel our physical appearance or sexuality is the primary, or only, currency we can trade in, that is where the problem lies.

'Being sexualised at such a young age, I ended up resigning myself to the fact that maybe this is just something I have to accept, maybe this is my only power,' Emma tells me. 'My followers are dropping now that I'm not posting nude content anymore, but I would rather have a smaller audience who follow me because I am posting things that are true to me. If you just want me to get naked all the time, then, I am sorry, there's more to me than that. Why should I feel the need to keep posting nudes or sexy pictures because it will appease the algorithm?'

*

'I am empowered by my body . . . I hope that through this platform I have been given, I can encourage the same empowerment for girls and women all over the world.' For Kim to write this whilst actively constructing her image into the ideal with countless painful and expensive procedures feels like a Pyrrhic victory.

Visibility is important and it's something we stress for minority groups – to be seen and heard, to be given a platform and a voice, is critical for true discussions and understanding of self-hood, identity and experience. In taking a selfie, we have the opportunity for reclamation – without a male photographer, lens or director dictating how we present – and yet here I am, showing you life through my lens, and I have chosen to replicate the very forces imposed on me, the very stereotypes that harm me. This is because the taking and publishing of the material is not without context. We post pictures consistent with conformist beauty standards to avoid being marginalised in spaces created by men and ruled by an inherently sexist algorithm. These are platforms that reward a specific type of acceptable sexuality and that convert those adherences into a tangible currency both online and off.

In an article for the *Independent*, journalist Victoria Smith wrote:

> *There have been carrots as well as sticks driving every manifestation of female oppression . . . there's always been something to sweeten the pill, enabling oppressors to repackage submission as choice. This is not proof of the absence of gender inequality; it's a demonstration of how it functions . . . Just because women get something out of a given situation does not mean that situation represents the way relations between men and women should be.*

I may be demanding that my sexuality be seen alongside my intelligence, kindness and humanity – but ultimately, these platforms flatten us into two-dimensional images. They reward us for the former and often dismiss the latter. Our digital world, much like the virgin/whore dichotomy of old, requires us to be reduced. Me demanding that my sexuality be seen is of little political value when I adhere so closely to the ideal – as Kim and Emily do. Not that I am comparable, but my point still stands. The same opportunities are not as liberating for other women; the intersecting gazes of colonialism, capitalism and misogyny cannot be simply ushered aside in favour of pseudo-celebratory empowerment discourses.

It is not surprising that in adhering to a sexy archetype you might feel sexier, that in wearing heels or shaving your legs you would feel more desirable. That is what we have been taught our whole lives, a message internalised since before we started school.

As much as we can claim these images are 'for us', they are posted to public platforms with an audience. They are, to some degree, a wider performance. A 2013 study found that when women were asked to make an online profile for an audience (versus no audience), they were more likely to self-objectify and self-sexualise. The more we anticipate feedback on our appearance, the more we adhere to beauty ideals from the male gaze. In our own private worlds, in our sacred safe spaces, we view ourselves as fully human, we allow ourselves more freedom in our expression. As soon as we know people are watching, we are flattened, reduced.

Not only is our digital realm censoring bodies that don't adhere to the binary ideal, it's also intensifying existing gender stereotypes and the sexualisation of young women. Studies have shown that selfies posted to Instagram reflect traditional gender roles and are even more gender stereotypical than magazine adverts. With pornographic images almost impossible to avoid online, as well as celebrities regularly posting semi-nude and posing seductively, women and girls post on social media to mimic the poses desired by the male gaze, with pouty lips, eyes wide, often looking up with their breasts and/or bum exposed. In almost every interview I did with women about their social media profiles, they knew that being 'sexier' online would result in more engagement – more likes, comments and followers. The platforms reward female sexuality but only in very specific ways – ways that reinforce our rigid feminine ideal and adhere to the beauty standard.

The more we are validated and rewarded for doing so, the more likely we are to keep posting, eventually becoming desensitised to the level of sexuality we're portraying as it becomes increasingly normalised. These media archetypes then become the prototype for femininity to which young women and girls are encouraged to emulate and aspire to – content that emphasises 'sexy' as critical to self-worth.

Charities I worked with told me about girls in primary school posting images of themselves in lingerie. Psychologists told me of parents expressing concern for their young daughters asking for vibrators – not for their own pleasure and self-exploration, but because a boy was asking for content. Friends came to me for advice when thirteen-year-old family members were found to be sending nudes to boys in their school. Social media, of course, didn't create sexualisation or objectification, but it has 'amplified age-old pressures for teenage girls to conform to certain sexualised narratives', according to a study published by the *American Journal of Psychiatry*.

In 2015, we celebrated when Page 3, criticised as an overly accessible form of objectification, in which nude women were placed next to stories of male world leaders discussing the big issues of the day, was removed from the *Sun*. Only a few years later, it seems as if we've reintroduced the concept via our digital feeds, on an even more prolific scale. Online, you can scroll for an hour and see a cute cat video, outfit inspiration, soft porn and extreme violence – usually directed at women. The flattening of our social realm means all facets of our lives previously separated and contained are collapsed into one profile that has to contain every aspect of ourselves and show it to the world. Not only that, but this sexualised content is readily available for young people of all ages to discover.

The genius of the virgin/whore dichotomy is that any attempt to question sexualisation makes you automatically prudish, naive and/or deeply unsexy, whilst any display of sexuality can be used to undermine our autonomy. Are we succumbing and submitting to the male gaze? Or creating this content for ourselves?

*

As I entered my twenties, the women I had followed from Tumblr to Blogspot to YouTube to Instagram added a new platform to their roster: OnlyFans, a popular site used by sex workers to sell their content to subscribers. We had grown up learning how to turn ourselves into digital products; what began as a hobby soon became monetisable, the transactional nature of creating content for an audience ever more explicit. Our bedrooms had become our sets, for an audience both imagined and, increasingly, actual. We curated backgrounds and broadcast from the inner sanctum, inviting the world in.

It's not a coincidence that the desire for DIY porn has risen alongside social media. In 2019, 'amateur' topped Pornhub's list of most-searched terms and in 2022 searches for 'real amateur homemade' grew by 310 per cent in the United States and 179 per cent worldwide. Over the past few years, we've seen a rise in platforms merging social media with the porn industry. OnlyFans had 60,000 creators in 2019. Now it has over 2 million.

Founded by Essex businessman Tim Stokely in 2016, OnlyFans differs from traditional webcamming sites in its mainstream adoption by those who have never engaged in sex work before. The site doesn't have its own algorithm promoting new creators, so those who start on the site need to tease their content on other channels in order to drive traffic to their page – adding another dimension to our already overflowing profiles. The result has been a huge increase in the number of sexualised images on platforms like Instagram, Snapchat, Facebook and Twitter, as new sex workers use their existing accounts to promote their OnlyFans content.

On OnlyFans, followers can see one of the only sides of their favourite influencers they haven't yet seen. It felt like a final frontier in content creation, a natural step when everything else about yourself was already for sale. One influencer I had followed for a decade, Naomi, made the move in 2021, posting semi-nude on her main feed but getting 'freakier' in private DMs with paying fans. In the pictures, she appears as a fantasy creature in cosplay-inspired lingerie, elven ears and an array of wigs – long silver tendrils, pink bunches and a bleached bob. In all images her body is hairless, tanned and smooth. In many, she is arching her back on all fours, submissive as she exaggerates her curves, looking doe-eyed up to the camera. An example caption on her posts reads, 'You have been so desperate to see my pussy, I wanted to spoil you all with this sexy vid!'

In a screenshot posted to her Instagram stories, Naomi shows one of her followers questioning her decision as a self-proclaimed feminist to start selling pornographic content. The user writes, 'Do you not realise that posting nudes and making an OnlyFans is literally ENCOURAGING the objectification of women. You're actually just making the problem worse. How can you complain about being objectified and then objectify yourself?'

Naomi emblazons the post with the caption 'This is a joke' before responding: 'Women are seen through the male gaze whether we like it or not. I've decided to cash my cheques and get compensation in a safe environment. Men want us to be sexy but only when it's on their terms. By capitalising on their desire, we take back the narrative and harness a potent source of power that defies patriarchal control.'

As I watched this interaction play out, it felt hard to agree with either side. Is this a source of power? Is it really safe? Can sexy ever truly be on our terms? Is this what it means to escape control?

The pandemic led to record levels of lay-offs and heightened job instability, with unemployment disproportionately affecting women. A Pew Research Center study conducted in January 2021 found that two-thirds of unemployed adults had 'seriously considered' changing their careers to something potentially better-paying. The rise in unemployment directly paralleled a loss of IRL intimacy. The creator economy and the emerging accessibility of digital sex work were ready and waiting to sell them a dream. Sex work, for many, became a side hustle with the promise of huge success.

That's exactly how Rebecca started on OnlyFans.

'I was single for the first time in my adult life and I sent a lot of images and videos to men on dating apps, as you can imagine,' she tells me, sitting on the floor in her bedroom, surrounded by dreamcatchers and vases of dried flowers.

'My ex had an affair. So, for me, messaging these men and getting all this attention back made me feel good about myself. I know it's not a very healthy relationship to have, needing that validation from somebody else, but in the end, they would never be satisfied. I'd send one thing and they'd always push for something more. It got really intense and I started to wonder why I was creating and sending all of this content for free – men should be paying for this! You'd hear so many good stories about how people were making so much money, it felt like I had an opportunity to change my life. I thought it would be a really big thing.'

I told Rebecca that I could relate. To this day, there are photographs and videos of me on men's phones that I will never be able to trace, remove or retrieve. I only have my blind faith in their morality that these images will not be shared or shown to anyone else, or that they were deleted the moment we stopped having contact. I doubt they have been. That's not to say I regret sending them – I felt good about my body and I was acting on the emotions I had at the time – but what frustrates me is the power imbalance they create. Most of the time, the content sharing was not reciprocated and these men now possess parts of me in a way that I do not possess them. It is the lack of control that concerns me – that I may forever be a pocket porn star used eternally against my will.

In their digital form, our bodies became something else: content. The transference of our corporeal selves to pixelated equivalents feels like a new, more intense form of objectification. We are no longer mere 3D objects but 2D images. These versions of our bodies could be passed around without consent, viewed, used and shared eternally. We consent once and circulate forever – real unreal things, no longer in control of our own image. Other women told me that as they got sexually harassed at work anyway, or they risked being sexualised on their commute, on a night out or online, they might as well make some money and feel in control of what was happening to their bodies, digital and physical.

When sexy photos online get more comments and likes, when being sexy and submissive and constructing your body for the male gaze results in more status, when we're rewarded the more of ourselves we reveal, the internet makes sex workers of all of us, just to varying degrees. We're all competing in the market of sex and you're already for sale. Whether it's your face, your body, your outfits, your thoughts, your interactions, your relationships with others, your photo albums, your most intimate moments, your attention – it's all being monetised by tech companies with little to no regard for your humanity.

From e-girlfriends to cam girls, sharing nudes or creating personalised porn, girls all over the internet are seeing if they can make money from the very thing they'd been told their bodies were for – being sexually desirable to men. Hundreds of videos have circulated online of women speaking about joining sex work sites and making thousands of dollars in the first week. Digital sex work was lauded as a miracle solution to our modern-day money problems whilst simultaneously offering a shortcut to social media success and the destigmatisation of sex work.

But it's not as easy as it appeared. One data scientist estimated that the median OnlyFans creator makes $180 per month, with the top 10 per cent of active OnlyFans accounts making 73 percent of all the money on the site. For those who are unsuccessful on OnlyFans, publicly engaging in sex work can still have serious consequences. As the *Guardian* reports, it has been known to affect job prospects in non-sex work industries, can affect court decisions in child custody cases and, in extreme cases, has resulted in housing discrimination. Engaging in online sex work also comes with risks, including the potential for revenge porn, the unauthorised release of intimate images, blackmail, harassment, and stalking. Whilst all women face these dangers online, sex workers are particularly vulnerable.

'You have to make $20 before you can withdraw any funds and I made $17,' Rebecca told me. 'It's not even close to minimum wage and you have to put so much effort into it. You have to be vulnerable, you have to be on it constantly and just be willing to put everything out there. I felt like I had to say yes to everything but that's not me. I felt so much pressure to provide more and more extreme content for them, and not disappoint. With video content, it's much harder to edit what you look like and I just felt so much pressure to look a certain way that it made me uncomfortable.'

The wage gap between white sex workers and sex workers of colour persists online, mirroring the inequalities present in the offline world. Actress and sex worker Erika Heidewald has explained how Black sex workers are discriminated against by social media algorithms that often reward white people and light-skinned people. 'There's just a discriminatory stereotype of how much different sex workers can charge based on their looks,' she told Okayplayer in 2020. 'If you're Black it can be harder to fight for the higher prices that you deserve.'

More people turn to sex work in times of economic instability – often out of force and necessity. If your income depends on sex work and your appearance then you aren't going to take any risk in deviating from the fantasies and fetishes established by beauty standards. The same goes for posting sexualised images online. When your body is a commodity from which you need to profit, you are going to create the most reliable source of income – which means adhering to the patriarchal norm of a hairless, poreless, submissive being at the mercy of her masters.

'Editing apps are amazing at transforming you from one thing to something completely different,' says Rebecca. 'I always shave everything before creating content. I would do my makeup, false eyelashes, and my hair. I would use a filter to make my lips look a bit more plump, smooth the skin on my body and erase my stretch marks. They want to pay for a polished product, and you see the other girls do it and they look like models – all tanned and toned with perfect teeth and filler and all that stuff. I did start thinking that if I was going to do videos, I would want to lose some weight. And it is because you are looking at yourself so much more, and then looking at an edited version of yourself. It is tempting to get work done, I've thought about it a lot.'

Whilst the creator economy has boomed, the money and opportunities it has created are disproportionately given to those who embody the beauty standard. Algorithms built with the inherent bias towards slim, white women who adhere to the ideal make it much easier for those who fit these standards to monetise their bodies. In recent years, we've seen an intensification of focus on sculpting the female form to an ever-narrower sexual expectation – from the recent trend of big lips to the worrying rise of labiaplasty among women.

In reality, 'hotness' by the beauty standard's definition is not the only, or even a primary, marker of sexual desirability. Biologically and psychologically, our sex drive is an innate, animal instinct that makes us desire a wide range of bodies in a wide range of circumstances. All bodies, by nature, are desirable and good. Beauty does not equal attraction and sexual desirability does not equal 'hot'. Meeting the beauty standard of any given period should not correlate to more joyful sex – all bodies hold sexual desirability and all deserve to be sexual beings, giving and receiving pleasure as they wish. The conflation of physical appearance and sexuality is detrimental to women on individual, interpersonal and systemic levels, and it ultimately sustains gender-based oppression.

We grew up with porn – with men masturbating over us on chat sites, with padded bras and sexy music videos – our sexual awakening aligning exactly with access to more sexual content than any human has ever seen. This porn was never meant to replicate reality but the male fantasy it projected seeped into our real lives. To be desirable, to have sex, we thought, meant to submit – to want rough, often degrading sex and to make loud, obnoxious noises, despite the fact that we often felt no pleasure at all. Porn wasn't created with women's pleasure in mind and, thus, neither was our sexual experience. Porn seeped into mainstream culture, and the lines blurred between fantasy and reality, between acting and agency, between desirability and what we actually desire.

I would love to be able to view the sexualised selfies I and other women are posting as evidence of a new sexual age, in which women's agency and pleasure are foregrounded, or even considered an equal priority in a heterosexual encounter. However, the research would suggest otherwise. Posting self-sexualising photos is not associated with actual sexual agency in offline encounters. The rise in the sexualisation of young girls hasn't correlated to an increase in sexual pleasure and agency in the same group. The orgasm gap still proliferates. The objectification and denigration of women's bodies is still rife. Young men and boys still feel entitled to nudes, as well as physical access to women's bodies and sexual pleasure. For most, sex still ends when the man finishes, with little regard to the woman's experience.

John Berger wrote that there's a difference between being naked and being nude – when you post a sexy selfie, you're nude, gaining status. When you engage in sexual relations with a partner, you're naked. The two experiences live in different domains. Sex should be fun – an exploration of bodies between partners that is pleasurable for everyone involved. You should feel prioritised, you should feel like you matter and that your pleasure matters. You should, above all, feel comfortable and safe.

Having a high level of body confidence is directly correlated to feeling entitled to sexual pleasure and, therefore, greater sexual satisfaction and safety. Our bodies are exposed and vulnerable during sex, and so the way we feel about ourselves has a huge impact on sexuality. Instead of focusing on how we look in the eyes of our partner, and how our partner is thinking during sexual activity, women with higher body confidence are able to focus on their own pleasure. That we break free of expectations and raise young women and girls to have an unwavering sense of self is not only beneficial, it is essential for safety and sexual agency – whether it's saying no to unwanted sex, asking for what you want or advocating for condom use. It's horrifying to think how a patriarchal structure might benefit from the low self-esteem and body image of young women, who in turn feel less able to say no to sexual advances and are more vulnerable to manipulation.

'All of this propaganda around sexualised activities being good for girls and women, as being sex positive and feminist, it's all driven by a market culture,' Dr Choukas-Bradley tells me. 'True positive sexuality involves being in touch with what one wants sexually, who one wants to have sex with, the types of sex she wants to have. It's connected with the ability to experience desire, sexual lubrication, arousal and orgasm. None of that is increasing for adolescent girls. Instead, we see a rise, mostly anecdotally, in unwanted rough sex in young adults. A rise in young women and girls having a lot of sex that they don't actually want to have.'

When I heard those last words something shifted within me and I started to cry. All of a sudden, I was confronted with every time I had said yes when I really meant no, when I had hypersexualised myself to feel wanted and desired. At times in my life, I had wanted nothing more than to be someone else's fantasy come to life, the love interest – I preened my body for hours before a sexual encounter, I watched YouTube videos on how to give the best blowjob, I bought sex toys and lingerie, I took nude pictures and sent them to men I had never met, I analysed men's social channels to figure out their fantasies and I would mould myself as such, posting provocative selfies to get attention. But in all of that submitting and serving I lost sight of my own sense of self, my own sense of desire. I let men humiliate me, degrade me, hurt me and then dismiss me – all whilst pretending I was totally chill and enjoying myself.

When I felt trapped and like I couldn't say no, I would perform. When a man said he didn't want me, I would dangle my body like a carrot, knowing he would be unable to resist. When a man didn't immediately want to have sex with me I would be offended. When a man I dated told me it was weird to bring up sex on the first date, I thought he was the one with issues. In reality, none of these men cared for me once it was over. When I needed them, they didn't show up. Giving them my body and every ounce of self-respect I could muster meant nothing. They would take someone else for dinner and I would be left feeling used and alone. I told them they could do whatever they wanted to me in the hope that they would love me in return. That they would see that I was everything they ever wanted and tell me I would be special forever.

As I started to cry, Dr Choukas-Bradley began to tear up too. It felt all too familiar – this sense of exhaustion, self-questioning and regret for our former selves. We sat in silence for a minute, both of us at our desks in our bedrooms sobbing quietly, both of us transported, temporarily, back to girlhood.

'Girls have been socialised by porn, by memes and by TV shows to think that sexual relationships with boys and men, or even with folks of other genders, involve rough slapping and choking, which has an actual risk of death and asphyxiation,' Dr Choukas-Bradley continued. 'All of that messaging can be internalised as something that she really likes. Of course, there are adolescent girls who if raised with no media at all would naturally want these things. But it's not a coincidence that there's been this enormous rise in how many girls and women report that this is the sex they are having without the concomitant rise in enjoyment of those things. The vast majority of girls have performed oral sex without receiving it. When asked to describe the experience, they would describe feeling powerful, but almost none of the girls reported anything about their own sexual desire – being wet or excited beyond the sense of empowerment that comes from satisfying men, which we are socialised to believe is the number one implicit goal.'

After our call, Dr Choukas-Bradley introduced me to Dr Debby Hebernick, an internationally recognised sexual and reproductive health professor. She told me of a study she published that showed on average, women are twenty-six before they feel like their pleasure matters to a partner. Considering that, on average, girls are sexually active with a partner for the first time from around fifteen or sixteen, that means women are having sex for a *decade* before they feel like their pleasure is a consideration, let alone a priority.

'It takes a long time for people to say, "If my pleasure doesn't matter to this person, I shouldn't be with them,"' Dr Hebernick explains. 'And it's not just sexual pleasure, right? It can be about general desires – where I want to eat or what movie I want to watch.' It's about being seen as a living, breathing, desiring thing with thoughts and feelings and opinions – rather than a glorified sex toy for someone to fuck.

I told Debby about a recent encounter I'd had. A few months ago, I invited a man I'd known for a few years to my house for the weekend. We had recently begun dating despite the fact that he lived a few hours away. He was a kind and humble man, a gentle giant. Not long out of a traumatic relationship, I craved the safety and simplicity of his company. My prep, as usual, started a few days before. By the time he arrived, I was exfoliated, tanned, shaved from armpit to toe, moisturised, oiled, hair styled, lips scrubbed, makeup done, matching lingerie and outfits selected. I was glossy and glowing and soft to the touch.

We had sex as soon as we got in the door, and despite months of build-up, I didn't cum.

'Sorry, I haven't showered today,' he said afterwards, sitting down on my new green velvet sofa in the stained jogging bottoms he'd brought to relax in. He grabbed the TV remote, put his feet on my coffee table and loaded up my Netflix account to *Breaking Bad*, season three, episode five.

'Oh, I've already seen *Breaking Bad*,' I said, walking over in my brand-new underwear and silk shirt to sit next to him on the couch.

'Yeah, me too. I'm watching it again,' he said, making himself comfortable. 'This is where I got up to at home.'

I was about to formulate a response about how, actually, it was *my* house and *my* TV and I didn't really feel like rewatching a series I'd already seen before, and if *I* were in somebody's house who had just made me cum *I* would simply watch whatever they wanted to watch or, you know, maybe *talk* to them, when I noticed he'd already helped himself to food from my kitchen. I looked down at my pedicured toes and across at his holey socks and I wanted to scream. I never saw or spoke to him again.

In the weeks after, I tried to assess the need within me that felt so inherent – the need to be a prize. Why did I feel I owed him attractiveness? And not only attractiveness but perfection. In reality, many of my partners have expressed a total lack of judgement around body hair or weight gain or period sex or 'imperfections', telling me my desirability went deeper than that. Of course, I convinced myself they were just being nice, that it couldn't possibly be true. I couldn't fathom not putting effort in, having a single hair out of place. I was angry at myself for wasting so much time but it also felt like a cycle I was doomed to repeat.

The truly insidious thing about these sexual experiences, about sexual violence defined and undefined, is that they are private and intimate – nobody sees them and so nobody knows to ask if you're okay. As we know from our teen years spent in chatrooms, taking webcam selfies and blogging our lives away, the very nature of digital beauty culture is that it's built on personal, embodied practices that take place in other worlds, in online communities, often hidden from view. In both universes there is so much space for secrecy, shame, deception and distortion.

As the internet and social media took hold, the boundaries between our private and public worlds collapsed around us. Every space was invaded, every facet of our faces and bodies converted into content. I thought about the sacred spaces that our bedrooms had once been and how that place of sanctity had now become something disturbed. The simple mention of a girl's sleepover now prompts raised eyebrows – the image instantly sexualised, pornified through the lens of the male gaze. We are no longer 'acting something out' in search of ourselves but performing for something else entirely, someone else entirely. A never-ending negotiation of the ideas that men project onto us – a play that isn't for us.

We perform in our private spaces, in our intimate moments, so much so that we've lost a sense of who we really are and what we want, even when nobody's watching. We perform pleasure and keep up the pretence of living for ourselves, giving each other the illusion that everything is totally fine. But once I started to ask questions it soon became apparent that for many women and girls, the trauma they have experienced around body image, sex and sexual agency is palpable. More women cried to me during the research for this chapter than any other in the book – their bedrooms no longer safe havens or playgrounds but at times a stage, a snare, a false sense of security. I was forced to work through my experiences in real time, stories I had buried, others I had convinced myself were harmless experiences I had to accept.

Getting to know your body, what brings you joy and makes you feel comfortable and confident is your greatest sexual power, not learning how to push your feelings aside in favour of somebody else's pleasure. We are all trying to be desirable but the biggest question to ask above all is – desirable to who?

How can we create a more beautiful future for women and girls?

'We need to de-centre men, because until we do that, we will forever be trying to please them. Our appearance is the first step. There's always this expectation to be attractive based on what the patriarchy has said is attractive. I think dismantling that and starting to find our own self-worth in the world, in how we show up in the world – how we contribute to society, how confident we are, what good friends we are – if we could prioritise that, versus what some random man thinks, then that's what we need to do.'

Alya Mooro,
author of *The Greater Freedom*

4

Coloniser Culture

On a Friday night in London's Piccadilly Circus, Sarah was performing again. Her pictures had recently gone viral across Europe and tonight was another sold-out show, another audience of gaping mouths and eyes aghast. She squeezed into her skintight garments, adorned herself with beads and feathers and stepped out onto the stage. Sarah was tired but she performed as if her life depended on it, as if there was a man standing close to the stage with a bamboo cane, threatening to whip her from behind the curtains if she stopped singing. She twerked, she rolled her hips and shook her now-famous bum, as those who had paid extra fought their way to the front to grope at her undergarments and poke her with sticks. Sarah couldn't tell how many hands were on her at once, too many to count. When she flinched away from their fingernails, from their feverish attacks, the man emerged from behind the curtain with his hand held up, threatening to strike Sarah with his fist, and the audience laughed and cheered as she resigned herself to her fate. When he reemerged to place a collar around Sarah's neck, she got on all fours and the richest in the audience sat on her back as if she were an animal, hitting her until she crawled around.

Sarah Baartman was born about fifty miles north of the Gamtoos Valley in the Eastern Cape of what is now South Africa in 1789, and sold into slavery at sixteen after colonists murdered her father. She was brought to London by a physician and despite the passing of the Slave Trade Act in 1807, Sarah was exhibited for years, whipped if she didn't want to be touched, prostituted and sold from owner to owner.

The image of Sarah, with her large backside, breasts and lips, went viral in the nineteenth century. Sarah's body became an obsession of white audiences, and she became known as the Hottentot Venus. 'Hottentot' was a derogatory term created to mock the language spoken by the Khoikhoi people of South Africa, ridiculing the clicks and staccato pronunciation considered strange and bestial by colonisers. The word is now considered a highly offensive way to describe the Khoikhoi. By combining it with 'Venus', an icon of idealised beauty throughout Western culture, Sarah Baartman's moniker points to a beauty that needed to be caged, owned and controlled – one that was a spectacle, othered and degraded. Paraded and exposed around the world as though an animal in a zoo or a circus freak show, Sarah Baartman was dehumanised so much that her entire existence was reduced to her body and its ability to be consumed by white audiences – for the creation of content and spectacle. She was made to be less than the sum of her parts, her body then used to inform a reductive stereotype of Black womanhood. Her beauty was considered savage, oversexed, sub-human, and she was marketed as the 'missing link between man and beast'.

Sarah Baartman never consented to performing nude due to her culture's stance on modesty, despite bribes and calls for her to remove the small undergarment she wore to conceal her genitalia. However, upon her death, Sarah's body was bought by Dr Georges Cuvier, who used her corpse to write a thesis comparing her genitalia to that of an ape. His work formed racist theories that positioned Black women as hypersexual and subhuman – shaping European science on 'savage women', seen as distinct from the 'civilised' females of Europe, and embedding a hierarchy of races with white men at the top and Black women at the bottom. Not only that, he dissected her body, cut out her brain and her labia and preserved them in jars of formaldehyde. The jars of Sarah's dissected body parts remained on display at the Musée de l'Homme in Paris up until the 1980s.

*

A hair salon in New York City, but really we could've been anywhere in the world. Venus and I sit together in this liminal space, this site of self-expression. The music is loud but women sit chatting with their babies asleep in their arms, duplicated infinitely in the mirrors behind them, each one in the process of being transformed.

The salon is one of the few sites left largely unchanged by the digital – proof that we still need the unbroken physical touch of strangers, the ritual and the care of others. For a few moments, we can surrender ourselves to another being, to knowing hands, to ancient algorithms carried out by our ancestors over centuries – the geometry of braiding, the alchemy of dye, the parting, weaving, combing, sectioning, scrunching, bathing and oiling of our hair.

Women have created spaces similar to salons for centuries, whether sat on the floor with their head cradled in the lap of an auntie or upright in a faux leather chair. The original meaning of the word 'salon' referred to a conversational gathering of intellectuals, artists and activists. They would meet in salons to discuss the ideas of the day and we recreate that here, in this sacred space, surrounded by chemicals and deft hands. We intellectuals meet and we talk about beauty.

Venus is the founder of underground club nights GHE20G0THIK, a now global movement championing inclusivity and self-expression. We first bonded over beauty culture when I worked in beauty salons – Venus's approach to beauty always fascinated me, a blend of her Black and Latino heritage; she is self-directed and endlessly inspiring.

'One of my most formative experiences was getting ready for my aunt's wedding when I was around eleven years old,' Venus tells me. 'The whole wedding party – me, fifteen of my cousins, my mum and my grandma were in this Dominican woman's salon. It was very loud, full of music, and we were probably there for six or seven hours, but that was a normal thing for us. I don't recall anything as clearly as I do that day. I just remember realising that this is the culture of women in my community. Beauty culture in a lot of communities is a very private thing, but in mine it's a very public and shared experience, it's like another playground or marketplace. Women talk and they connect in so many ways at their salon, and in my neighbourhood that was a real place where we spent every Saturday morning. We were taught what it was to be a woman and given space to design our personalities. It really moulded who I am today.'

I worked in salons during the earliest years of my career, running events and creating communities around beauty. I saw firsthand how these spaces become sites of culture, self-expression and self-indulgence – often directed by women working around their family lives. I came to think of salons as spiritual places – places for tangible connection, a microcosm of culture, of femininity, of beauty, of womanhood, an instant and inherent sorority. We'd have girls coming in to get ready for major life events, we'd have women run in off the streets of central London looking for a sanctuary mid-panic attack, we'd have girls asking to sit and charge their phones so they could get home safely, we'd hear stories of grief and girlhood, we'd hear giggles and gossip and we'd therapise one another over treatments, holding space for what typically went unsaid. In the busyness of day-to-day life, salons are static, an unchanging in-between space and a constant cornerstone of womanhood. Some of our clients had been with their beauty professional longer than any romantic partner, whilst others spoke of salons as grounding in new cities, places they sought out for connection to their culture, for a sense of belonging.

But the belonging felt bittersweet for many, because how much you belonged, even in your own cultural space, hinged on your ability to conform. Whilst we learnt the warmth of womanhood we also learnt the cold reality: that our value and our worth was conditional, even in the spaces we created for ourselves.

Venus describes her experience in salons as an 'indoctrination into good hair'. The measure of 'good' being defined by the Eurocentric beauty standards imposed on her as straight, long and fine. 'Ever since I was six years old, beauty meant going to the hair salon, sitting in hot dryers, getting my hair yanked so that it would be straight, my ears on fire from the chemical relaxers on my edges. No one ever thought that my natural curly hair was good enough for special occasions and my mum invested a lot of time into controlling the image of me as a child.'

When European colonists invaded non-white countries across Africa, Asia and Central/South America, they established themselves as superior and elevated European culture. Conceptions of beauty have long been aligned with prestige, wealth and social hierarchy, so the aesthetic of the colonists was enforced and adopted as the ideal. These Eurocentric beauty ideals were defined as fair skin; wide, light eyes; a small nose; slim body type; and straight, blonde hair.

'Eurocentric beauty ideals were my first encounter with a type of beauty standard,' twenty-four-year-old Zoe says candidly, leaning over from the salon seats next to us to join in the conversation. 'Coming from a dark-skinned Black woman's perspective, it was a painful introduction to beauty, because beauty was this thing that was not only exclusionary but then also just impossible for me to attain. It was a traumatic experience to realise that as a child, to realise not only that you aren't beautiful but that there is no way for you to *ever* be beautiful. I can remember saying to my mum on the way to school that I wished I was white. I look back now and think about how heartbreaking that statement is, how hard that must've been for my mum to hear from her eight-year-old daughter. In that way, self-hate was something that I learnt before self-love.'

As I researched this book, more women and girls added their stories to the conversation – telling me about their experiences growing up in the digital realm, their first memories of beauty. I heard recollections of racism in early digital interactions, of the impact of Eurocentric beauty standards and the near-total lack of representation in the beauty space. There was a repeated sense of being exorcised from your body – alienated from your physical self as it is discussed as separate to your humanity. Racism intensifies objectification because it creates a hierarchy of beauty – all women are objects but some are less desirable, less visible, than others.

'I would get called the N word. People would refuse to chat with me or play online with me. It got so bad that I deleted my account to recreate one with a white avatar,' one young woman tells me of her first digital memories of playing a game called Habbo Hotel. 'Even when it came to digital, pixelated images, I learnt at ten years old that Black was seen as inferior. That feeling then carried on when I got Tumblr.'

'I wish I never knew what Tumblr was,' agrees Sahana, a twenty-five-year-old with Indian heritage – a sentiment I'd heard numerous times by this point. If my research made one thing clear, it's that Tumblr owes *a lot* of women reparations. 'All I ever saw were images of white women and that warped my perception of myself. I had visions of what it meant to be beautiful and it wasn't me, it was a young white girl. It was the same on YouTube, and Pinterest is another equivalent. In all these images of beauty and aspiration, there are still no people of colour.'

In her book *Algorithms of Oppression*, Safiya Noble details how much this colonisation is a part of the internet's code – how bias has been built in by white, male tech monopolies to create a reductive image of women of colour and an experience that positions them as second-class citizens in the digital space.

'The ghosts of colonisation still haunt our digital realm,' says Jasmine Banks, an academic specialising in the psychology of Black women's online experience, when we meet over video call. 'I really try to emphasise that the internet is a new medium, but the things happening in it are not new. The ways that women are experiencing beauty and perceptions of beauty online are exactly the same as offline, but even more amplified because the bias is now much more explicit. Black women have to intentionally search for "curly hairstyles for Black women" or "red lipstick for Black women". It's seemingly small things like that, where the algorithms and the platforms have the dominant narrative of whiteness as the standard. And then we see dating profiles where men will literally write "no Black women", or we see the other side with fetishisation, where women describe the experience as feeling like they're being "conquered".'

Eurocentric beauty standards are also reinforced by digital technology. Many filters, editing presets and apps offer skin 'brightening' as standard – with platforms coming under fire for automating skin lightening in generic beauty filters, encoding an association between a fair complexion and desirability. Your phone camera itself was optimised for white skin and often distorts darker skin tones, and there are countless apps offering ways to edit and tweak nose, lip and eye shapes, underscored with a racialised subtext.

'It's a very consistent thing. And then we start to see women say, "Maybe I am the issue, maybe I'm not enough."

It makes women question their worth and question their own beauty,' says Jasmine. 'I see an acknowledgment of the fact that this is happening and a sense of hopelessness – of, well, if I'm not good enough for all these reasons and for all of these platforms, what am I good for? Where do I belong?'

It became clear that the digital world, like the salon, was a site of tension – where every virtue is a double-edged sword. Both social media and salon spaces are public performances full of smiles and 'wow I love it! I'm so confident! I look amazing!' before you log off or leave to cry in the car because you've never felt uglier in your whole entire life. Both are places of connection and therapy, places of supposed self-expression, where you can be anything you want to be, but where that freedom comes with its own consequences and constrictions – its own trappings of womanhood. Both keep up the illusion that change has come, that transformation is possible, but, ultimately, that it is you who needs to adapt.

'I was twelve years old when I made that link in my head. Rather than thinking "I'm doomed," I tried to say, "Okay, what can I do to make sure that I fit this standard?"' twenty-two-year-old Annabelle tells me from her London home. 'And it's not even just being dark-skinned, it's being dark-skinned and plus-size. I felt like I was the opposite of what beauty was, and when you're young, you feel like it's you who has to change, like you're not the permanent one here. I used products like Fair & Lovely and Caro White to try to lighten my skin. I had a massive issue with my hair texture and there was a time in my life when all I would watch on YouTube were videos on how to change your natural hair texture, how to go from a 4C (the most tightly coiled afro hair) to a 3C (a looser, defined coil curl), and how to lighten your skin naturally. There was so much self-hatred and self-loathing. It felt like my life was predestined for me, that I would be capped if I aspired to be anything. That's hard for a child to realise.'

Annabelle tells me about her own indoctrination into 'good hair', sitting in a salon as a five-year-old girl, her scalp burning, creating wounds that would later turn to scabs. She was told it was the only way to 'manage' and 'rectify' her natural 4C hair – a necessary process she must endure. Much of this conversation is framed as self-care strategies but, as Emma Dabiri writes in her book *Don't Touch My Hair*, 'The language once employed to describe Black people has not vanished. It has simply shifted to head height,' with products designed for hair that is 'unruly', 'coarse' and 'difficult to control'. Beauty is so close, so attainable, if only you buy this shiny new product to get you in line. The subordination of women of colour under coloniser culture continues, as it has for centuries, in the guise of beauty and self-improvement.

The more I spoke to women about their experiences with digital beauty culture, about their experiences in salons and on social media sites, it became clear that the hierarchy cemented by Dr Georges Cuvier, the one that left dark-skinned Black women at the bottom, remains largely intact. That even in these places of connection and self-expression, they felt judged, devalued and degraded. There were no places of belonging; there were no sites that were safe.

'A lot of the time, we are going to the hair salon to conceal the hair, to make it more "manageable, acceptable or palatable". That sort of mentality, that sort of action, can never be just left at the hair,' says Annabelle. 'I think it extends to the whole body. They look at me and everything that possesses me, and they deem that it is not worthy enough.'

Hairstyles have always been a significant part of African culture, signalling status, identifying tribes and even telling stories. In the microcosm of the salon, we see how Black hair becomes an emblem of racial and cultural tension in modern beauty culture, in which ancient algorithmic braiding rituals designed to protect and preserve afro hair exist alongside processes designed to cover, disguise or break down the same bonds.

'Engaging with beauty – via hair, for example – definitely means something, and what it means to me is a pathway to freedom,' says Annabelle. 'From back in captivity when braiding styles were used to map out escape routes to now, when you can relax your hair, sew on a weave or wear a wig – it's all about using what you have as a negotiation of power, as a way to obtain freedom.'

Our idea of femininity is intricately braided into our perception of hair. The feminine beauty ideal is seen from a Western perspective, in which beautiful hair is long, soft and silky, but Asian hair is also lusted after for its close proximity to the dominant ideology.

'I think people just look at the hair on your head and say, "You have such an amazing head of hair," but that's literally all over my body,' writer, model and South-East Asian influencer Simran Randhawa tells me. 'I remember being twelve years old and my mum would take me to the salon to wax my armpits. My hair was so thick that I would bleed whenever I was waxed. I resorted to shaving because I felt I had no other choice, but I was literally harming myself. Shaving left me with all these cuts and scabs on my legs – I'd have so many scars and ingrown hairs and open wounds. I was mutilating myself in the name of beauty because it was preferable to being hairy. When I started to earn money, the first thing I bought was a MacBook and then the second was laser hair removal.'

Beauty and technology – the two core tenets of a young girl's life – held in equal priority.

'For me, laser hair removal was one of the best things I ever invested in because it just took so much self-consciousness out of my body. But again, it's something you have to keep up with. It's something that I'll have to pay to top up for the rest of my life. I just think that's so sad, that something that's so completely normal and natural, that's literally my genetics, was considered so ugly that I ended up hurting myself and spending thousands of pounds to avoid it.'

Hairlessness is often seen as a cornerstone of the beauty standard and is becoming increasingly 'necessary' for women across the globe, despite the fact that it is one of the most unnatural requirements of the ideal. Whilst some women might be naturally slim, have large breasts, clear skin or straight hair, no woman is free from body hair. Annabelle's words echoed in my mind – beauty as a path to freedom, but freedom at what cost? In reality, freedom that comes with a price doesn't feel much like liberty at all.

'I just feel like there weren't women in beauty who represented my body or my skin tone, my lifestyle or my economic background when I was growing up,' says Venus as we leave the salon. 'I still don't. It feels like they are cosplaying with what we don't get to choose. Women who look like me are either watered down or just used as a reference.'

*

In plantation slavery, jealousy over beauty and male attention led white women to violate Black women's bodies, a cruel extension of the systemic sexual abuse already experienced by many. The result was that Black women were forced to cover their elaborate hairstyles or shave their heads – an issue deemed so critical it was formalised in law in Louisiana in 1786. But it didn't stop there. In *Don't Touch My Hair*, Emma Dabiri tells of a white mistress in Brazil who suspected her husband was having sexual relations with an attractive mulatto (biracial) slave noted for her beautiful eyes. The wife responded by removing the eyes of her 'competitor'.

Fetishised for her large backside, Sarah Baartman is thought to have informed the fashion trends of the time. The obsession with Sarah's body and the concerns of white women that their husbands desired a curvier body shape are thought to have led to the creation of the bustle in the mid-nineteenth century – a structured skirt designed to give the illusion of a larger bum. From the men who sold her into entertainment to the men profiting from her image, the manufacturers making bustle skirts and the merchants selling white women a fix for their jealousy, countless men profited from Sarah Baartman's body and its oppression. Sarah herself died penniless.

'Women were really anxious that their men were going to be lowered into wanting this sort of exotic, hypersexual African woman,' Dr Gordon-Chipembere told the Australian Broadcasting Corporation. So they tried to emulate her.

In November 2014, *Paper* magazine released a cover featuring Kim Kardashian that broke the internet. In the lead image, Kim is shown nude and oiled, with her back to camera, revealing her large bum. In other shots, she is completely naked, her enhanced curves emphasised. Another shows Kim balancing a champagne glass on her exaggerated behind, her mouth wide with theatre and spectacle. Many pointed to the similarities between Kim's nude profile and the depictions of Sarah Baartman, criticising the images for the exploitation and fetishisation of the Black female body.

The man behind the photo, Jean-Paul Goude, drew inspiration from his previous work 'Carolina Beaumont', a nude image of Grace Jones featured on the cover of his 1981 book *Jungle Fever*. 'Blacks are the premise of my work . . . I have jungle fever,' he told *People* in 1979. The image depicts Jones in a cage, naked and surrounded by raw meat. Cropped out of the cover image, but visible in other versions of the photograph, is a sign that reads 'DO NOT FEED THE ANIMAL'.

Kim's image – nude and digitally distorted – became one of the most viral images of all time, cementing her legacy as the beauty icon of the decade. Something had shifted in the 2010s when digital social media was adopted en masse. A new ideal emerged; exaggeration and ethnic ambiguity were in as we competed for global attention in tiny squares. As we saturated ourselves with images, we craved something new to catch our fleeting attention. Baartman's body type became an obsession of audiences once again.

The difference between Kim Kardashian's image and the ones of Sarah Baartman is that Kim is now able to profit from the very features that kept Sarah enslaved. The body parts are still fetishised and commodified, but this time they have been purchased by a light-skinned woman, further distorted by digital editing tools and published to create spectacle. Kim Kardashian, whilst half-Armenian, is a light-skinned, privileged woman. She has been able to capitalise on her body, aided by an aesthetic she has manufactured specifically based on Black women, in a way that Black women themselves have been historically unable to do.

Blackfishing, or mixed-fishing, is a twist on the concept of catfishing (pretending to be someone else online) and refers to the practice of (mostly) white women adopting Blackness or striving for proximity to Blackness by using makeup, hairstyles and surgical enhancements that originate from or mimic Black bodies and Black culture to gain financial or cultural benefits. From Jesy Nelson to Ariana Grande and the Kardashians, as well as countless influencers, this phenomenon has seen white women co-opting the features of women of colour to fit an emerging racially ambiguous beauty ideal.

Calls for increased diversity, alongside the rampant spread of capitalism and the homogenisation of our beauty culture under globalisation, have led to the creation of a new, ethnically ambiguous beauty standard within digital culture. In an online world in which everything was everywhere all at once and you could easily watch content from every continent in the space of a few minutes, the beauty standard began to evolve to represent someone who *could* be from anywhere.

Brands started to cotton on that a Eurocentric 'look' was becoming increasingly outdated as the world got smaller and women globally were using their digital channels to gain access to power and a voice. But this ethnically ambiguous global beauty standard did not emerge from a postfeminist, post-racial, post-misogynoir utopia. Despite appearing more diverse, it is in fact more insidious in its colonisation of women's bodies, in the way that manages to *appear* inclusive whilst maintaining a racial hierarchy that keeps women of colour, and especially dark-skinned women, at the bottom, whilst continuing the colonialist tradition of commodifying their features and dismembering their bodies.

This market shift is no real surprise. It was realised that a huge amount of spending power lies with women of colour, who historically have felt entirely neglected by the Western beauty industry and hadn't seen themselves in beauty at all. They could, all of a sudden, meet an ideal – if only they subscribed to a set of regimes and rituals to assimilate. Meanwhile, the industry gets credit for diversifying from a rigid archetype, whilst simply creating another and making millions in the process.

That mythical being, the most beautiful woman in the world, now has light skin chemically darkened with dihydroxyacetone, the chemical used in artificial tanner. (It is important that she begins as light before the darkening – she cannot simply be dark.) She has had her nose broken and reconstructed to be straight and small, and her lips injected with synthetic hyaluronic acid, whilst fat has been beaten out of her body and redistributed to her hips, bum and breasts to create a more exaggerated curve, not dissimilar to that of Sarah Baartman. Everywhere else she is athletic and lean – her stomach is flat and tight. She cannot simply be curvaceous or lean, she must be both and neither. She must be constructed. All of the hair on her body has been removed with a laser whilst her teeth have been filed down into fangs and replaced with porcelain, electric white. She wears the hair of an Asian woman sewn close to her scalp, and her eyes have been stapled up at the outer corner.

Where is she from, people ask. Where does the most beautiful woman in the world call home?

She laughs coyly, flashing her dazzling smile, but says nothing. She says nothing when women are murdered by their governments for showing their long, luscious hair. Or when dark-skinned women, the ones with no use for the chemical dye, are killed in their homes by those meant to protect them. She does not discuss the teeth knocked out of women's skulls by their partners or the little girls sexualised for the same features she parades, created from artifice. She is quiet when girls are bullied for their body hair, for their belly rolls and their burdensome bodies. She does not comment on the women of colour calling out for somewhere to belong, a space that's truly theirs. She claims nowhere whilst taking everywhere, and she says nothing. She has no politics, no culture, no real stance on anything. She consumes but she does not contend (unless it can be made into content). Why should she? She's the most beautiful woman in the world.

An ethnically ambiguous beauty ideal represents a middle ground – one that everyone can strive to achieve. For darker-skinned women, access can be achieved through skin bleaching, wearing wigs, relaxing afro hair, contouring the nose or getting surgery to erase ethnic features. For white women, a tan is a necessity. Despite the plethora of literature detailing the life-threatening consequences of sunbeds and tanning without SPF protection, sunbed use has skyrocketed in recent years. Searches for 'sunbeds' on Google increased by 260 per cent in the first six months of 2023, whilst 'how many sunbeds to get a tan' was up 180 per cent. The deadly beauty trend is also garnering millions of views on TikTok as young people strive for the aesthetic. BBLs and lip filler are also increasingly commonplace and squat challenges are prolific. TikTok Shop advertises padded shorts to give the illusion of a larger bum and more exaggerated curves, and schoolgirls stuff their pockets to create bustle-esque skirts. Whilst the influence of K-pop drives a new wave of thinness in the West and makeup tutorials show how to get an elongated eye, East Asian women invest in double eyelid surgery to create wider, more Western, eyes. South Asian women must remove all body hair whilst the hair on their head is coveted. Biracial women must have typically European features whilst boasting the large lips and curves associated with Black womanhood, or risk not being 'Black enough'. Biracial and brown-skinned women the world over must maintain the exact shade of toffee-brown complexion light enough to be white adjacent but dark enough to show the luxury of a 'tan'. This ethnically ambiguous beauty ideal leaves no one exempt from the need to self-improve. It is, in other words, a capitalist's dream.

This new beauty standard bears very little resemblance to women anywhere, yet it has colonised every woman's conscience and tells them how they are lacking. It is convenient to create a composite standard that fits nobody in a global market that profits from the sale of insecurities, as everybody needs to invest financially, physically or emotionally in order to be worthy.

The new, transcultural beauty standard is a homogeneous hybrid horror, a composite chimera of us all and a colonisation of every continent. However, the cherry-picking still means that lighter-skinned women with European features can assimilate far easier than darker-skinned women with African features. Everyone is flawed but some are more flawed than others. Everyone must work but for some, no amount of work will achieve the ideal.

Whilst a globalised capitalist beauty standard has us all augmenting our bodies, we don't do so from positions of equity. Unlike Black women, who can only ever embody Blackness, celebrities like Kim Kardashian and Ariana Grande can revel in this ambiguity whilst retaining the privileges that come with their race, reverting back to the comfort of whiteness (or white passing) when Blackness is no longer convenient or profitable, without ever having to deal with any of the challenges or forms of oppression that Black women cannot opt out of. They can try on the desirable parts of Black identity without having to confront the systemic oppression that shapes it.

'I find blackfishing quite traumatic, actually,' says Zoe. 'It's a mindfuck to see things that were originally seen as "too much" or "too ghetto" or "too ugly" on Black women be celebrated and prized on white women who take them. It hurts that white women can take on these features that we have been tormented for in order to advance themselves or benefit in some way. We don't actually have any power over Blackness; it doesn't feel like it belongs to us. It's more like something that white supremacy is entitled to manoeuvre and control and use. I feel alienated from my Blackness and alienated from my beauty in that way. I find it traumatic when I see all the content about white girls wanting to grow their bums. It feels painful and I get angry. Having a big bum is something that was made to be really gross and hypersexual and wrong for me, but now white women are doing it, it's sexy and something that we should all aspire to.'

It's a sentiment women of colour the world over seem to relate to – I spoke to many who voiced the same frustrations that the culture, complexion and customs that they were once ostracised for are now used as currency by white women. A currency that should be theirs but is worth more in white hands.

'I was at university and I met a white girl in a nightclub bathroom,' Simran tells me. 'She told me she loved my "tan" and then she pulled out her foundation, which was the same shade that I use. I know she didn't think of it with malice but to her, that skintone was a choice or a costume – when she washes her face she's literally six shades lighter than me. It hurts because I had such a hard time at university, I felt so ostracised. When I was younger, I did not see myself as beautiful. I did not see other brown women as beautiful. I didn't get to grow up thinking my mum was the most beautiful woman in the world. I've had to recondition my brain to be like, no, this is beautiful, I am beautiful.'

'It's just hilarious because my mother and my grandmother grew up using brown lip liner and brown lipstick because that's what looks good on brown skin tones,' says Sahana. 'Then Hailey Bieber does it and all of a sudden it's a trend called "Hailey Bieber lips". That was eye-opening for me because it only became socially acceptable when a white girl did it. Beauty trends always have to start with a white woman to gain traction online.'

The assessment of these power dynamics is crucial in understanding what qualifies as appropriation and what doesn't. Only light-skinned women have the ability to shapeshift successfully in this way, adapting their skin, hair and body to the trend *du jour* and reaping the rewards. That is not sharing because it does not share the experience as a whole. Whilst 'Bo Derek' braids are trending thanks to the appropriation of a white woman (or decades later, the Kardashians), Black women are still being reprimanded in court for 'unprofessional' hairstyles. We are not sharing, we're just *taking*. Coloniser culture repeats itself.

Through colonialism and imperialism, Europeans spent centuries stealing and subjugating, cementing themselves as superior. They took everything – bodies, culture, resources – and destroyed centuries of tradition, heritage and history in the process. That, inevitably, has repercussions. It creates the lens through which 'sharing' does not look equitable, where our continued 'taking' feels all the more cruel. Whilst racism, colourism and the subjugation of non-white bodies continue to fill the media and our social feeds, we cannot simply decide that we want to 'share' in the parts we deem pretty. That privilege must be earned.

I come to this after years of learning and unlearning – decoding what was programmed into my psyche – with an awareness that I am an embodiment of Eurocentric standards, the exact image that has been levelled against many women their entire lives. I can't ignore that and it would feel wrong to try. I believe I have a responsibility, as we all do, to approach this topic with empathy and a listening ear. A duty to hear and to act. It is important that white people reflect and engage critically with our own consumption of beauty culture – where 'trends' originate from and how the biases have been built into beauty standards. We need to look critically at how we might be supporting violence against women of colour, through the appropriation of culture or consumption of content.

As much as I feel pressure to maintain a tan under current beauty ideals and am less confident wearing shorts or a sleeveless top that exposes my pale skin, my natural skin tone is not politicised in the same way. I don't face active discrimination or oppression for not wearing fake tan. I might feel a bit uncomfortable but my safety is not at risk, I won't be accused of being unprofessional or unkempt, and I won't be discriminated against in the job market or in my access to resources and opportunities. I may tan for the aesthetic but millions of women across the world are bleaching their skin for a better life.

We are seeing what appears to be an increase in diversity online but it isn't translating into economic or social power. The risk of inflating the progress made, of getting complacent, is that many will use it as proof that racism is over, whilst a racial hierarchy remains largely intact. What we are witnessing now is a surface-level display of tokenized representation that conceals the fact that we have failed to create structural change. In reality, brands will still pay more for a white woman co-opting the features of women of colour than they will for women of colour who possess those features naturally.

Charlotte Stavrou, a colleague I met in my years working in beauty salons, went on to found SevenSix, an influencer marketing agency that specialises in working with diverse talent for digital campaigns. In 2022, SevenSix created a landmark report on the influencer pay gap, after being routinely shocked at brands' reluctance to extend their budgets to darker-skinned creators.

'We've seen cases where brands will offer about 25–30 per cent of the budget they originally had for a light-skinned influencer with European features for a dark-skinned influencer with African features – despite them both having the same following, the same levels of engagement and both posting high-quality content,' she tells me. 'To be a Black woman is trendy as long as you're not actually Black, and that is very confusing. We see brands who will work with creators who use fake tan to create a skin tone darker than mine, who have lip filler, who are augmenting their bodies to create a stereotypically African woman's shape, but it's really sexy on them because they're white. Brands will pay them more than if they were paying someone who naturally looked like that. Without realising it, we create this hierarchy of worth when it comes to beauty. We like Black beauty but it's more valuable if it's taken and put on white women.'

According to the 2022 report, in the UK there is, on average, an 18.7 per cent pay gap between white influencers and influencers of colour. This increases to 21.5 per cent when comparing white influencers and Black influencers. In North America, a similar report by communications agency MSL showed that the pay gap between white and Black influencers was 35 per cent, the most significant racial pay gap in any industry.

We see the legacy of the treatment of Sarah Baartman in the hypersexualisation of Black women's bodies, in the commodification of Black features, in the parading of Black as an aesthetic before the novelty wears off and it switches to another owner. It can be found in the permissiveness towards Black women's bodies, the ease with which people feel they can touch without consent, fat-shame or denigrate. On social media, on dating apps and on TV, we see that Black women's bodies still seem to belong to everyone but themselves. In every single inaugural 'coupling' ceremony of the first six seasons of *Love Island*, a non-white contestant was picked last. Every single one. The features that women of colour were once mocked for (in both political propaganda and on the playground) have now become assets white women are paying to achieve. Women of colour are repeatedly sidelined, picked last, asked to twerk and perform, to create shock and spectacle, but cast aside when they demand their humanity be seen alongside their bodies. Sarah Baartman's experience is still being echoed in the heightened experience of violence, entitlement and fetishisation – Black women's bodies are still figuratively caged and literally uncared for, whilst being bought and sold for profit by those in positions of power.

'To be considered beautiful and attractive as a Black woman, you now need to change yourself to fit that Kim Kardashian trope,' says Annabelle. The commodification of a body type that some Black women naturally possess – as well as the distortion of what that looks like – reinforces the phenomenon of appropriation. In her co-option and exaggeration of Black womanhood and Black features, Kim Kardashian set a new standard for women of colour, essentialising Blackness into a hypersexualised, exaggerated curvy body. She becomes the blueprint for a woman of colour and sets the expectation for women's bodies across the globe.

You may think that biracial (notably Black/white) women are revelling in this standard shift, but the conflict persists.

'Being a biracial woman, I grew up with the biggest lips of anybody I knew and it was always a point of insecurity for me,' one beauty influencer with over a million followers tells me. 'I remember trying to google how to fix it when I was eleven because I was made to feel so different, but fast-forward a decade and everybody is getting lip filler. I was constantly being accused of blackfishing even though I'm half Black. The things that I had been insecure about when I was growing up were now things that people were leveraging against me, saying I was trying to look like Kylie Jenner or Kim Kardashian. It was just such a discomforting feeling for me. I felt like the only identifier of me being Black was the fact that my lips are naturally big, which was such a screwed-up way of thinking, but it felt like my only defence against people who thought I was trying to look a certain way. As the trend persisted, my lips became so unremarkable among my peers in the beauty industry that I ended up getting lip filler. It was such a weird psychological game I was playing with myself. They did four injections and I just freaked out – I stopped midway through my appointment because I just had to leave the salon.'

But the choice of how we present ourselves feels, at times, like it is coming back to us, like we have some semblance of control. In 2015, Marissa Rei started #TheBlackout on Tumblr, a day where Black women were encouraged to post their selfies onto the platform – feeds were filled with dark-skinned women racking up hundreds of thousands of positive notes. It was a moment of visibility that became a recurring celebration of Black beauty, subverting the beauty standard for countless young women, including Zoe.

'It basically blew up my Tumblr. Ever since that happened, my dashboard was just full of Black and brown people, and what I consumed was just completely flipped on its head. I always think of that as the closest we've come to a digital revolution. To see something that I consumed on a daily basis change so drastically simplified my self-love and healing journey tenfold. Representation is powerful – it's very simple but it's powerful, especially now when at such a young age you can be consuming positive representations of Black women. Even boring representation! I love seeing Black people and brown people just living their everyday life and taking up space – doing outfit videos, or vlogs. It means everything.'

In the 2010s, Chizi Duru, an African-American YouTuber, cut off all her hair to start afresh without any chemicals, relaxers or dyes. 'The Big Chop', as it became known online, signified a ritual of rebirth, renewal and resistance for Black women. The natural hair movement flourished on social media, and whilst it quickly became co-opted by companies selling products, fronted by loose-curled, light-skinned women, with campaigns almost entirely devoid of tighter 4C textures, we were starting to see glimmers of what could be.

'We see a lot of women of colour curating their digital spaces very intentionally, following hashtags like Black Beauty and Black Girl Magic in order to create safe harbours where they're validated and seen, curating places of belonging,' says Jasmine. 'Although it's additional labour that they have to engage in, it's a way to exist beyond the stereotypes and to find pockets of hope and self-love in the digital.'

When I interviewed Claire Barnett, former executive director of UN Women UK, she spoke about the importance of differentiating 'freedom from' and 'freedom to'. 'Both are important,' she told me. 'In these digital spaces, we have the freedom *to* post whatever we want, to say whatever we want, to present ourselves however we want, but we don't have freedom *from* oppression and abuse. And so, if we create more and more spaces where we can do whatever we want, but we don't have any protection from dangerous influences, are we really free?'

I thought again about Annabelle's path to freedom, about how beauty practices and social media allowed us 'freedom to' express ourselves, curate our worlds and decide how we want to present, how they can be tools to leverage what relative power we might have, but they haven't provided freedom *from* the oppressive structures that are ingrained in their institutions – the bias, the beauty standards and the bigotry that have become part of the fabric of the code.

'You have to constantly remind yourself that your features are there for a reason,' says Annabelle as we say goodbye, and I know it is a battleground, a mantra she is repeating for her own benefit as well as Venus's, Simran's and Zoe's, as well as yours and mine. 'You represent your ancestors, your history and the beauty that has been seen in those features over millennia. You are here for a reason and I think once you decentre yourself, you begin to cherish your beauty in ways unimaginable. You are here on a mission. You're an ancestor in the making.'

In the early 2000s, after almost a decade of debate, Sarah Baartman's remains were returned to her homeland. On 9 August 2002, National Women's Day in South Africa, thousands attended Baartman's centuries-delayed funeral in Cape Town. The fight to reclaim Sarah's body is over but the fight for the reclamation of the bodies of women of colour all over the world continues.

How can we create a more beautiful future for women and girls?

'We live in an ever-evolving digital world, which has its pros and cons. I believe honesty and transparency online are integral factors into making the world a more beautiful place for women and girls, particularly when it comes to disclosing plastic surgery or aesthetic treatments.'

Alizey Mirza,
influencer and Head of Marketing and VIP Relations at Biolite

5

The Power of Pretty

The ritual takes place over the course of three days. When it begins, we are alone, but we come together on the last evening to prepare ourselves for the main event. It is different for every woman and girl, each of us differing in our schedules and preferences, needs and desires, but I like to start with my skin.

I scrub it at first, forcing it to shed and make me anew. My reddened epidermis is then covered in oils which I sleep in and wash off the next day. Next, my self-tanning process begins and I walk around for hours sticky and incapable before showering. In that same shower I will also wash my hair – because day-two hair is easier to style than fluffy and unreliable day-one hair. When the main event comes we want compliant hair and freshly tanned skin.

It is at this point, on day two, that we share our plans in an assembly of group chat pictures both posed and unposed, taken in front of beds smothered by discarded outfits. We send options, a couple each, and the group votes. We try to assimilate, to coordinate – are you wearing heels? Because I'll wear heels if you do. What about lashes? Sometimes, in secret, we take videos of ourselves in our hypothetical outfits and we practise our existence for the night. We prop up the camera on our nightstands and walk away as if unwitting, turn to buy a drink from a pretend bartender, who definitely fancies us, chat animatedly to our invisible friends and break out into a dance sequence just in case the mood takes us. We then return to our device and assess the footage – what we look like from each angle, how the dress holds our flesh, whether we should attempt the dancing or spend as much of the night as possible with our clutch bags held over our stomachs.

They had chosen me for this particular event because of my social media profiles – the pictures and videos I had posed for and curated. The final edits whittled down from 300 takes. There was a lot of pressure to live up to my own hype.

On the day, we meet in the afternoon, this time at my house. It is just me and Eliza so we turn the music up loud and the ceremony begins. I start with a shower, removing any visible hair on my body whilst being careful not to wet the hair on my head. It is a careful balance – my leg up on the bath edge, folding over myself to check I've eliminated every possible strand, just in case. Sometimes I get so tired in these showers I have to sit down. I'm not sure it's possible to sweat under water but I feel like I do, emerging too hot, too fed up, somehow feeling less clean.

I do my hair next because I want to give it time to cool and set before I step outside. I place an iron primed at 200 degrees celsius by my face and I wrap sections around it, occasionally burning my neck and leaving red welts. Steam billows from the back of my head and I hold still for as long as I dare.

The music still blares and we sip on our cheap wine, but Eliza and I are largely focused on ourselves, breaking for tiny moments to check in and ask for feedback. Is my eyeliner okay? Do you have a spare brush? I'm hungry! But eating is cheating.

Makeup is next – primer, corrector, concealer, foundation, more concealer, cream blush, cream contour, even more concealer, setting powder, powder blush, bronzer, eyeshadow, eyeliner, mascara, lip liner, lipstick, setting spray. It takes about forty-five minutes to apply. Me on a chair at my windowsill and Eliza on the floor by the big mirror, the contents of her makeup bag spread across the laminate like the puzzle pieces of her face. We both pick through each other's things – it feels primal – testing and cooing and excitedly swatching shiny new things, each a potential key to unlock another level of ourselves.

If I were to cost up everything I had done to my body for this event, the total would be somewhere over £600; with my bleached hair included the figure is over £800. It seems stark to add it all up, to quantify just how much beauty work I engage in on a regular basis, but this is how the world works. The average woman spends just under an hour a day on beauty prep, over two full weeks a year. Financially, we spend an estimated $300,000 in our lifetimes – just on our faces alone. In making the choice between my corporeal home and the possibility of owning bricks and mortar, I had chosen my body every time. Mortgaging my beauty for privilege and wealth, exchanging my efforts for capital.

This may be a special event but this is a ritual I complete multiple times a month – it feels essential before dates, parties, days out and holidays. Every month a series of mental gymnastics as I assess which events I have coming up and which beauty rituals I need on each day to make the most of my purchases – to look as perfect as possible at each one. I got my nails done regularly, my eyebrows waxed, I shaved multiple times a week, I got my hair bleached every eight weeks like clockwork – each appointment costing over £150. Once you started, it felt impossible to stop – once you knew how you *could* look, once you tried a new product, once you reaped the rewards, it was added to the routine. Before you knew it, you had to complete a twenty-seven-step process before you could leave the house. I'd spent hours and hours, thousands and thousands of pounds on beauty – but I had never really sat down to question why. Why did this feel like a necessity? Why did it feel worth the effort? Was it truly worth it?

Eliza asks me to help with her eyeshadow. I'm thrilled and pad over with my brand-new palette. She closes her eyelids and, resting my hand to her face, I tap ever so gently, her delicate skin picking up pigment, her hollows deepening. I feel conscious of the smell of cheap prosecco on my breath and realise that, in my concentration, I hadn't exhaled. I hold her face a little longer than I need to, her eyelids closed and trembling. 'My masterpiece!' I whisper as I take a step back to assess what I've done. She looks in the mirror, eyes widening, and I tell her that she is beautiful. It feels genuine and true. This is the most connected we've felt in a while, sharing and touching and shimmering. I remember how much I love being a woman, how much I love these safe spaces we create for ourselves. How much I love holding her face in my hands.

I'd chosen Eliza for this particular club night because of her new face. We are heading to an exclusive London venue, one of the many that only permit entry to women who meet the beauty standard, those who have maintained the feminine ideal and appear in the image of Venus. Of all my closest friends, Eliza is the closest to the mark. She'd agreed to come with me to help me research. If we get in, we'll get free drinks all night and I'll get to meet the darlings of the city – those who have been certified beautiful and therefore more worthy of free things and luxury experiences.

The day before the event, I'd had to send in pictures of Eliza and I, along with our social accounts, for approval. I'd heard there was a group chat that girls' profiles were assessed in – each member of the majority-male group giving a yes or no, a ranking out of ten. I'd never looked at Eliza in that way until now and it had felt wrong to pull her face and body away as if separate from her soul. Much to my relief, they'd said we could both come but we would be judged on the door for the final say.

I can tell Eliza is getting nervous. The dread sits in my gut, heavy and foul. I don't know how we'll feel if they tell us we aren't enough – if they say only one of us was worthy. But we smile at each other, finish our wine and get into the taxi nonetheless. Later, I will wish I'd kept us there in my apartment, glittery and safe.

*

Beauty has always been seen as women's work – degraded and devalued, whilst simultaneously lauded as a necessary mandate for our humanity. Beauty is both required and stigmatised, but to dismiss its importance is a way of reinforcing stereotypes and systems that keep white men in power. We, as women, are not inherently more beautiful or more intent on beautification than men, but we have been conditioned and encouraged to become so. It is convenient to play down the significance of beauty in our lives, to mark it as frivolous and trivial, denying its entrenchment in our social, cultural and economic standing. But we can't keep up the pretence any longer.

That beauty is a path to freedom, a negotiation of power, extends beyond conversations of race and into the intricacies of wealth, class and access to opportunity for all women. The notion that 'what is beautiful is good' is as old as time – ancient philosophers positioned beauty as a virtue akin to truth, love and the divine. But in an increasingly visual digital culture, where image is everything and adherence is rewarded with platform and status, beauty as a currency, as a tool for social mobility, is only gaining value. The more beauty you possess, the more wealth – of all kinds – you can accumulate.

Now more than ever, beauty can be bought, cultivated, curated and attained with an investment of time, money and energy. With the rise of technology, our perceived attractiveness is not a fixed constant but a changeable variable that can be manipulated with makeup, injectables, surgery, filters and editing apps to achieve desirable outcomes – from increased credibility, status, power, and followers, to better health and employment outcomes. The benefits that come with being attractive can then create palpable disparities in wealth and opportunity – online and in real life. The time and money we invest in beauty, therefore, is no insignificant matter.

*

We arrive early and take our place in the queue on the busy London side street. Wet cobblestones illuminated by city lights. We want this so badly – every girl supposedly wants to post on their profiles and tag this venue. It is sparkly and exclusive, full of influencers, celebrities and the lucky few. We've done our best to fit the ideal, cosplaying *Love Island* contestants with our blow-dried hair, nail extensions, tanned skin and heels. I feel sick to my stomach. Eliza fidgets from side to side, tugging at her dress.

'What if we don't get in?' she whispers. 'What if I have to pay and you don't?'

A guy comes over to confirm we are wearing heels; we dutifully lift our feet in a girlish kick. I feel myself smile, breathe in. I worry about my makeup, how it looks under the neon lights. I find myself looking at the other girls, casting my eyes up and down, assessing how they'd interpreted the dress code ('we like our ladies to look elegant and classy – heels are strongly advised'), comparing every inch of them with every inch of me.

In the queue we meet Ava and Mila – best friends who tell us they've taken all day getting ready. Their DMs are full of these invites, Ava tells me, for intoxicating experiences at exclusive venues. She says this makes her feel special, that she has been chosen for something, that for a few fleeting moments she feels shiny and rare in an endless scroll of identical faces. It's a sentiment that doesn't last long – in the queue, she tells me, she can't stop comparing herself to the other girls, that she feels it was 'set up this way'. With each pretty girl paying different prices, the pecking order is set from the moment you walk in the door. Unfortunately, in the competitive nature of girlhood, I think that makes us want to be chosen even more.

We get to the front of the queue. A woman looks us up and down, handing us each a playing card – the Jack of hearts, a ranking. She waves us through to the entrance and we present our cards at the till.

'£10 each.'

'Could be worse,' I say but Eliza is upset.

'Does that mean we're ugly?' she asks, audibly.

The guy smirks: 'If you were ugly, we wouldn't let you in at all.'

Whilst so-called ugly girls might be denied entry, the most beautiful got in for free.

These promoters, as they are called, promise the world to a select few. An invite-only network created exclusively for beautiful people. This is where the digital and physical benefits of pretty privilege collide. Those whose profiles are deemed worthy – who have invested in Instagram Face and have perfected their self-portraits – are granted access to club nights, restaurants, hotels and experiences in exchange for attractive faces in their venues and on their social media channels.

We are escorted to a red leather booth – one of about ten, each with a table in the centre. On the table sits a large silver bucket full of ice with an oversized bottle of vodka that is all ours. Next to it, carafes of orange and cranberry juice. The promoter stands and pours us drinks on demand, watching over us as we take our seats atop the booth, our heels piercing dents into the seats. This is where we must stay for the night –

in a line with the other girls. Our phones' flashes bright. Our lips pouting, bodies posing.

We may have paid £10 to get in but we will have free drinks all night in this exclusive London venue. A night that would usually cost well over £100 will cost us 10 per cent of that. Not only does being beautiful open physical doors for us but symbolic ones too. In the status games of social media, there is a currency in being here, in being able to post your photos and tag the location, in being seen to live a luxurious life. To be granted entry is to be confirmed as beautiful, to rub shoulders with influencers and celebrities, to be ordained with a level of importance in a society that values aesthetics over everything. Most of the girls here have been scouted online. The men have each paid upwards of £5,000 for their booths, furnished with beautiful women plied with free alcohol. Sat pretty and posing, we are their reward.

What we are doing is defined as aesthetic labour – work for which you are compensated, directly or indirectly, for your body's appearance. This may include sex work, modelling and social media influencing. In our highly visual online world, aesthetic labour is becoming a more common line of work and lifestyle. When everyone can strive to be professionally beautiful, we increasingly choose to do so, with certain aesthetics (such as Instagram Face) creating currency in the digital world. Adherence to the digital beauty standard can lead to an incredibly lucrative career at best – despite the outlay on procedures, products and enhancements – and a dopamine hit at worst, with the possibility of free trips, dinners, club nights, products and brand deals too.

This aesthetic labour we are performing is an extension of a long history of women as sexualised display objects – from Victorian barmaids to the glamorous uniforms of air hostesses – that blur the line between aesthetics and sexualised labour. Despite some progress in professional arenas, the digital age has led to the aestheticisation of more and more sectors of the economy as we focus increasingly on appearance and our bodies become products both on- and offline.

Aesthetic labour is a gendered practice, one that reinforces the idea of beauty as 'women's work' and compounds the currency associated with beauty ideals. Our bodies are used to bestow status upon venues and organisations in ways male or non-conforming bodies could not. For our part, we perform as we should, as pretty, sexy, available objects; visible and contained.

We sit in a line on the booth, pressed against each other shoulder to shoulder, like a row of dolls on a shelf. Me and Eliza, with Ava, Mila, Leah, Zara and Nadia – each a regular on the club scene, each beautiful, none older than twenty-two. Nadia, Leah and Zara had gotten in for free. Ava and Mila had had to pay.

Leah is twenty-one and an intern, doing what she refers to as 'slave labour' for luxury fashion brands – often sewing in basements, returning garments and working until 5am, all for no pay. She has a degree in economics, but, as a recent graduate, is living in a small room in Marylebone without any windows. When a man slid into her DMs one night, not long after she'd moved to London from Stuttgart, complimenting her profile and asking if she wanted to dine at a Mayfair restaurant for free that evening, it seemed too good to be true. She ate five courses there four times a week, each meal worth more than her weekly rent. She never paid for a thing.

Nadia tells a similar story – she's a student, originally from Manchester with Scandinavian and Pakistani parents; she moved here for university to study business. There were times when she would go out with the promoters every night for a week. She tells me proudly that during her first week in London she didn't pay for a single meal – her fridge was empty but her Instagram DMs were full of offers for free food at the most expensive restaurants in the city. Her profiles are awash with high-flash images and designer shopping bags, expensive interiors and nightclub toilets. You would never guess she is broke, that the carrier bags are empty, that she buys expensive makeup to use once a month and the rest of the time is frugal with her routine. You'd never know that the beautiful life she leads is smoke and mirrors, an artful deception of ultimate influence.

'It's like manifesting,' she tells me. 'You have to present yourself a certain way and then you attract the type of life that gets you into these expensive places. I just post really sexy pictures in clubs and I edit the pictures so I look better. I use airbrush, I'll smooth my skin, I'll put on digital makeup, and I'll make my waist a bit smaller than it actually is. The better you look, the more opportunities you unlock, so you have to finesse the system.'

Other times, it wasn't only dinners. Leah would be invited to entire weekends away – rich men who own crypto-currency or kids of the super-rich visit the city for a few days and want people around to party with, to entertain on their yachts and accompany them to bars. Leah doesn't think of herself as any more beautiful than the average woman; I think most people would disagree. When she's insecure, her boyfriend will tell her she's blind. She tells me now that she's finally in a place where she no longer looks in the mirror and cries.

Nadia tells me about her getting-ready rituals, and she adds that she hasn't eaten all day – that she went to the gym this morning and spent the whole day in bed to avoid having to waste any energy and risk getting hungry. Sometimes she'll go three days without any food (just vapes) so that she can look skinny in her dress.

'I'll go to stand up and I'll feel like fainting, but if my dress is tight there's no way I'm eating anything,' she says.

She tells me how one time, she and her friends had starved themselves for three days before a night out but got so hungry that they devoured a Nando's on the way to the club. Filled with instant regret, they spent hours throwing it all up, crowding the toilets until their throats hurt. She says it as if it's nothing and I ask if she does that often. She nods, as if it's the most obvious thing in the world, and I glance down at the two glasses of vodka in her hands.

Leah had asked to bring someone with her to the events at first, but after the promoters requested to see her friend's profile, they told her to come alone. This was a VIP venue and they had to keep the standards high – they didn't say it explicitly but the message was clear: her friend was not beautiful enough. Leah didn't know how to tell her friend this, so instead insisted that the restaurant had simply run out of space.

Beauty is a constant negotiation of power and privilege – these girls are the lucky ones, the ones whose beauty opened doors and opportunities. They have pretty privilege and social platforms that other girls crave. In the battle of the beauty haves and have-nots, they are winning but, once again, it feels like winning in these beauty status games comes with no prize at all. The cost – both psychological and physical – seems too high to stomach.

Nadia has plans to go to Turkey to get a nose job. 'I don't like people taking pictures of me from certain angles,' she says. 'The one I want is £12,500 but I've been researching this since I was twelve.' She tells me she would break up with her abusive boyfriend but he's agreed to buy it for her. She only has to stick it out till the summer, she says.

*

A few weeks later, just a few miles away from that Mayfair club, on the Dollis Valley estate in Barnet, north London, I sit waiting in the Art Against Knives community nail salon.

Before the girls arrive, I flick through the charity's latest project – a zine created by eight- to fourteen-year-olds, covering the issues they care about the most: gentrification, LGBTQ+ rights, racism, feminism and the qualities of a healthy relationship. There are four pages on beauty: candyfloss-coloured paper peppered with faces cut from magazines and inspirational quotes complete with spelling mistakes. To the lefthand side, one of the young people has written in purple pen 'even the prettiest people think there not good enough' whilst another scrawled 'everyone is different and unique in there own way. No one is perfect'.

Open every Tuesday, Dollis Dolls is a space for vulnerable young women to get beauty treatments done for free whilst accessing a range of creative activities and social care. In the salon, specialist staff offer support on issues from domestic violence to street harassment. To my right, an older woman sits to get a manicure done before a job interview, her nails now a glossy nude. Founder Katy Dawe created the space after noticing that some of the most marginalised women were prioritising beauty treatments over necessary purchases.

In the age of the digital, beauty standards are creating a beauty tax that is higher than ever. With cosmetic procedures readily available and the ideal intensifying, there is now an expectation for women to undergo not only the usual roster of 'maintenance' treatments – hair, nails, eyebrows, lashes, teeth – but also 'tweakments' like injectables and surgeries. Those who are celebrated for their beauty both on and offline are increasingly people who have undergone various surgeries and treatments. The 'I'm not ugly, I'm just poor' meme format is a reflection of this change: using before and after pictures of high-profile celebrities like Bella Hadid, Kylie Jenner and influencers Simi and Haze, it demonstrates how money rather than genetics is all that's necessary to create a face that's deemed beautiful.

This is significant because now, more than ever, our appearance has become our most valuable commodity. Thanks to social media, selfies and Zoom calls, our faces and bodies are always front and centre and have become something we 'should' invest in. Middle- and upper-class women have the financial freedom to view an expensive and risky surgical procedure as a 'treat' to allow them to fit the beauty standard and reap the rewards of adherence.

'When I first started working with young women, one of the biggest things that shocked me was that I'd often feel like the least glamorous person in the room,' Katy Dawe tells me. 'But this was my privilege playing out. I would think, "How come you've got your nails and lashes done but you're on free school meals?" And then I took a step back. What is possible for people who have no hope or opportunity? You still need to find the strength to present yourself to the world and you have to consider what has social currency in your community – what can improve your experience, and what might make the difference between you getting home safely or not being bullied.'

As the cost of beauty increases – the jump between a manicure and a nose job is significant – people are being priced out and putting themselves at risk financially in order to participate. An article in *Refinery29* detailed how women are racking up thousands of pounds in credit card debt in order to get Botox and filler. The pressures levelled against women to retain and maintain the perfect face, resist the effects of ageing, remove their body hair and groom themselves to perfection mean that beauty treatments are often paid for over other 'essential' items.

Beauty and wealth have always been inextricably linked. Throughout history, the beauty standard of any given period has served the ideological interests of the ruling class, with our perception of ugliness so often intertwined with disability, queer identity, race and poverty. Whilst the beauty standard is entirely undemocratic, its impact is universal. Women and girls are given little choice but to chase this elusive quality in order to get a better slice of the world, or even to simply feel *human*. Adhering to the beauty standard requires privilege but also generates privilege, creating a vicious cycle in which those without the economic freedom to participate are heavily penalised, financially and socially. The ideal is more attainable for women who already closely resemble the standard but marginalises those who are already less privileged. The result is a new beauty class system in which there are those who can afford to participate and those who cannot.

Beauty elicits what is referred to as a 'halo' effect – in which we automatically assign positive traits to an attractive person, assuming they are more confident, competent and socially skilled than the average person, simply because they are beautiful. Attractive people are almost 12 per cent more likely to be successful in applying for loans, are more likely to win arguments, to persuade others to change their opinions, and to be offered help and assistance. Multiple studies also found that beautiful people are seen as healthier and more credible.

This beauty premium is apparent in the legal system, in which attractive offenders are less likely to be caught, less likely to be reported and face more lenient treatment if their case makes it to court. At work, individuals are more likely to evaluate work done by beautiful people favourably, even if their work is inferior. Attractive people are more likely to be called back for an interview, more likely to be hired and promoted, and they earn higher salaries. It's a phenomenon that transcends industries and geographical borders – being beautiful is aligned with higher salaries among American lawyers and beauty salon employees in East Asia. A beauty premium has been documented in fields as diverse as education, politics, charity, finance and strategy.

Our online world is no different. On social media, beauty plays a role in structuring opportunity, returning significant benefits to those who are deemed attractive. Those rewards may be likes, follows or lucrative brand deals and sponsorships.

But what we're talking about here isn't just naturally attributed beauty. In the labour market, being attractive is not enough, it is *doing* attractiveness appropriately that gets rewarded. Consistent with Naomi Wolf's argument in *The Beauty Myth* that the 'beauty myth is always actually prescribing behaviour and not appearance', the more effort, money and time women spend on their appearance, the more they are rewarded. The more obedient we are to the status quo, the more we will be compensated.

In the workplace, being poorly groomed resulted in a 28 per cent penalty on earnings, whilst being very well groomed led to a 45 per cent premium. Studies show that less attractive but well-groomed women earn more than attractive or very attractive women who don't invest in beautification. This supports Wolf's argument that the beauty standard is ultimately a mechanism for controlling women's behaviour: in making the effort, in showing willingness to conform to the social cues and adhering to the standard, women are granted access to a privilege readily available for men. Whilst good grooming is beneficial for men, it is made vital for women, giving women of all levels of beauty access to the premiums, if they're willing to spend the time, money and effort in adhering.

*

Katy started coming to the estate in 2012, when other youth workers identified that whilst there were initiatives in place to support young men and boys, there were countless young women on the periphery who were equally at risk. She started showing up every Tuesday, sitting outside, in stairwells, in cafes and community centres, and she'd pull out her nail polish and offer free manicures. A couple of girls soon turned into twenty – the nail art becoming a point of connection between generations and cultural groups. It was the girls themselves who decided they wanted to set up the salon – and it's been open forty-eight weeks a year for the past ten years.

'As a society, we've now got some celebrity representation that has expanded beyond the traditional forms of beauty, right? But still, they have celebrity status, that freedom still feels far removed from us down here. The same rules don't apply. We still have this aspirational, unachievable, unrealistic idea of what you need to look like in order to be successful,' Katy says. 'If you've got good nails, everyone thinks you have your shit together. As a young woman, it felt like a powerful tool and form of currency: when I had no money, I could paint my nails, walk into any room and gain some respect.'

This reminded of what Ruth Holliday, professor of gender and culture at the University of Leeds, said to me when I spoke to her about the relationship between beauty and class for an article for *Dazed* magazine: 'If you're white, middle class and you've got a good job, you don't need these things as much. It's when you're marginalised that this beauty work becomes so much more important.' Those with privilege have long been able to use their wealth to communicate their social 'value' and set themselves apart. As a result, beauty reflects a class hierarchy and a site of social struggle. Beauty is used by many as self-care but when this desire turns into a need, just to feel seen and respected as a human being, that is when we have a problem.

The value assigned to women's beauty is steeped in class inequalities, ageism, ableism, racial prejudices and colonial impacts – and is therefore not equally available for all women. Bodies hold value in their social context and thus their value cannot solely be determined by individual will or work. The notion of beauty as a virtue, akin to truth, still exists today in our determination to be perceived as naturally and effortlessly attractive. To employ artificial means in order to achieve beauty, you have engaged in deception, which is marked as vulgar. Hence why so many celebrities who profit from their appearance refuse to acknowledge the beauty work they have had done. To do so would be to admit effort and would automatically lower their level of perceived beauty. The result is a paradox, in which women are valued for their beauty and physical attractiveness, but often penalised and judged for putting effort in to enhance their appearance. Women are expected to employ rigorous self-discipline and monitoring, whilst appearing nonchalant and unconcerned by beauty at all.

Whilst beauty work done well can act as a form of social advancement, when done badly these procedures can have the reverse effect. Whether it's larger lips, poorly applied filler or too-white veneers, the way beauty treatments are performed is adding another layer of social separation. 'For middle-class people, seeing somebody who has obviously had work done can evoke a bit of disgust,' says Professor Holliday. 'Working-class bodies are nearly always marked as excessive, as too much, and lip filler would be a classic example. However, working-class people might not see it in the same way. Bigger is better because it's the obviousness of it that shows you are a body of value, and that you should be included in society. By working on your own body, you're showing your skill, your resources and your labour, which is more valued in working-class culture.'

We see this in digital beauty culture regularly, when influential women employ beauty work in order to achieve a level of fame before reversing their beauty work once they have reached an unassailable level of success. Whether it was Molly-Mae dissolving her filler and having her veneers removed, or Kylie Jenner supposedly removing the filler from her lips after making millions from her pout, we see beauty work used as a means to an end to achieve visibility and move from one cultural class to another, at which point it must be abandoned and exchanged for something more 'effortless'. Once the look that they have profited from and popularised is achieved by the masses, they must distance themselves so as not to be associated with a now 'common' aesthetic.

*

At the club, every time we leave the booth – to take selfies in the bathroom or chat in the smoking area – my phone lights up with a message from the promoter.

'Hey, where did you go?'

'When are you coming back to the booth?'

'Come back soon'

It's easy to forget that our drinks aren't actually free – that our attendance comes at a price. We must be on display. We must be sat in the line on top of the booth. We must be visible and we couldn't hide.

'It's like ownership,' says Zara when I show her the texts. 'They think because they've given you free drinks that you're theirs for the night. Sometimes the promoters expect you to go home with them because they've treated you nicely in the club.'

This was something I'd heard from other sources – that once the men paying for their tables had made their selection of girls, the promoters would take their pick from who was left. We spend our night trying to avoid these interchangeable men, gravitating instead to the electric sanctuary of the nightclub bathroom. Every girl knows that there are fewer places more magical than this. Here, we converge in a sacred space that transcends the trappings of our ordinary encounters. Amidst a backdrop of soft beats and sticky floors, we let go of our inhibitions and centuries of indoctrination – gone is the competition, the hierarchy and the jealousy. The curtain drops and we see each other, emerging from the stalls, as human beings, as sisters once more. We are instantly transported back to nights spent effervescent under duvet covers, high-pitched giggles echoing from sugar-frosted lips. We were mere strangers moments ago, but all of a sudden, a transcendent sisterhood is formed.

'You look so hot!' Eliza gushes at the two girls taking mirror pics as we enter.

'Are you joking?! Look at YOU!' they reply. 'Your lipstick looks AMAZING! You're so beautiful, honestly.'

'Oh my god, it's this one!' Eliza says as she empties the contents of her clutch bag by the side of the sinks to find the lipstick, before offering it for everyone to try. 'It looks so good on you, you have to keep it,' she says, refusing to take the lipstick back from Mila's hands.

When Leah starts crying because her ex-boyfriend has recently soft-launched a new girl on his social accounts, Eliza is ready to take a taxi to his house and smash his windows. 'We can't believe it, you deserve so much better. You're so beautiful and kind and smart and lovely,' we coo, as she wipes the tears from her face and my phone buzzes with more messages from my promoter, asking us to resume our positions on the booth. 'Now let's get this girl some drinks!'

We knock on the stall doors; we check everyone is okay. We make it our mission to fetch water for the girls who are stumbling – we nurture one another and stroke each other's hair. Before we know it, I've invited everyone to my birthday party and we've all agreed we absolutely must go on an all-inclusive holiday to Greece.

As we push our way through the club, the girls each reach back in the dark, our fingers interlacing like ribbons under iridescent lights. We hold onto each other tightly as we loop through the crowds – Zara, Leah, Ava and Nadia all checking back to confirm we are still one indivisible thread. Once we arrive at our booth, we pose together for selfies, kissing each other's cheeks and telling each other how beautiful we are – not just for our makeup and pretty dresses but for our auras, our souls, our energies. We follow each other's accounts, we like all of the photos, we spam our stories with our new best friends and vow to watch over each other forever.

As we break away from one another, I sit down next to Zara; a twenty-two-year-old originally from Belgium, she travelled to London to study civil engineering. I tell her she looks beautiful and she replies with a knowing look. 'I've realised I have to look a certain way to get into these spaces,' she tells me. 'As a dark-skinned Black woman, I have to straighten my hair, I have to dress up when other girls can get away with putting in less effort. We know we can't go out as a group of Black girls; we just get denied entry even if we look the part. There's favouritism towards lighter-skinned girls for sure. One promoter told me that it's just due to what the clients like – that the majority of men buying tables prefer Latin, Asian or white women, but not Black girls. They need the client to spend money, they want to impress them, even if it's at our expense.'

Zara spends £300 a month on her beauty regime. Beauty products for darker-skinned women are notoriously more expensive and despite progress on behalf of brands, are still limited as to what is available at an affordable price. And still, after investing so much, she finds herself overlooked.

'I try to just accept myself as much as I can, but there are times when I am out with lighter-skinned friends and the staff will ask if they want anything to drink but will miss me out.'

I ask why she comes back often and she tells me it's like networking, that it's a way to open doors to affluent spaces and influential people. Whilst the hyper-visibility of the female body and the use of women as display objects in venues like these clubs assign power to the men orchestrating these scenes, we have to consider the agency of these women too. Zara views this evening as a strategic move, in which she is playing the game in pursuit of her own goals. She carefully balances manipulation, subjugation and resistance in the hope that she will ultimately leave better off. Her friend already got a job from a contact she met in a club; Zara is hoping for the same.

The idea of beauty work being a form of 'investment' came up in almost every interview I did with young women about the treatments they had had done or the products they bought. It's also a prevalent marketing message used by cosmetic companies, aesthetic clinics and practitioners to sell these products and services to us – positioning them as 'empowering' tools to help our confidence and social standing. The difficulty, however, in viewing beauty as an investment is that much of the beauty work women undertake is viewed as essential mandates for our humanity or femininity – not an additional form of capital.

Many aestheticians are also now offering payment plans, or 'buy now, pay later' services. As a generation, we have given up almost all hope of owning a property. We have more student debt, lower incomes and fewer assets than any other age group. We grew up during a global recession and are entering our adult years with the prospect of another. And yet we spend more on beauty, self-care and wellness than any other demographic – outspending baby boomers two to one.

'If you weigh the emotional risk of thousands of pounds of unattainable debt against the emotional risk of feeling undesirable, you'll probably find that the idea of being undesirable seems worse,' Charlotte Fox Weber, psychotherapist and author, said in an article for *Dazed*.

In our individualistic, capitalist and patriarchal culture, the beauty standard is acting as a tool to keep those with less privilege at the bottom of the social hierarchy. It is a way for those with privilege to keep and increase their advantage, whilst those who can't participate are given little choice but to cut corners in order to do so. Unless we work to change things, we are approaching a future in which our beauty standard evolves to an ever-expensive ideal, further increasing the opportunity gap between classes. 'I'm not ugly, I'm just poor' may only be a meme but the reality behind the satire paints a terrifying vision for the future.

*

As the school day comes to a close, a few girls filter through the door at the Dollis Valley Nail Salon. They sit huddled together, all on their phones. They each offer to show me their channels and their favourite filters (they would never post without one). I nod, horrified by the videos they swiped to show me – young teen girls blurred and sculpted to similarity by AR, dancing and pouting to music.

Katy had told me about the complexity of working with young women whose lives exist so pervasively online. Social media has created a huge challenge – and when the charity set up their own accounts, they all of a sudden had access to what the girls were posting.

'Typical things I would hear on any given day would be fourteen-year-old girls talking about men they've met online and have arranged to meet,' says Katy. 'But we also see them posting about wanting to commit suicide or I see twelve-year-old girls posting photos in lingerie.'

Whilst the girls get their nails done by volunteers, learn how to braid hair on a mannequin, paint self-portraits and eat snacks from the spread laid out for them on a fold-out table, they start to open up. They each tell me, individually, that they don't feel pretty. That they aren't beautiful. I ask them what they think beauty is, if not themselves. Without blinking, they simply reply 'the popular girls online'.

I look back at the zine still on my lap and realise it is a script, a series of empowering quotes they had memorised but not internalised. A marketing spiel they had seen in countless pastel posts on Instagram, empty platitudes they were now regurgitating. These are the lies we tell ourselves in order to live. To say that you are beautiful no matter what and that self-love is all that matters entirely ignores the impact that beauty has on our actual, physical lives. It is to pretend that pretty privilege does not exist, that opportunities don't correlate to physical appearance and that the way you look makes no difference to the way you are treated by others. The pursuit of beauty is an entirely rational one. One that we are given little choice but to pursue. These girls know it at thirteen, just as I know it at twenty-eight.

As I sit there, I repeat the script I too had learnt is useful to say in the face of self-doubt. I remind them that the 'popular' girls they're following are all feeling the same, that they use filters too, and don't always look as picture-perfect as social media would make it seem. I am thinking about Nadia and her friends in the toilets at Nando's. Of Leah crying at her reflection. But I have to physically stop myself from telling them that none of it matters, that beauty is irrelevant or just harmless fun. Because we all know it is a lie. Every scroll, every day spent in school, every minute spent online reaffirms what they already know. That now, more than ever, there is a privilege that comes with being pretty. And they want in.

As I leave, I ask them what they'd like to do the next time I come to visit. Perhaps we could create collages like they had in their zine? They respond unanimously with the same idea: they want to learn how to do makeup like mine.

*

It's hard to disentangle the enjoyment women get from beauty practices from the pressure society puts on us to pursue the ideal. Beauty work can be a fun and intimate exchange, often creating a space for bonding and connection that transcends generational and cultural barriers, but we can't remove ourselves from the culture that tells us that it is necessary or advantageous.

Beauty, after all, is a multi-billion-dollar industry, with 70 per cent controlled by major conglomerates, only one of which currently has a female CEO. It is in their best interest to keep us hooked, to damage our self-esteem and convince us that we must buy their products in order to be worthy. If we feel good, it's because they want us to feel good. They want us to relish our own subjugation. Beauty – cultural, intimate, symbolic and joyful – is something we are taught to love. It is then sold back to us for profit, at our own expense.

Whilst attractiveness matters for men, it is essential for women. Whether it's gaining weight or ageing, we see men given more social latitude as they deviate from the beauty ideal, whilst women are harshly penalised. Alongside the extraordinary pressure that women face to be slim, obese women suffer greater financial penalties than obese men, and are judged as less sexually attractive. When it comes to gendered expectations of the feminine performance, such as shaving, women are also penalised for not adhering to the social standard. Women who do not remove body hair are not only rated as unattractive but also as less intelligent, less happy, and less sociable than women who do shave their legs and underarms.

This work we do to our bodies for the pursuit of a better life is what French philosopher Foucault described as 'technologies of the self' – actions we take to transform ourselves 'in order to attain a state of happiness, purity, wisdom, perfection or immortality'. Our desire to make these 'investments' into our appearance is neither an irrational nor a passive response to patriarchal culture, but rather a reflection of our agency within a predetermined set of constraints. A desire to get dermal filler injections can simultaneously come from a feeling of insecurity inflicted by a prescriptive beauty standard and a very rational understanding that adhering to the standard can result in a better life and a subsequent return on investment – whether the reward is psychological, social or financial.

What's interesting, however, is that according to economists' research, men are rewarded more for putting effort into their appearance than women (despite the much longer list of requirements, products and expectations placed on women's beauty regimes). This means that women's 'investment' into beauty work is not translating into their relative earning potential. This is further compounded by the gender pay gap – the idea of 'investment' in the self is a false promise when women are already disadvantaged in terms of earnings and the cost of grooming requirements for women is ever increasing. We begin at a net negative but are told we must 'invest' in our appearance in order to better our career development and achieve a parity status to that of men. Whilst we pay for beauty rituals, men are afforded the ability to invest their spare cash into long-term financial planning.

Our belief in beauty becomes a self-fulfilling prophecy. If we believe that it is our primary social currency, then we are more likely to support an environment where this currency is accepted and worth the effort. We look to legitimise our beauty work and inadvertently bolster the unequal system that requires it. In reality, when we consider the constant self-monitoring, psychological labour and time expended, we likely receive a negative return on what is sold to us as a so-called 'investment'. Multiple studies into the cost-benefit analysis of investing in beauty work have shown that, for most people, it is not worth the time, money and effort expended. Women face several contradictions when they perform beauty work. If we fail at beauty conformity, we are powerless and condemned as ugly; if we are successful, we are still powerless in a regime that defines our value and worth by our appearance. In our attempts, we also reinforce unequal economic structures and a multi-billion-dollar-a-year beauty industry profits from our efforts.

Studies have found that having more followers on social media increases the pressure to be beautiful, but only for women. The more you adhere to the internet's standard of beauty, the more successful you become online. The more successful you become online, the worse you feel about your appearance. The cycle is vicious and feels impossible to escape.

For us to succeed long-term, we must think and work as a collective, taking actions for the betterment of womanhood as a whole. However, this creates a double bind. On an individual and short-term level, the benefits of conforming to current beauty culture *seem* worthwhile. There is the instant dopamine hit, the very real rewards – from Instagram likes to free nights out and employment opportunities – that make beauty a very rational pursuit for many.

Despite our changing role in society and increased earning potential, our beauty standards are more prescriptive than ever. The gender status quo is largely preserved, if not worsened, by the increasing aestheticisation of our world and the ever-increasing beauty tax women are faced with. We are told over and over again by digital beauty culture that disempowerment is power. In truth, there are no good strategies in a game that is rigged from the start; there is no way to win without resetting the entire board.

*

Across the haze of the darkened club I see Mila holding Ava by the waist, her head drooped to the side, mouth open. Mila's eyes hold mine, wide with panic. She is buckling.

'You need to get her out of here, she's too drunk,' a bouncer yells over the music.

'She's had one drink all night!' Mila is incredulous. 'I think she left it on the stage at one point.'

We look at one another – instantly sober. We all know what that means. She has been poisoned. Spiked. It is something that has long happened – sometimes by dropping substances into women's drinks, but most recently through injections to exposed skin.

Beauty may have promised us power but we know now more than ever that misogyny always prevails.

Eliza and I take the weight of Ava's body in our arms and we help Mila to carry her up the stairs, the promoters looking on. I think about the open carafes on the table, the oversized bottles we'd shared. I think about how easy it would be to take us all out, to have a booth of beautiful girls lifeless and unmoving.

Outside, night stains the sky and our tiny outfits feel suddenly absurd. We collapse onto the pavement, falling over each other like tongues trying to tie up a cherry stem. Attempting to keep Ava safe at our core. Next to us, shivering girls await their judgement.

Mila tries calling for a taxi, rejected over and over again as they see us huddled on the tarmac. Ava lies with her head on the ground, her mouth foaming with tiny bubbles, her eyes white and rolling back into her glistening skull. Mila tries to stand her up but her limbs collapse under her, a paralysed and beautiful marionette.

We promise we will text when everyone is home safe, and the next morning when Ava comes to. We will hold contact with Mila in our palms and wait feverishly for confirmation until the call comes at midday. She is okay, she will be okay.

A few months later, Ava appears on my screens again, the camera flash holding her in an angelic glow. She is wearing another tiny outfit, looking back over her shoulder in the same club, and she looks, to all of us, like she is living her most luxurious life.

How can we create a more beautiful future for women and girls?

'I think empathy is a huge part of it. I don't think we can make any progress if we are all just shouting at each other. I think the future is all about nuance and understanding why people feel they need to do these things or get these treatments, understanding that people are multi-faceted. I think only then are we ever going to make any kind of progress when it comes to unravelling these issues.'

Scarlett Curtis,
writer and activist

6

Build a Body

I couldn't tell you when it started. It might've been with Sarah Baartman, when her body was sliced up, dissected and preserved in parts. It might've been in the 1950s when Sylvia Plath wrote: 'I know pretty much what I like and dislike; but please, don't ask me who I am. A passionate, fragmentary girl, maybe?' Or it might've been in 1972, when Susan Sontag wrote: 'Men present themselves as face-and-body, a physical whole. Women are split, as men are not, into a body and a face – each judged by somewhat different standards.' By now, it is so much worse than that.

I might not know when it started, but I can tell you that we felt it all the same. It might've been the paper dolls, the ring-bound picture books with the girls sliced into thirds that we'd play with, flipping through options of legs and torsos to line up with their heads. Or the large, bodiless dolls we made over, cutting off their hair with delight, or the Betty Spaghetty toys we tore limb from limb. It might've been the body shape books, the makeover shows. Perhaps it was our mothers and their laundry list of body hang-ups, the workouts to get Olivia Wilde's abs or Miley Cyrus's legs. Or even the men chuckling over 'breast or thigh?' as they served us meat. I couldn't tell you when it started, but dismemberment followed us growing up.

I remember playing a game when I was twelve on school buses and at sleepovers, just like we'd seen in the movie *Angus*,

Thongs and Perfect Snogging. We'd tear a piece of paper from felted spiral notepads and create a grid, writing our name at the very top and our features down the side, leaving space for each person in the group to assign a rating, anonymously, in the columns to the right.

Hair

Eyes

Nose

Lips

Boobs

Stomach

Legs

We'd pass the papers along, as pieces of our soft young selves were anatomised, quantified, analysed and criticised as separate from the whole to which they belonged. Once the rounds were complete, our eyes would flicker over the final judgements and we'd laugh nervously at our dismemberment.

When the internet arrived, we continued to assign each other ratings, even pre-social media. Websites like 'Hot or Not' allowed us to judge one another, and we became accustomed to ranking each other from one to ten. In *Angus, Thongs and Perfect Snogging*, Georgia got a six for her nose and in girl-world that was a dagger to the heart. A social homicide. We all knew that a six was as close to a one as you could get, and a nine wasn't really a nine, it was a heart-shaped badge that said 'you are loved, you are my favourite and I will forever sit next to you at lunch'.

Not only did our bodies fragment, ruptures appeared *between* bodies, divorcing us from each other. There will always be a part of another woman that I want, that she is unable to give to me. Someone will always score higher. I am destined to live in envy, resenting the parts of her that I covet, failing to see the parts of myself she would trade if she could. We look each other up and down in the street, we glare across the void. In order to make ourselves feel better about our dismembered parts we take our knives to one another. We dissect, we discuss, we dehumanise – we separate our sisters from their souls and selves, assuming we're the only ones suffering. At night, we imagine they sleep peacefully, their perfect, whole bodies unworried, unbroken, no scalpels under their sheets. We hate that they're happy. They are not like us, those perfect other girls. We feel feral when they fall, when they inevitably break down, and we welcome them into the fractured girls club with a smug smile, making eyes at one another as we bring them in for an embrace. We feel unthreatened here, at the bottom together.

Ask any woman or girl and she will produce, with ease, a list of her own body parts that are defective. She may be able to tell you that some parts of herself are 'okay' and perhaps name one or two that she actually likes, but this is often rare. Research has shown that when asked to describe their bodies, women tend to break themselves down into a series of pull-apart components that need to be fixed. Men, on the other hand, view their bodies as single units. As whole, holistic entities.

Perhaps most importantly, men think much more about their bodies' capabilities. Every single man asked to describe their body in a study by the University of Sussex talked about it in terms of what it could *do.* Not a single woman did. Instead, the women in the study assessed the value of their body solely as a decorative object, based only on aesthetic value. The fragmentation extended past their physical selves and into their sentient selves – a fracture between the body and its entitlement to value purely for *being*.

Stomach

The bath was too hot but I didn't mind. I lowered one foot in, letting out a series of short, sharp exhales. Everything tingled as I forced myself in through clenched teeth. I lay back, trying to relax. Toes gripping on to the mottled faucet.

I was thirteen and my body was still soft, half-formed. I stared at the concertina of flesh between my hips and chest – lines seared into my skin where my body insisted on bending. I sat up straight. I leant back. I curled forwards. All the time glaring at the opening and closing, opening and closing of the folds.

This is the first part of myself I remember hating, viscerally hating. I liked my eyes and my hair. That was it. My nose was too angular, my skin too pale, my under-eyes too dark, my ribcage too wide and my legs too short. But my stomach I hated with a vengeance.

I remember scowling at my torso, I remember wishing I could just cut chunks of myself off. I wanted to know why my middle looked so different to the women I saw on the screens, why mine needed to bend this way, why it needed to bend at all.

When the bath started to cool, I added more hot water until it threatened the lip of the tub. They say that if you put a frog in boiling water, it jumps out straight away. But if you put a frog in warm water that slowly begins to boil, the frog will sit there, unknowingly cooking to death.

*

Fifteen-year-old Karen stands in front of a large, gilded mirror.

'God, my hips are huge!'

'Oh, please. I hate my calves.' Gretchen moves to stand beside her.

'At least you guys can wear halters. I've got man shoulders,' Regina joins in.

The three girls – all incredibly beautiful – stand in front of the mirror looking their bodies up and down, fidgeting, their hands on their faces, then rearranging their hair.

'My hairline is so weird.'

'My pores are huge.'

'My nail beds suck.'

The girls turn to Cady, sat on the bed, expectantly waiting to hear her confess her flaws.

'I have really bad breath in the morning,' she shrugs.

'Ew,' Regina replies.

I couldn't tell you how many times I have watched this scene from the 2004 cult-classic movie *Mean Girls*, how many times I saw it and didn't blink, didn't bat an eyelid at the girls' commentary on their still-developing selves. I realise now it is meant as satire but for us this was the norm, to break ourselves down in front of our friends, to seek validation and reassurance, and then to refuse to believe any that came our way. The girls were stunning, yes, but it didn't shock me to hear them complain. I had learnt by the time I was a teenager that there will always be something wrong – even if you're the most beautiful girl in school.

Cady, a previously home-schooled 'jungle freak', transgresses the social order by stating a flaw that is a universal, short-term problem. To admit to having bad breath is not to fragment the self but to humanise the self. That is not the game. Women are simultaneously objectified fantasies and imperfect projects under development, self-loathing beings always looking to evolve towards perfection. For Cady to name a natural issue that's easy to fix, one that should have already been dealt with in secret, shatters the illusions of femininity and defies the rules. You should hate something about your body that is difficult, or nigh on impossible, to fix; something that requires extensive labour to work on or through. To hate what can easily be changed gets the beauty industrial complex nowhere. You must hate your bones, your muscles, your sinew, your flesh. You must hate yourself for how you have been constructed. It's like, the rules of feminism.

And so, we became the girlbosses of our own bodies. As the digital blurred the boundaries between the public, private and professional domains, our selves became a site of labour. We took a knife to our 2D pictures and said 'Oh, crop me out of that one, will you?', flattened ourselves into mere objects – decorative pretty pictures and props. We chopped off our heads, cut ourselves down to size, deformed ourselves in the digital. We were scared to live in 3D – to take up space with our physical bodies, to allow ourselves depth of feeling, to express anything other than a 'smile, love, it might never happen'. We broke ourselves down in every dimension, tearing ourselves apart evermore intensely until we were left with nothing but a pile of pixels and particles on the cutting room floor.

We worked on ourselves instead of working on the culture. We turned inwards, becoming entrepreneurs of the self; positioning ourselves as the prototype, assessing our inventory, recording our previous performance and logging how much we needed to invest in order to increase our returns – professionally, privately and personally. Which fix would make the biggest difference? Where can we maximise our potential?

It became increasingly apparent that no part of us was too trivial to be torn apart. Each aspect of ourselves zoomed into, placed under a microscope and dominated by a forensic dissection. Our flaws became more and more specific, our list of ailments more intensive and extensive. We thought about our cellulite, cankles, stretch marks, strawberry legs, thread veins, skin tone, calves, kneecaps, hip dips, ribcage, bellybutton, nipple size, smile lines, armpit fat, waist-to-hip ratio, wide torso, double chin, uneven breasts, too-large breasts, too-small breasts, too-large thighs, too-small thighs, the roundness of our bum, the colour of our arm hair, the length of our nail beds, the balance of our chins, the length of our legs, the sharpness of our shoulders, the hollows under our eyes, the angle of our nose, the length of our labia, our upper arms, our cupid's bow, our foot arch, the length of our neck, the size of our hands. We imagined each part magnified, red circles highlighting what we needed to fix. We stepped outside of ourselves to view our bodies through the cosmetic gaze, mercilessly breaking ourselves apart into a factory of detachable pieces, analysed, assessed and ready to be rebuilt. Eventually, we became so detached from our own bodies that I think we lost the ability to see.

Eyes

Lately, Mira has spent a lot of time considering a blepharoplasty to 'fix' her hooded eyes and give her 'that snatched look'. She's convinced most celebrities have had one and now she wants one too. When Mira was a toddler, her mum entered her into baby pageants and she'd always win sashes for 'best eyes'.

'Yes, I'm holding onto those accolades for dear life – sue me,' she says. 'The eyebrow lift is something I believe would improve my face. Since turning thirty, I've been experiencing noticeable ageing and sadly – or more so predictably – it's been stressing me out. Botox, retinols, face massages can only do so much. The one thing they can't do is lift my brows – surgery is my only option. Having hooded eyes feels like a curse sometimes; I just hate the way it looks in photos.'

Mira uses filters and editing apps to augment her eyes, fixating on the fold of skin above her lid. Multiple times a day, she stands in front of the mirror lifting her brows with her hands to see what she would look like post-surgery. The temptation to go under the knife becoming increasingly hard to ignore.

'I can imagine feeling so much better about the way I look. I think I'd feel invincible. Though the likelihood I then fixate on something else is almost 100 per cent. I also want a breast lift and a mini face lift once I'm over forty. I spend a lot of time thinking about these procedures. The more cosmetic procedure content I consume, the more I feel like I need to start preparing to get things done to ensure that I age gracefully, as if ageing is a sin.'

The main thing stopping Mira is the fear of it all going wrong. She's scared of the risks of surgery but she's not sure which fear is worse: 'A permanent improvement is so enticing but horror stories and the possibility of ruining my face is debilitating. Almost as debilitating as my insecurities.'

*

There are many ways to build a body but cosmetic surgery represents the ultimate form of bodily invasion in the pursuit of beauty. It shows the lengths we are willing to go to for the sake of transformation. It sits in a category that seems worlds apart from exercise, makeup, hair styling or even dieting – one that requires us to subjugate fully, to quite literally put our life in another's hands. Those who undertake cosmetic surgery are viewed as the most dedicated to their vanity, the most extreme evangelists in the pursuit of perfection.

Despite the risks, there was more than a 20 per cent increase worldwide in cosmetic surgical procedures between 2015 and 2019. The industry is set to almost double in value from 2019 to 2026. According to the Aesthetic Surgery Society, surgical procedures increased by 54 per cent in the US alone in 2021, whilst in South Korea approximately 20 per cent of the population undergoes cosmetic surgery each year. Recent reports also highlight a growing number of adolescents undergoing plastic surgery, with rhinoplasty being the most popular procedure.

When I say cosmetic surgery, I'm referring to the specific branch of plastic surgery concerned with enhancing physical appearance, such as breast augmentations, liposuction, bum lifts and rhinoplasty – not reconstructive plastic surgeries designed to restore appearance or function after an accident or disease. But to define what constitutes cosmetic surgery is more difficult than you'd think. Throughout my travels and research for this book, I've noticed a fluidity in terms that is often used as a way to evade acknowledgement of procedures or to minimise their pervasiveness. In South Korea, double eyelid surgery is so common that it is not considered cosmetic surgery, despite requiring anaesthetic and a surgeon. Similarly, Kim Kardashian went to great lengths, including getting an X-ray, to prove she didn't have butt *implants*, despite the widespread rumour that she'd actually had fat transferred to her bum (which wouldn't show up on a scan). Injectables, lasers, fat freezing and invasive skincare treatments are considered 'non-surgical' but often lead to dramatic transformations in appearance. Those who undertake such procedures can (and often do) claim they haven't had any cosmetic surgery at all, as technically, their augmentations wouldn't count. Whilst we get caught up in semantics as a way of evading admission of the extent of our beauty work, the industry continues to grow.

Cosmetic surgery casts the body as a mutative state, in a continuous act of becoming, rather than simply being. The types of surgeries available began to extend as we fragmented ourselves further. Parts of us previously considered irrelevant to beauty now came with their own fix – from labiaplasty to buccal fat removal, areola reduction to dimple creation, the beauty industrial complex expanded its offerings, fuelling our fragmentation, driving up the number of patients and increasing profits. It is convenient, this fragmentation of our bodies, to an industry and a society that profit from us breaking down in order to be rebuilt, at great risk and expense, in the image of the ideal. This is an industry that depends on us perceiving ourselves as defective – and that will continuously find ways to encourage us to do so. In this way, cosmetic surgery becomes not only a means by which to comply with modern beauty standards but also an active agent in determining the standard.

The plastic surgery industry originally flourished in the name of restorative care. There is evidence of reconstructive surgery going back to antiquity – from prosthetic toes in ancient Egypt to cleft lip surgeries by fourth-century Chinese doctors. Progress in the field was slow for centuries but in the early 1900s, the advent of global warfare, along with increased knowledge of medicine, anaesthetics and infection control, fuelled possibilities and innovation. After the First World War, thousands of soldiers needed reconstructive work, prompting some of the best minds in medicine to devote themselves to restoring bodies, treating the disfigurements caused by modern weaponry, from burns to smashed skulls and missing limbs. But surgeons eventually ran out of patients on which to use their skills, and thus began the commercial shift into women's psyches. By 2005, the number of cosmetic surgery procedures performed in the US was almost double that of reconstructive procedures, according to data from the American Society of Plastic Surgeons.

When 90 per cent of board-certified plastic surgeons are men who remake our bodies, and 94 per cent of patients are now women, our beauty both is and isn't ours. Hyper-visible celebrities such as Kim Kardashian have, as Wolf writes in *The Beauty Myth*, processed their 'bodies into man-made women'.

*

The arrival of social media has fuelled the fragmentation of self. A study of teen profile pictures found that girls tend to choose close-up pictures (showing only their face or upper torso), whereas boys prefer pictures in which they are further away. For me, this poses a question about who gets to be whole – to be seen for all that they are – not just a pretty face, cute smile, nice hair, teeth, lips, eyes, cheeks and chin. Who gets to pose with their full body in frame, as if to say: take it or leave it. In posting their whole selves, boys are able to be both unfragmented and unfragmentable. In a tiny profile picture, an entire body appears pixelated and undefined, it is not worth the critique. It is only when a face is cropped off, zoomed in, that we can start to dissect it fully.

Just as the images that promote Kylie packages or other aesthetic procedures make fragmented parts of our faces and bodies the entire focus of each photo, we post images that break ourselves down into component parts, perfecting images of ever-closer crops. We post a pair of lips, collar-bones, breasts, a ribcage, a bum – treating our body parts like display objects rather than acknowledging ourselves as whole human beings. By capturing specific separate body parts, we intensify the beauty standard applied to that particular piece of ourselves, creating the blueprint for how we 'should' look. Beauty becomes a jigsaw puzzle of perfect pieces, all of which must come together – a feed of images, full of dismembered women.

Social media use, and particularly viewing content of women who have had work done, makes teenagers more likely to want to undergo cosmetic surgery. The more invested you are in your selfies and the response they receive, the more heightened your body surveillance, and the more likely you are to be unhappy with your body. Filters also support this popularisation of cosmetic surgery in adolescents, but only among girls, who feel more pressure to comply with a beauty ideal, and therefore are more inclined to use filters to augment their digital self as such. Our hyper-visual platforms have reinforced forensic self-scrutiny to the point where the nano-surveillance of women's faces and bodies has become a normal practice – whether you're thirteen years old fixating on your stomach rolls or thirty and focused on your eyelids. The fragmentation then intensifies past self-loathing and into self-correcting.

Arms

'I bet you have a lot of girls coming here,' I prompted the lady in the mask and faux scrubs. She didn't say anything as she prepared the machines. 'I bet so many women come here even though they don't need it. It's sad, really; there are so many beautiful women who just don't realise it.'

'Body dysmorphia is a very real thing,' she replied, curtly, bringing the fat freezing tubes up towards me. 'So, it was the lower tummy and upper arms for you, wasn't it?'

I nodded in reply. I was in my early twenties and had been working in beauty for a number of years at this point.

'This will be uncomfortable but it won't hurt.'

The woman in the mask proceeded to place a device over the pouch at the bottom of my stomach (the one I later learnt is strategically placed fat my body needs to protect my reproductive organs). It gripped onto the skin and sucked my stomach into its mouth, before beginning to freeze its fatty prey. I bit my lip as the woman moved to attach a similar, but smaller device to my upper arms. She placed the opening of the tube above my elbow and turned the machine on, letting it whirr before turning, perplexed, back to my arm. She tried again, pushing the tube hard into the flesh. Nothing. She grabbed me harder, willing the machine to bite as it continued to whirr. But there was no suction, no grip.

'This isn't going to work,' she said, turning to me. 'There isn't enough fat on your arms. This is my smallest attachment but you're too thin.'

I heard what she said and I felt the repeated failure of the machine as it attempted to force my body fat into submission. The size of my arms, inflated in my mind's eye, was undeniable. People could, and did, tell me otherwise, dismissing my feelings as ridiculous, but it didn't untie the logic in my mind. I didn't leave the clinic that day with a sense of confidence or reassurance, but with a sense of loss, of hopelessness. Realising I was simultaneously too much and not enough, that nothing would fix me, despite the fact that I felt I so desperately needed to be fixed. It wasn't even a pursuit of beauty at this point, I just wanted to feel comfortable in clothes. I wanted to wear strappy tops in summer or formal dresses without sleeves. I wanted to navigate my life without feelings of self-loathing and self-consciousness, to look at photographs of myself and not want to cry.

*

In many ways, I also feel fragmented from my politics. Once again, I am caught in the endless in-fighting of the opposing things I know to be true. Those treatments were painful but so was the anguish of self-loathing. I knew I was only contributing to a wider problem and yet my problems consumed my entire world. The pursuit of beauty was both freedom and enslavement. I knew I'd likely never be happy, but I still thought I might be happier. I wanted to be beautiful more than anything and that might have been one of the ugliest parts of me. But in order to survive in twenty-first century, late-stage capitalism, a woman must hold all of these things up in the air at once. Psychologically, my mind felt like it was built almost entirely of paradoxical fragmented parts – parts that couldn't fit together, nor could they be taken apart.

Beauty theorist Kathy Davis argued that women are not blind victims adhering mindlessly to a patriarchal beauty standard but instead make considered and informed decisions in navigating oppressive forces. In taking control of their self-image, women are agents making the most of a tyrannical system. Beauty work is a negotiation 'in the context of many promises and few options'. Women who opt for cosmetic surgery often do so as a result of psychological suffering: self-consciousness over small breasts, embarrassment over a crooked nose and even self-loathing as a result of protruding ears. For some of us, cosmetic surgery feels like the best or only option to alleviate suffering that has gone beyond the point of endurance.

Multiple studies have shown that many women get cosmetic surgery not necessarily to look beautiful but to become 'normal'. For these women, the desire to have a tummy tuck, breast lift or liposuction does not arise from a longing to have the perfect body but rather to no longer feel atypical. A fact surely more terrifying, as it implies that the ideal has become so pervasive that any deviations are considered abnormalities, deformities that need to be fixed. The women I interviewed described feeling more 'womanly' and 'confident' after undergoing cosmetic procedures. The surgery provided positive results, but only within a highly restrictive culture of beauty and ideal femininity that functions more as a system of control. We can't ignore the analysis of this system that prompts us to turn inwards rather than outwards in looking for what needs to be fixed.

Not only has our beauty ideal intensified but it's also led to the medicalisation of our bodies within a surgical industrial complex that profits from the pathologising of natural bodily deviation. To have an ageing face, small breasts, hip dips, protruding labia minora, cellulite or a rounder stomach is not to have a medical concern that requires treatment, but we are increasingly taught to view our unique features as unnatural deformities.

If I've learnt anything over the course of this research, it is that we are *tired*. Tired of feeling this way, tired of having ever more things to think about, body parts to fixate on, feminist debates to wrangle in our minds over what is and isn't morally acceptable when it comes to what we do to our own bodies. We are tired of it all. I am tired of it all. But the notion of empowerment obscures our social and cultural realities, in which there are huge industrial and political forces that stand to profit from breaking us down to be rebuilt in the image of an ever-changing ideal.

In surveilling, slicing and shapeshifting into the archetypal feminine, we reify cultural hegemony. We reinforce the reconstructed standard for all others. Whilst we should respect the agency of women to make their own choices for their own bodies, we should also take our microscope, our critical, forensic lens, and apply it not to ourselves but to the larger cultural and social context in which personal choices occur.

Nose

Alizey Mirza had already had her first nose job when we met at university, aged eighteen. Even as a student, she was incredibly glamorous, put-together in a palette of neutrals and splitting her time between London and Dubai. Alizey had been famous online since her early teens. Among the first young influencers to grace the internet, she and her twin sister, Lailli, were catapulted into hyper-visibility, their formative years spent documenting their lives, appearing in glossy magazines and being invited to exclusive industry events. 'We were fourteen and we'd compare ourselves to women who were obviously much older, who had more experience when it came to makeup, and who had had a lot of work done but weren't necessarily disclosing it,' Alizey told me when we met in London recently. It wasn't long before the self-scrutiny intensified – consumed by comments breaking down their appearance, comparing the teenage twins to one another, and the ever-narrower ideal.

'I actually had my dad's nose and my dad's family is all Iranian,' Alizey said. 'My nose was a prominent feature, but then it's funny because I go to Iran now and all the girls have these tiny little upturned pixie noses. I feel like everyone does look like clones of each other, especially in this region; it's crazy.'

In 2022, supermodel Bella Hadid admitted to getting a nose job at fourteen, after years of speculation and denying any cosmetic work. Despite the fact that it inevitably contributed to her illustrious career, Bella, who is part-Palestinian, expressed regret: 'I wish I had kept the nose of my ancestors. I think I would have grown into it.'

Once exchanged, these features can't be taken back. It was a modern-day Faustian bargain, in which she traded part of her soul in exchange for the privileges that came from adherence to the hegemonic ideal. In so many ways, it paid off – Bella is considered one of the most beautiful women of her generation. In 'erasing' her Arab nose, Bella drew herself closer to the Eurocentric standard and also undeniably closer to the fame she now enjoys, but that success comes with a sense of historic loss.

Often, in undertaking body modification, but especially when it comes to noses, we not only fragment ourselves but we fracture ancestral lines, erasing millennia of cultural history from our faces and bodies. Given that our beauty standards have historically pedestalled white beauty ideals, our surgical techniques often focus on the elimination of stereotypically racial or cultural features in favour of a Eurocentric beauty standard. When so many surgeons are white men, knowledge of non-white features can be sparse. Inevitably, white supremacy is still embedded in our approach to crafting the ideal. Unlike other features, which typically allow for more deviation, we know what an ideal nose is supposed to look like. To request a hooked nose, a bump, a wide bridge, or a crooked tip would prompt psychiatric referral.

Now in her mid-twenties, Alizey has just had her second nose job. Her twin sister is on her third. 'I felt because I had very thick skin, when my nose healed the first time, it didn't go back to being contoured,' Alizey said. 'It was just quite bulbous still.' Alizey's second nose job was focused just on the tip of her nose – on perfecting her nostrils, her columella, her alar rim and infratip lobule. Her face in ever-finer fragments, being intricately rebuilt.

'I had my first nose job done just before Snapchat came out – we didn't have all these crazy beauty filters,' she told me. 'I think that's why I did my second one, because when the filters came out, I realised, "Oh, wait, my nose is still not the way that I want it to look – maybe I need another nose job." But honestly, it's never-ending.'

Rhinoplasties are the most sought-after cosmetic surgery for adolescents, a phenomenon that's being exacerbated by the digital. One TikTok trend saw millions of users analysing their side profiles, placing their index fingers over their noses to create the illusion of a small, straight slope, before revealing what their noses truly looked like beneath. The majority of people who participated in the trend mimed their upset at their real nose, at the ways it deviated from the ideal.

'There is a noted relationship between the increase in selfie photographs and an increase in rhinoplasty requests, particularly among younger patients,' said Dr Bardia Amirlak, who led a study on digital nasal distortion after noticing a rise in patients requesting nose jobs in response to social media. His work found that the close-up perspective of selfies, paired with a phone camera's typically wider lens, mean that noses in selfies appear up to 30 per cent wider than they do in real life. Here, colonialist beauty ideals are compounded by technological distortion as we aim to create features for the digital gaze.

'Once you start there's just so much more to fixate on,' Alizey said, shaking her head. 'I always tell my friends that if you haven't had any cosmetic surgery, don't do it because you're not going to want to stop. It really becomes so addictive.'

*

Cosmetic surgery sits within a paradox of its own – it remains stigmatised and secretive, despite its surging popularity. Our increasingly unrealistic beauty standard practically demands surgical enhancement and yet we still condemn women who achieve their beauty through artifice. You must look as if you've had cosmetic surgery, but you must never do so. Whilst attitudes appear to be changing, wealthy, high-profile women still shy away from admitting to invasive beauty work, whilst overt surgery continues to be associated with lower culture. A 2020 study of 985 adults in the USA still found that recipients of cosmetic surgery were considered less warm, competent, moral and even human than non-recipients.

In response to this, makeover culture shifted from the private domain to the public and back again. Now, before and after images are shared as a commercial tool by cosmetic companies but are not posted by individuals as a personal win. The issue with before and after images is that 'during' is obfuscated. We move from origin to destination almost seamlessly. The signs of labour, the gruesome reality and risk of surgical intervention, are rendered invisible. The transformation appears to happen as if by magic – feeding the mythology of a quick and easy fix by those who want you to purchase it.

'When I get my nose job, I'll just delete all my old pictures and never tell anyone,' Nadia had told me in the nightclub. 'If anyone accuses me of having it done I'd deny it, how would they ever find out?'

I believe that the deception that surrounds the ways we build our bodies is one of the most harmful aspects of our modern beauty culture. The Kardashian's describe themselves as promoting only a 'healthy' body image with emphasis on 'working for their bodies' to 'take care of themselves'. Influencer and friend of the family Jordyn Woods started a fitness app in 2019 when she unveiled her 'new body', and insisted that she hadn't undergone surgical procedures to achieve what many commentators thought was too extreme a transformation to be achieved through exercise alone. Meanwhile, models are putting padding in their trousers to give the illusion of bigger bums in photo and video shoots, aggravating body image issues further. The result is a demographic of young women and girls who feel constantly lacking, stuck in a pursuit of remedies or in a spiral of self-loathing as they struggle to pin the needle on their insecurities.

Even in South Korea, one of the plastic surgery capitals of the world, recent research has found that amongst women, cosmetic surgery is largely only considered acceptable when the outcome of surgery looks 'natural'. They found that women who'd had cosmetic surgery who *look* as though they have undergone cosmetic surgery face social stigmatisation, whereas those who look 'natural' do not face the same judgement. That women must be pure and unaltered in their physical appearance acts as an aesthetic extension of the virgin/whore dichotomy used to essentialise and condemn women for their sexuality and sexual agency. There is an inherent patriarchal entitlement to our bodies that continues to claim moral superiority over our choices. It's a system used to denigrate and divide women

– judging the act of cosmetic surgery whilst upholding and sexualising a beauty standard that makes most women feel undesirable without surgical intervention. There is a reason the majority of female *Love Island* contestants each year have undergone breast augmentations, facial filler and extensive diet regimes, despite only being in their early twenties.

Even though low self-esteem directly predicts women's likelihood to undergo cosmetic surgery, research has indicated that self-esteem improvements post-surgery are either small or largely insignificant. Whilst cosmetic surgery *does* in fact prompt significant immediate improvements to body image amongst its recipients, society's generally negative view of surgically altered bodies plays a role in negating any positive impact. It is important to note that whilst body image is improved post-surgery, it is still worse for recipients than for groups who do not seek surgery. Cosmetic surgery, it seems, cannot restore you to a secure sense of self; what would be better would be to find ways to safeguard women and girls from body dissatisfaction in the first place.

When 94 per cent of cosmetic surgery recipients are women, we must look critically at why a society might pressure women into choosing a painful, dangerous and expensive procedure in the hope of a better life, only to use it as an excuse to dehumanise them. Why might a patriarchal culture want to view women as less competent and more morally corrupt? And how do we, as women, reinforce that view of each other?

Bum

On a 2021 flight out of Miami, a woman sat perplexed in her seat thousands of feet in the air. Surrounding her were women kneeling on the aeroplane floor, with their heads resting in their hands. Some were on their hands and knees in the aisle, others spread over two chairs, their bums lifted in the air. The women didn't know each other but they all had one thing in common. They were recovering from a BBL surgery.

No cosmetic procedure has defined the beauty culture of the last decade like the Brazilian butt lift, a cosmetic procedure in which fat is removed from the stomach, lower back or thighs and then strategically injected into the buttocks. A resurgence of our cultural obsession with big bums after the ultra-thin ideal of the nineties was seeded in mainstream pop culture in the early noughties by celebrities such as Jennifer Lopez, but became a widespread cultural phenomenon by the mid-2010s. In 2014, *Vogue* declared: 'We're Officially in the Era of the Big Booty', citing Kim Kardashian, Nicki Minaj and even Miley Cyrus's 2013 VMAs performance as bastions of the new age. Later that year, Kim Kardashian broke the internet with her *Paper* magazine cover, flashing her bare derrière and tiny waist to the camera. Gone were the days when 'her butt looks big in that' could be taken as an insult – for the rest of the 2010s, the bigger the butt, the better.

Between 2015 and 2019, the number of BBL procedures performed increased by 90 per cent. From 2019 to 2020, the US saw a further 37 per cent increase in butt augmentations and in 2021, the BBL reached its apex as the fastest-growing cosmetic surgery in the world. Egypt Rodriguez, a twenty-seven-year-old from Atlanta, Georgia, was one of these patients. When I interviewed Egypt for an article for *The Face*, she told me she'd had two BBL procedures within three months in 2018 and has spent upwards of $15,000 on her surgeries.

'I remember being as young as fifteen years old growing up in Miami and passing by a billboard outside of Aventura mall with a doctor showing the BBL before and after results. Before I had any surgery, I would try a lot of diets and workouts, but I always had love handles or certain things I wanted to change,' she said. 'Nicki Minaj was very popular and she had a big, beautiful butt. I loved that look and once I realised I could achieve it through surgery, I knew that was what I wanted to do.'

Despite being the fastest-growing cosmetic procedure, the BBL is also one of the deadliest. One 2017 study placed the worldwide mortality rate at a staggering 1 in 3,000, although through increased awareness and education the ratio is widening. Still, thousands of women fly to Turkey, Miami, the Dominican Republic or Mexico in order to get cheaper treatments, with TikTok showing videos of long lines of BBL patients waiting at airports in their wheelchairs, or on their knees during a flight. In March this year, Nicki Minaj confessed to receiving butt injections from a 'random person' and celebs such as Cardi B have been open about how unsafe their BBL surgeries were.

As with any trend, once the BBL became popular in the beauty mainstream, it began to lose its social and financial capital. The exaggerated proportions no longer had the same impact that they had just a few years earlier.

'The BBL is a relatively new procedure,' says Dr Alan Matarasso, New York cosmetic surgeon and immediate past president of the American Society of Plastic Surgeons when I interviewed him for *The Face* article. 'Often, these things take time to find their place in our society and culture. People get excited initially because it's a relatively new concept and then we see where it fits in. Both surgeons and patients are becoming more conservative in their approach.'

Like the exaggerated breast augmentations of the 1990s, the overt BBL look will inevitably die down. The procedure will find its place in the beauty ecosystem, settling into itself and becoming increasingly commonplace and undetectable.

Influencers with privilege, like the Kardashians, can trade on this, moving from one trending ideal to the next, morphing their physical selves into whichever mould is most desirable. Women with less privilege, power and wealth, however, do not have the same luxury. When we consider the risk associated with BBL procedures, the very fact that women are willing to undergo multiple rounds of the surgery, before potentially getting a reversal just years later, sparks huge concern. Despite only having her surgeries in 2018, and spending thousands, Egypt is already considering a BBL reduction.

'I have what's called a vixen look, which is a super-tiny waist and big hips,' Egypt says. 'I gained about forty pounds after having surgery. It looks more dramatic and the areas just keep on growing. I researched reductions for over a year and paid a deposit with a doctor who does reconstructive surgery, but I'm just not at ease about it. I don't want to get a BBL reduction and then risk needing another surgery to fix contours and irregularities, but I don't know if I can maintain the look throughout my entire life. I might have to go ahead with the reduction.'

The BBL's absorption into the zeitgeist and the widespread popularisation of the procedure as a 'solution' for women has many finding fault in their body where perhaps they would not have done before. The BBL boom might now be dying down but we can't retract the accessibility of the procedure or the scar it has left on women's consciousnesses. In 2022, a UK nationwide 'Body Image Study' by OriGym found that one in five sixteen- to twenty-four-year-olds want to change their derrière with either implants or a bum lift. These findings are reinforced by Google search data, which shows that searches for 'bum lift' were up 69 per cent in 2021–22.

Bodyshape trends do not change so much now as accumulate, each new one adding to the shopping list of attributes to acquire in order to become acceptable. As capitalism moves on to colonise another area of the female consciousness, the BBL in its more subdued form will simply be added to the roster of treatments and procedures women are expected to partake in in order to achieve the beauty standard.

I wasn't immune either. A week before a holiday to Spain in 2019, I took the day off work to get two trains and a taxi to a salon above a shop just outside of Birmingham. I didn't tell anyone I was going and I haven't told anyone since. The journey took me six hours in total, three hours there and back. I was in the salon for no more than forty-five minutes. I'd seen it on Instagram but the reality was a lot less polished than the pictures had made it seem. I walked through an empty hair-dressers and up a narrow carpeted stairwell to reach the main door, one covered in promotional pamphlets that were peeling off at the corners.

Once inside, I removed my jeans and lay face down on the beauty bed whilst a beautician massaged a machine from my thighs up to my butt cheeks. I fantasised about my new body as she repeated the process over and over again, forcing the fat up to its most desirable location.

The truth is, I could not bear to be in a swimsuit in front of people, my insecurities on show. I wasn't entirely sure why I cared so much about random people I'd never see again, about my friends, but I would have paid any amount of money to dis-solve the dread that was accumulating in the pit of my stomach.

Once my thighs were starting to bruise from the pressure, the machines stopped whirring and I was instructed to stand in my underwear by the photo backdrop. The beautician moved around me with her phone before placing my before and after images side by side. I could see no discernible difference. Heartbroken and ashamed, I began my long journey home.

As the sun scorched the Spanish desert, I sat in an ankle-length skirt and watched as my friends cooled off in the pool. I wondered what it was like not to care, willing myself to stand up and jump into the water as my hips welded themselves to the seat.

Body

Jess was twenty when she bought her body. She maxed out her credit cards and saved up her student loans to pay for the procedures – a breast augmentation, a BBL, fat-freezing treatments in her arms, filler in her lips, chin, jaw and cheeks, a rhinoplasty and microblading on her brows. In total, she spent over £25,000 with one goal in mind: to get on *Love Island*.

To be successful, Jess understood, she had to fit the archetypal ideal. The stereotypical reality TV vixen had a flat stomach, large boobs, a round perky bum and a symmetrical face with big lips. Getting on the show would mean weeks spent almost exclusively wearing a bikini, and Jess wanted to be prepared. Being cast would mean a fast-track to a life of social media influencing, brand deals and a potential career as a content creator. Jess spent months crafting her body to generate the kind of currency she imagined would get her on the show – weeks spent in hospital, bandaged and bruised. When the time came to submit her application, Jess had been transformed, broken down and rebuilt, entirely anew.

But she didn't get in.

Despite investing everything she had in reconstructing herself, Jess's application was rejected and she was left with a body that carries little currency offline. The archetypal exaggerated beauty of reality TV may hold currency on social media, in sex work and on shows such as *Love Island* but can often be a penalising factor in applications for blue-collar jobs in more 'professional' offline industries. Jess broke down, she couldn't cope. In her eyes, she had done everything she could to be accepted and still fell short.

*

To be a woman is to exist in a changeling body, always on the brink of transformation. 'We are all chimeras, theorised and fabricated hybrids of machine and organism; in short, we are cyborgs,' Donna Haraway wrote in her 1985 essay 'The Cyborg Manifesto'. Haraway imagined technology as a pathway to freedom for women, a tool to create unrestricted and defiant identities – bodies created on our own terms. What has ultimately happened is the opposite. Haraway described the cyborg as 'a cybernetic organism, a hybrid of machine and organism, a creature of social reality as well as a creature of fiction'. Fiction, instead of an opportunity for creativity, has become the ideal beauty – the beauty we create from artifice with surgical innovation and technological advancements. From this perspective, every implant augmenting our body, every redistribution of fat with metal cannulas, every digital distortion can be interpreted as a transformation of the human body from its original state, inching us nearer to the convergence of human and machine. As the cosmetic industry continues to grow, and is fuelled increasingly by digital technology, melding to create a hybrid beauty ideal that transcends the physical realm, the question we must now face is: how will this end?

Using Haraway's model, media theorists, such as mj corey of the Kardashian Kolloquium, have positioned the Kardashians, our archetypal beauty ideal, as cyborgs.

'I really think that the Kardashians are cyborgs not only in the way they use cosmetic surgery – though that is the most visible example – but in every way that they construct their powerful and far-reaching hyper-reality,' corey tells me. 'The Kardashians fuse fiction and nonfiction in the way they stage their TV show and media content. They're also fusing their bodies with literal technologies: their phones are attached to their hands. To the makeup and cosmetic surgery point, they are engaging with ever-advancing technologies to create their ever-evolving looks. Instagram Face is a formula. A code. That's as good as having "technology" as a concept embedded on the body. When people critique "Kardashian Face" and its dizzying homogeny, they often express having experienced what could be best described as "uncanny valley", which is the psychological effect some humans experience when looking at artificial intelligence in action. Whether the Kardashians inspire aspirational imitation in their audiences or uncanny valley, their brand only benefits. Mimicry is a sign of power. So is the ability to induce nausea.'

As cosmetic enhancements become increasingly popular, we are crafting our bodies into cyborgs, forever transforming under cultural, social and historical contexts. Philosopher Elizabeth Grosz describes the body as 'plastic', stating the female body 'can no longer be regarded as a fixed, concrete substance, a pre-cultural given', rather, it gains its 'determinate form only by being socially inscribed'. The body is both a symbol of identity and of our unlimited capacity for alteration and modification. The body becomes a commodity that can be continuously upgraded and modified in line with trends and resources. We are shaped, ultimately, by our capacity for consumption.

In this sense, our bodies no longer stop at the boundary of our skin. We extend ourselves prosthetically with technology, accessories, external objects and fragments that we incorporate into our self-image. What constitutes a whole body, or a whole self, becomes increasingly elusive – at the mercy of trend cycles and consumer culture. We start buying new things to feel complete, to fill the void and scream 'this is who I am' over and over again. And then the meaning of the purchase changes, becomes passé, devalued, and we find ourselves once more in a state of flux. Being the ideal self is no longer just about the body corporeal, but the body as a consumer, the body as a curator and collector. Under capitalism, we acquire evermore things and feel ever emptier.

The standards of fast fashion, hype culture and micro-trends then apply to our bodies, as we shapeshift into the ideal. Makeover is present tense: it was never about the finished product; the goal, truly, is endless reconstruction. We were never meant to feel complete. Makeover became a ceaseless list of improvements to be made, of ever-finer fragmentation. When the next dramatic shift in the ideal fashionable body type inevitably arrives, people could be undergoing their third round of trend-chasing procedures, even with the risks that come with doing so. What we are left with is a generation of cyborgs, constantly cutting away at their own bodies.

'There's an argument that it's empowering, in a neoliberal feminist sense, to use the technologies and resources available to "affirm" an aspirational vision of yourself,' says corey. 'The Kardashians as cyborgs have managed to endlessly "optimise" but, naturally, there are follies to this quest. It's proof alone that we've internalised the capitalist system. The "cyborg question" around the Kardashians causes us to question whether it empowers women – are we more bionic with these additions to our beauty arsenals? Or do they fragment us into bits and pieces?'

Are we augmented and enhanced, or have we been sold for parts? We are all fragmented, split into more pieces than we can count, but can our inevitably fragmented bodies be unified? Can we make each other whole?

How can we create a more beautiful future for women and girls?

'There should be more support, and we should have safe spaces where we can talk about these issues. Being a young woman can feel really isolating. Even though social media connects us, it also feels incredibly lonely and competitive. I think it would be so great to have spaces where collaboration and community were rewarded for everyone, so that it encourages people to work together, to promote each other and be happy for each other. I think that's incredibly lacking with social media at the moment.'

Zara Ward,
specialist at the UK Revenge Porn Helpline

7

Everything Is Content and Reality Is a Myth

Across millennia, there have been legends of those who lived between realms. Tales of chameleon souls, shapeshifters, demigods or *sídhe* walking among us. They still walk amongst us now. At the point when the digital world glitched its way into the mortal world, Snitchery emerged. A chromatic symphony of a shapeshifter, Snitchery had many faces, all illuminated by LED lights and the lunar tones of teeth.

In the mortal realm, whispers of Snitchery's existence spread like wildfire. Faithful to the algorithmic oracle, she was elevated to a heavenly status, deified in the digital. Worshippers sat with faces lit by the soft glow of screens, eyes gleaming with a feral intensity. People from all over the world congregated to marvel at her and the wonder of her gifts. Over a million followers came to her platforms to leave offerings in the form of likes, giving tiny sacrificial hearts and anointing her as their goddess or their queen in the comments below. Some created shrines of her pictures and reproduced themselves in her image, sharing photographs of themselves echoing her looks, mimicking her poses in the mirror. They spoke of how she inspired them, how she ignited creativity and self-expression with her idealised reality. Her stories became parables, her wisdom, gospel. In this new age, the pursuit of beauty became a sacred quest and influencers guided us mortals through the labyrinth of existence.

Yet, in the quiet moments, when the world was still and the screens were dim, Snitchery would take her face off entirely. Beneath the pixels and the pigment and the polish was Eleanor Barnes – a twenty-five-year-old woman from Virginia.

*

Eleanor Barnes sat in a hotel room surrounded by beauty products. They covered the bed and the bathroom, they lined every cabinet; every surface was a stage for display, every little detail constructed and considered. More than a hotel room, this was a living set, a dreamscape that she was encapsulated within. Next to personalised gifts were selfie lights and promotional pamphlets, a script to learn about the products. Outside, a camera crew waited by the door, eager for her to transform.

Eleanor was taking part in a trip organised by a beauty brand, one of many in which the most beautiful girls are taken to the most beautiful locations to do the most beautiful things and eat the most beautiful food, all in the name of content. As a beauty influencer with over a million followers, Eleanor had been flown out business class. Her plus one had to sit alone in economy.

Eleanor was part of the generation whose childhood began outside. As she grew up, she was gradually drawn in. Reality shifting further away. Just as I did, she became a teen in the age of indie sleaze. Of Tumblr girls, tie dye and *i bet that you look good on the dancefloor* <3. It was the first time she had fallen into a visual digital world, headfirst down the rabbit hole, her particles transferred to pixels. It was obsessive, consuming and compulsive; her hands filled with the jewels of the instant. She devoured the pictures that tasted like bile and stirred that feeling in her stomach. Belonging?

Eleanor remembers that era as the first time she had wanted to look a certain way, attaching a look to an entire existence. She chose her aesthetics and assimilated – a heady blend of mixed metals, thigh gaps, swallow tattoos and studded bags. Her outfits an imitation of a repost. It was over-the-knee socks, off-the-shoulder tops and denim cut offs. Collarbones and stretched navels.

In this new religious paradigm, consumption has become a central act of devotion. Followers eagerly purchase the products, services and experiences recommended by their chosen influencers, seeking to align themselves with the ideals they represent. This act of consumption serves as a tangible expression of faith, a means of forging a connection with the modern divine. But Eleanor was increasingly unsure if she believed in any of this, if she believed in herself.

Eleanor's days now revolved around the creation of content. What had started on Photobooth at sleepovers as a teenager now became a full production. A complete and utter transformation. It was for the same reason that there were now entire shops in malls across the world that sold nothing other than the space to create content, selfie museums and factories from Westfield London to Dallas, Texas offering countless empty sets for us to capture artificial moments. All uncannily alike. A single seat on a 'private jet' with cotton-wool clouds painted onto the window. A ball pit with a podium in the centre for posing. Pink train carriages covered in posters screaming 'Girl Power'. Visitors are allowed sixty minutes in the 'factory' to do as much creative labour as possible.

Eleanor's first viral images were monochromatic, her various wigs edited to the same pastel tones as the bedroom wall behind her, her makeup done in a cutesy e-girl glam. But she could feel her face getting stuck.

'I was certainly more original before I immersed myself in the digital,' she says. 'Now I'm stuck in this hellscape that has homogenised me in a way I never used to be. Once it became my job, I had to follow trends, and nobody looked like a real person. Everybody's eyes were like these sparkling little whitened diamonds. Nobody's teeth were anything other than pearly blue-white. There were no fine lines, no imperfections. Everybody was poreless.'

Eleanor graduated to Instagram in 2015 and after a year and a half of posting beauty images as Snitchery, she had over 200,000 followers. Now, she has over a million.

These brand trips are where the fantasy of the digital realm comes to life for a few days. Once 'Snitchery' arrived, a lavish itinerary awaited, a crew following her every move, always ready to capture her in the moment. After all, this paid vacation wasn't only designed to sell a product but also to promote an ideal, creating a real-life 'highlight reel' full to the brim with photographable moments. According to leaked emails, four-to-five day brand trips like this cost upwards of $800,000.

But in real life, nothing was quite as it seemed. Eleanor could recognise her fellow influencers, but not because their faces looked like theirs.

'We all looked like *Sims* characters,' she tells me when we meet. 'Even though I knew that I was editing my photos, I was *still* so baffled when I saw other content creators and they didn't look like their pictures. We were all editing the fuck out of our faces. You'd meet these people in real life and no one would look like themselves, it was comical.'

At the height of her influencing career, Eleanor had spent between $5,000 and $10,000 on beauty procedures – from filler to Botox – and was using Facetune to edit all of her images, changing her face further. 'I was so taken by this idea that I could just change my face if I wanted to, it's so dystopian, but also really tempting to somebody like me, who was being rewarded for having an ever-changing aesthetic. I knew it didn't have a happy ending.'

Eleanor was a living paradox. To be in this world at the crossroads of existence, somewhere between the digital and the physical, was to live in a different dimension. There were many others in this universe, of course. Whilst Kylie remained the epitome of the ideal, Eleanor was on a different plane to her friends back home in Michigan, but they were all ascending into an augmented reality. One that required ring lights and exaggerated photo-ready makeup – where faces were constructed and everyone was always in character, always on theme.

'Online, everyone was so angular, with perfect skin, perfect chins, perfect lips, perfect cheeks, but when you would see these people in real life, it was just uncanny. In a 360 view, no one looked like a real person. I definitely got to that point with my face as well. You could recognise influencers immediately in the wild because their faces just didn't look like human faces.'

In a world where looking like a human woman was becoming increasingly repulsive, we were forced into becoming something else. Perhaps it was a prophecy, a warning sign of what was to come.

*

Within the luminous realm of the screens, shadows lurked. There was previously more of a separation between the stars of Hollywood and our own individual lives – a border between the fantasy beauty standards of TV and film and our domestic reality. Shooting, editing and curating images is no longer a Hollywood exclusive; it has become an intimate part of our everyday existence – both private and public, further blurring the line between the two. Whilst once we might have seen edited, airbrushed, highly produced images a couple of times a day, we now see hundreds daily, often with no knowledge they've been manipulated at all.

We carry the ability to augment ourselves everywhere, the opportunity to capture and curate our lives – the tools to unlock our most beautiful selves are always in our pockets. Within a few seconds, whilst out for dinner, at a bus stop or in the comfort of our own homes, we can see what we might look like with a rhinoplasty or a shaved-down jaw, bigger lips or flawless skin, and we can publish that version of ourselves to the world. Now, we live in an augmented reality, creating the most heightened beauty expectations women have ever experienced.

According to research carried out by beauty brand Dove in 2021, 80 per cent of girls have used filters or photo editing apps to change their appearance online by the age of thirteen. The same research found that 67 per cent of girls aged ten to seventeen try to change or hide at least one body part or feature before posting a photo of themselves on social media. Their still-forming faces and bodies are seen as defective before they've even reached adulthood. At a youth organisation I volunteer at, ten- to twelve-year-old girls tell me that 'selfies are a must', holding up their photo albums full of filtered images, glowing and horrifying. One thirteen-year-old girl told me she doesn't leave the house after school anymore because she isn't pretty enough in real life, her friends nodding in agreement as she detailed how she looks so much better online and doesn't want people to 'have to see' her natural face any more than they already do.

Researchers at City University London found that 90 per cent of young women (with an average age of twenty) reported using filters or editing their photos. The most common filters they used were designed to even out and brighten skin tone, whiten teeth, bronze skin and reduce body size. Participants also used filters on social media to reshape jaws or noses, make their lips look fuller and their eyes appear bigger. Of those who used filters, 94 per cent reported feeling pressured to look a particular way and more than half described that pressure as 'intense'.

Not only are we seeing more faces than we were ever meant to see, we are now judging ourselves based on an artificial reality, whether we are aware of it or not. Not only is the Hollywood star system colliding with our own, cyberspace is becoming inextricable from the real world. Editing apps, filters, AI and AR are creating a hyper-augmented digital beauty standard that is impossible to live up to in real life, waging a form of psychological warfare on young women and girls worldwide.

'It's growing out of control,' says Dr Asalet, an NHS surgeon and aesthetic complications expert. 'Filters and unrealistic expectations of beauty are seen by everyone now – children see it, men expect women to look that way, women are expecting every other woman to look that way, parents are filtering images of their kids. There's a huge psychological impact to all of this.'

In her study of ten- to eleven-year-olds, early years specialist Dr Claire Pescott was shocked to hear about young girls consciously using filters and feeling pressure to exist as perfect beings online. They weren't technically even old enough to be on the platforms yet and still they had already internalised the ideal. Boys of the same age were totally oblivious to the pressures they faced.

'The gender divide around social media use was so significant that it became the focus of my work,' she tells me. 'To hear girls that young use phrases like "smooth out my imperfections" and "contour my features" was horrifying. They are comparing themselves to people who don't even exist like that in real life.'

In addition to the male gaze, we are now filtering our existence through a digital gaze – curating ourselves for a world that only exists online, living for a dimension beyond the physical world. Already pressured to perform as the ideal feminine, girls are feeling the compounded weight of existing in multiple realities and needing to be perfect in them all. 'I wish I was wearing a filter right now,' one ten-year-old girl had said.

*

We, as followers, as disciples, also feel the pull of the possibility of maybe one day being ordained. By simply existing in the digital realm, it feels as if we are always on the precipice of a big break, of being hand-picked by the gods.

We were on our way to the beach on our first girls' holiday – Sienna, Eliza and I – with other girls from our friendship group. We stopped at regular intervals to take photos – everyone needed a different background, so we spent our walks scanning the landscape for optimal spots. A nicely tiled floor, a distressed wall, the architecture you just don't get back home. Sienna had a Pinterest board of images she wanted to replicate – references for poses, angles and walls for us to use as a guide – she'd been prepping it for weeks before the trip. We took hundreds, thousands of pictures, but the aim wasn't to look posed, it was to be caught mid-stroll, to be captured casually, beautiful and unaware. So we'd walk back and forth, back and forth, sunglasses on, sunglasses off. Our journey took double the time but we'd captured our holiday looks to perfection, and everyone was content. All of us drowning in the thirst of an ideal.

There's a unique pressure that comes from an all-girls holiday. An all-girls existence. The pressure to be picturesque. The pressure to be perfect. The pressure to have fun. Not only for our real selves but our digital selves too. Not getting the 'right' pictures could ruin entire days. 'Pics or it didn't happen' circulated as a meme – but it felt increasingly true. Did we exist if we didn't prove it? If we weren't perfect? 'I was here,

I was here, I was here' started to feel less like a reclamation and more like a looming threat.

We'd spend our downtime once again in our ritual of self-curation – making our selects and doing our edits, annoying each other with impossible choices between almost identical yet entirely different pictures. None of us had a large following but it didn't really matter, what mattered was the fantasy we could create. The rush that came with the illusion of a beautiful life and the power we had to turn real things into unreal things. None of us believed in God but we still wanted to be watched. To have our existence ordained with a certain sense of importance. Attention was holy and we wanted to be anointed. Every performance still stands, archived and saved, to be watched for all eternity. To never have to die.

Through a meticulous process we had perfected over years, we knew how to highlight our best features and hide our imperfections. We knew our angles, our best sides, our go-to tools to curate the version of ourselves that was as close as possible to the ideal, without creating an image that appeared too edited, too curated or too much. To be heavenly, to be truly digitally good, we toed the line between intense curation and maintaining an acceptable level of authenticity. Often, this meant walking the tightrope between sexy but not too sexy, posed but not too posed, edited but not obviously so.

We all had an aesthetic – a personal brand that we subscribed to in order to elevate our presence online. It was normal for us, native internet girls, to express our identities with themes, brands and a niche. As writer and internet princess Rayne Fisher-Quann described, we each had an artfully curated list of things we consumed, or aspired to consume, and we crafted ourselves around them. Sienna's was Manhattan city girl – high contrast, low exposure imagery and sunglasses with everything; Eliza's was vintage cool, smoking for the aesthetic and Frank Ocean vinyl on repeat; mine was cool-toned, pink and pastel with stylised quotes and baby-face pouts. Even our saved folders were organised by themes and tones, our private spheres colour-coded and aestheticised.

These digital skins were responsive to trends and referential of subcultures, photography styles and brand affinity. One easily identifiable viral aesthetic – the VSCO girl – shot to internet fame in honour of the eponymous editing app. The look, thought to derive from Oregon, is associated with a suburban girl who wears oversized t-shirts and barely visible shorts. She's a laid-back, effortlessly cool beach babe who edits her photos with a preset and buys her clothes from Urban Outfitters or Brandy Melville, owns a HydroFlask, loves Glossier and accessorises with a cowrie shell necklace, an anklet and a Fjällräven backpack. As the vicious satirisation that follows internet fame proclaims, she's likely chasing sunsets and live, laugh, loving until nightfall.

I was lucky enough to meet an original VSCO girl. 'Lee from America', known in the mortal realm as Lee Tilghman, is a former wellness influencer who was based Los Angeles but now lives in New York. Lee from America was part of an echelon of influencers who were so powerful that they could herald the arrival of seasons – Lee's pronouncements of pumpkins in late September marked the start of fall for the masses. Her personal brand was an easy breezy approach to health and fitness, natural skincare and smoothie bowls. In the 2010s, she was deified as a health goddess for her visionary way of capturing lifestyle content. 'I kind of started this trend,' she told me as she showed me a series of images shot from above by a windowsill, a sea of plants surrounding a brightly coloured smoothie bowl in the centre, held above Lee's legs adorned with expensive activewear. 'But as you can see, everything's kind of orange.'

Lee's personal brand relied on VSCO K3 – a warm-toned orange filter – to maintain her aesthetic across her feed.

Everything was filtered in this hue – not only the images themselves but Lee's wardrobe, the clothes she wore, her apartment and the food she ate all had to be on brand. In a growing trend, influencers are now creating and selling their own preset filters so that their followers can easily replicate their aesthetic and create cohesive content grids in their image.

As with everything, social media has intensified our collective need for belonging. Whilst teen magazines would invite us to define our style with flowchart quizzes, digital channels invite you to filter and curate your existence into a single cohesive aesthetic. Whilst we resist labels in almost every other category, we relish tagging ourselves or our friends in aesthetics from art hoe to e-girl, pastel goth to dark academia.

A few weeks after our girls' holiday, we were all invited to a 'tonal'-themed birthday party. The birthday girl had made it that way to match her Instagram aesthetic. I wasn't exactly sure what tonals meant but the answer seemed to be beige. Everywhere we looked there were shimmering champagne silks and crisp linens. Bowls of crackers, fruit, chips and dip artfully sculpted into landscapes of edible decoration. Brunch boards to be consumed by the eyes only.

It wasn't a large or formal event but a small gathering in a patioed back garden in Hackney. I wasn't usually a tonal girl, so I wore white and ordered extra clothes especially for the event, sending the options into the group chat for the collective vote. On arrival, I saw that those who'd missed the memo were promptly swept into a bedroom by the front door and forced to change. One girl arrived in a red dress. A shock of violence in this serene sea. I widened my eyes at the others as she was swiftly remade in a taupe smock dress, a tonal girl now. We accepted her with open arms.

The rest of the party was a sea of flash photography, of smeared golden light against aesthetic walls. We smiled. We shimmered. We felt like we did not exist. Group pictures were taken – all of us girls smiling with our tongues pressed to the roofs of our mouths, mewing with our buccal fat pulled in. The pictures were then passed around to each girl, displayed and tweaked to their desired effect – our usual pattern of edits copied and pasted until each of us was happy with how we were to be perceived. Then, and only then, could the photo be published.

Our desire to be seen and understood is no new phenomenon, but the intense pressure that comes with maintaining this visual virtual identity is often less a fun experiment in self-expression and rather another confinement within which to place ourselves. To cultivate a personal brand is to transform ourselves into commodities, which is often a gendered practice that involves labour to curate and maintain. There is always a thin line to be walked between visibility and vulnerability, the authentic and the unflattering, the enhanced and the relatable, the curated and the fake. As women, our bodies are already more susceptible to being criticised and questioned, and for our online personas it is no different, if not worse.

We were the girls who had filtered our lives through the gaze of consumers. Who wrote diaries for future generations to find. Who placed a wet hand dramatically on the shower wall as we sang. Who performed makeup tutorials to our own reflection. Who had no idea how to exist as something unsellable, unobserved.

It began with a revelation, a collective yearning for connection in a world that felt increasingly fragmented. People sought solace in the glow of screens, where the boundaries of time and space melted away. They found fellowship in virtual tribes, united by shared beliefs and aspirations. We longed to be a part of something – but for connection and community to require a specific aesthetic, a certain face, body or product, creates an exclusionary system. Can we only embrace each other in the image of an ideal?

In the digital realm, where everything seems to evaporate quickly, we're left trying to grasp a semblance of something tangible, something that we can hold on to, something we can keep. We seem to long for a sense of community but these aesthetics will not be our salvation.

The fact that each identity is so connected to specific brands or products is key. In creating an ever-faster trend cycle, social media algorithms are enacting a particularly insidious form of control over our identity. Our hyper-categorisation only leads to increased self-surveillance and performance as we're fragmented into algorithmic subsets. Once categorised, we are easily targeted by ads and content that drives us deeper into our visual echo chamber. It doesn't matter which style you choose to assimilate to, we're all being sculpted into the same thing – ideal consumers. The result is a vicious cycle in which our identities are being managed and enabled, but also commodified, by big tech. What may seem like a fun and expressive tool is actually also a far-reaching form of control over our ability to craft and sustain a sense of self.

These platforms, these algorithmic oracles, are not neutral forces. They're a dictatorship. The result is often less a sense of increased connection and more an inflated sense of self-importance. That the platforms are more social the more you use them is, in itself, a myth.

'I was honestly thinking about myself too much,' says Lee. 'My whole page was about *my* journey, *my* wellness, *my* exercise, *my* diet. I wasn't ever featuring anyone else. When I was at that level of Instagram fame, I didn't have any friends because I was on my phone all the time. Imagine us hanging out right now but I wouldn't actually be here.' She gestures as if capturing the invisible threads between us with her hands.

'I'd just be waiting for you to stop talking so I can ask you to take a picture of me down the street. I was always thinking like, what would my brand do on vacation? Who would "Lee from America" date? What I wore, what music I listened to, it was all through the lens of this character I created. It was me, but only one part of me.'

Despite the internet's endless possibilities for performance and play, the profile structure of most platforms insists on a single, quantifiable self. Meta CEO Mark Zuckerberg maintains 'you have one identity'. We expect our favourite influencers to stay static, constant beacons of beauty. Scandinavian viral influencer Matilda Djerf, who is famed for her luscious layered hair and bombshell blowdries, has followers reminding her to cut her hair when it gets too long. Her image must be immortalised, as if we are disappointed in her humanness, her lack of divinity.

The idea of having to select and present a commercial facet of the self is a concept that came up time and time again in my research – whether from women who made a living online or those who wanted to replicate them. Women with hundreds of thousands of followers to women with a few hundred all spoke about the idea of limiting and distilling themselves to a specific essence, one that, once presented, they couldn't deviate from.

'Social media has really accentuated the boxes we put ourselves in,' says writer and feminist activist Scarlett Curtis. 'The internet only wants me to be one thing, a single pixel. We're all turning ourselves into these zeros and ones.'

I was reminded of something Venus had said to me in the hair salon in New York: 'I want to control the way that I'm consumed,' she told me. 'I don't want to wake up every day trying to figure out what's going to generate the most impressions, but I made a choice to prostitute this version of myself for this app. I can see the matrix and the impact it is having on me but I don't get to escape it because this is where my work and my community is. I'm a woman in the creative industry, I have an unstable income, I have the gender wage gap, I'm operating inside of an economy that's predominantly white men, so opting out of these platforms isn't really an option. A huge part of my value is how I look, not how well I play music or any of the contributions I've made culturally, and I have to mediate that, and enter the digital space understanding the compromises that I make and understanding the image that I'm going to put into the world. What worries me now is that most people don't have the time to develop a sense of self before they start to be controlled by the algorithms.'

At a discussion group I chaired on beauty and aesthetics, a young Black woman in her mid-twenties spoke of her frustration with this pressure to choose which side of herself to cultivate online, calling to the room but also to the ether: 'Which part of me do you want?!'

Despite the internet's rallies for activism and girl power, asserting that girls should do 'whatever the fuck they want', and our constant insistence on being our 'true selves', we only want it when packaged in a convenient and commercial way. We must be beautiful but 2D, filtered physically and politically.

Internet researchers have drawn on sociologist Erving Goffman's dramaturgical metaphor of 'collapsed contexts' to describe social media environments in which everyone in our lives is exposed to the same digital persona, now that the public and private have become indivisible, intertwined. This is particularly difficult for marginalised people, or those with stigmatised identity facets, who don't want to disclose every aspect of themselves to every possible onlooker. The result is a highly considered process of concealing and revealing, of fragmenting our identities across channels, creating 'finstas' (fake Instagram accounts) to post in an unfiltered way. This underscores the notion that 'fake' is default online and 'real' images are ancillary, the content you use to construct your image. In reality, our fake accounts are the most true representation of us, but these too are curated, designed to appear effortless but in a stylised way. In order to slightly expand our self-presentation bandwidth, we have to engage in twice the effort. We have to take, edit and curate more images, and manage our identity performance and the public perception of all aspects of ourselves to these varying audiences. Even apps like BeReal, which champion an unfiltered life, demand we capture ourselves daily, prompting us to look at ourselves and immortalise our image.

The pressure to be a 'personal brand' online creates yet another constriction that women have to place their identities within. Another ideal to keep up with and maintain. The idea of curating our personas online, in engaging in social media self-presentation, is not only a gendered issue but an individualistic endeavour that ultimately limits our propensity for collective action. To be successful in the digital realm is to focus on the self, intensely investing time and energy into self-perception and curation. Our peers are pitched as competition, or as data points to increase our virtual success. Group photos perform worse than individual selfies; edited images are more appealing than those left untouched. Post-feminism flourishes as we focus on personal responsibility, self-empowerment, entrepreneurialism and individual choice, but as we do so, we limit conversations around broader influences on gender inequality.

Requiring women to maintain impossible standards of beauty, perfection and curation (whether in the home or at work) is of course nothing new – it's an extension of the 'good girl' virginal archetype. Instead of (or in a lot of cases, as well as) being the perfect housewife and mother, women must now present as the perfect online woman. We must keep our profiles neat and tidy, meticulously curated with a palatable balance of humour, sexuality and authenticity. Both our digital and real selves must be immaculately kept and they must align as closely as possible – otherwise we have failed, both as a fantasy and in reality.

According to the internet's mythology, we should be discovering our true selves whilst performing our best selves and commodifying ourselves as objects. As social media takes a hold of our lives, more and more of us perform as micro celebrities, engaging in aspirational performance regardless of our personal reach. We all engage in the strategy of curating which content to share about ourselves and what we want that performance to say to our audience, no matter how big or small.

Goffman's idea that life is 'spaces where reality is being performed' takes on an even more literal meaning in the digital realm. Authenticity in the digital world is an impossible feat, a parody that we have learnt to accept. And yet it is still considered a core moral principle of our online spaces, a virtue we should all be striving for. We are aware that social media is a performance of a performance, yet we still call on our idols and friends to be 'real'. We ask for transparency whilst keeping our real bodies hidden. We claim to distrust image manipulation but prefer content that has been edited. We fear the repercussions of showing our real faces, bodies and selves whilst demanding absolute authenticity from everyone else. Overuse of filters is distasteful but not using any editing tools at all is likely to render an image flat and unappealing. In our highly curated online spaces, the calls for authenticity present a paradox, in which we are encouraged to be our 'real' selves, whilst those who conform to an unreal standard and formula of behaviour are fast-tracked to success and popularity.

'Everyone is performing at all times,' says Eleanor, of the influencers on the brand trip. 'Even though nobody looked like their Instagram photos, everyone acted like their YouTube personalities.'

Whilst the early internet (Web 2.0) focused on the online world needing to replicate real life, a space to discover niche communities and be your true self, the ever-evolving realms of the new digital frontier (Web 3.0) raise questions about what our 'true' self actually means. I would argue that our current reality exists in a limbo state between the two – we are left with performances of 'real' selves, whilst covert falsities masquerade as authentic.

Aesthetics come before everything, and it is now more important to show a beautiful life than to actually live one.

*

Just a few months before my holiday with Sienna and Eliza, a photograph of Khloé Kardashian in a leopard-print bikini had gone viral. The image showed the then-thirty-six-year-old smiling by the pool, phone in her right hand, hip cocked to the side and hair pulled back in a relaxed ponytail. It was a seemingly lovely holiday photo but Khloé spent weeks trying to remove it from the internet. The Kardashian family, our ultimate creators, threatened to sue anyone who reposted the image.

The photo had been uploaded by Khloé's grandmother, unfiltered and unedited. Although largely praised online for its beauty, the image was a stark contrast to Khloé's usual photos, in which her face and body are edited into a CGI fantasy.

In response to the image being shared, Khloé posted a video of herself in more flattering lighting to show her body wasn't 'photoshopped' and then released a statement to her Instagram, saying that whilst the image was 'beautiful' she had the right to ask for it to be removed.

'In truth, the pressure, constant ridicule and judgement my entire life to be perfect and to meet other's standards of how I should look has been too much to bear . . . My body, my image and how I choose to look and what I want to share is my choice. It's not for anyone to decide or judge what is acceptable or not anymore . . . We are all unique and perfect in our own way. Whichever way one chooses to be seen.'

Even those with access to all of the money, all of the surgery, all of the beauty treatments and personal trainers, nutritionists, private cosmetic doctors and at-home beauty tech still can't live up to the ideal in real life. Even those we deify can't keep up with the standards they're setting. Each picture Khloé posts is seen by millions of women worldwide. When the unedited photo went viral, many expressed relief at seeing a 'real' body, especially from a celebrity who has made an entire brand out of body positivity, but Khloé doubled down.

Khloé compared Instagram filters, good lighting and editing to makeup and having her nails done, adding that she used them to 'present myself to the world the way I want to be seen and it's exactly what I will continue to do unapologetically'. She said she was not asking for sympathy but, somewhat ironically, 'to be acknowledged for being human'.

But you can't have both. Khloé wanted us to acknowledge her humanity whilst simultaneously upholding the illusion that she wasn't one of us. In a way, I understood. I didn't have the same access to beauty resources but I worried so much that I didn't match up to the version of myself that I presented on the apps, a deep-rooted fear that I would never get a true answer to. It became a question I asked over and over again, on first dates, with friends old and new – do I look like my photos? When you stare into this black mirror is it a reflection of me that you see? I wanted to be that version of myself so badly. The most beautiful, most cohesive, most perfect version I portrayed online. I wanted so badly for someone to say yes yes yes, you are still that luminous without the blue light. That was all we ever wanted, I think.

But if Khloé, one of the most influential women in the world, a woman with access to all of the resources necessary to maintain the beauty ideal, still couldn't post one 'real' image – how were we, mere mortals, supposed to exist?

*

It is reported that 600 million people use AR filters every month on Instagram or Facebook, with 76 per cent of Snapchat users using a filter every single day. Popular filters include 'perfect face filter' on Instagram, that adjusts your face to 'ideal' proportions, 'touch up my appearance' on Zoom, 'Pretty Face' and 'Big Lips' on Snapchat, and 'the Skinny Filter' on TikTok, which slims your facial structure. Other popular apps, such as Facetune, FaceApp and Perfect365 allow you to smooth skin, erase blemishes, whiten your teeth, apply digital makeup, and reshape or refine your face and body shape. Since Snapchat first debuted AR filters in 2015, they've evolved from the silly and overt to the almost undetectable. The app now has a whole roster of 'beautifying' filters to choose from.

ABI Research, a global tech market advisory firm, estimates the AR market in retail, commerce and marketing will surpass $12 billion in 2025. According to The Information, Facebook is accelerating its efforts in the space, with nearly one-fifth of the social media platform's 10,000 employees working on AR and virtual reality (VR) devices.

'The internet is freakishly curated right now,' Eleanor tells me. 'There's an illusion that people are editing less but they're just editing more meticulously. It's the equivalent of a messy bun – you end up spending two hours creating something that looks effortless and natural. At least with our highly edited pictures in 2016, the production was more obvious. Now, people have photo dumps of the most casual mirror pics, or selfies of them lying in bed – the whole point of the photos is that they're not stylised but they'll have edited their faces in every single image. It's getting so much harder for our brains to parse out these super-casual lifestyle images as highly curated. That's what gets me, they just look perfect, their faces are pristine. And I am like, "I have never looked like that one day in my life," but of course, it's all edited.'

The bulk of the critical conversation around digital photo manipulation is rooted in a discourse around beauty filters, which are often marked as such by platforms or are, to an extent, detectable. What I see less critique of, but which scares me more, is the subtle and covert image tweaking that thousands of women are undertaking in apps such as Facetune or FaceApp – making their waist slightly smaller, their eyes or lips bigger and smoothing out any imperfections. According to Eleanor, the experience of being a woman online is only getting more 'complicated'.

'On top of everything else, we now have FaceApp. I actually haven't tried it because I'm genuinely afraid that if I do, it will become a problem for me,' she says. 'I have influencer friends who use FaceApp to edit their faces every single day and nobody's talking about it, nobody's acknowledging it.'

Studies have shown that AR beauty filters and photo editing can support self-expression and identity experimentation, but that this is largely done in private, not posted publicly. We may browse and try filters to explore new sides of ourselves, but we don't share the results.

Spencer Burnham, an AR creator who's made popular effects for TikTok and Instagram, admits that skin retouching is a standard in all filters; even if they aren't explicitly for 'beauty' or are intended just for 'fun', they will likely have some level of face editing.

'We're getting to a new place where it's not just augmenting reality, it's replacing reality. It kind of scares me,' he told *The Verge*, as editing technology is improving to encompass real-time augmentation on live videos and AI filters that won't glitch. Although the platforms keep the actual technology behind these filters relatively secret, many have speculated that they now use machine deep-learning tech that regenerates every pixel on a face based on a dataset of images. The results are so realistic it's going to become increasingly difficult to distinguish what's real from what's not, creating what Burnham worries could become a 'breeding ground for body dysmorphia'.

Those with low self-esteem are more likely to use filters, which only reinforces the belief that their real appearance isn't good enough. The longer girls spend editing their photos, the more their self-esteem decreases. What starts out as an exhilarating realm of new possibilities soon becomes anaesthetising – a numbness that comes with detaching from yourself to view your face as an image, and a desensitivity to augmented faces and bodies.

I was scheduled to interview representatives from Snapchat on three occasions during the research process for this book. Each time, the meeting was rescheduled. In our last communication, they asked for a few months to prepare their answers to my questions about the mental health impacts of their filters, while stating that this issue was 'incredibly important to them'. The interview never took place and the answers never came.

In response to concerns about their AI filters, a TikTok spokesperson provided a statement to *Glamour* that read, 'Being true to yourself is celebrated and encouraged on TikTok. Creative Effects are a part of what makes it fun to create content, empowering self-expression and creativity. Transparency is built into the effect experience, as all videos using them are clearly marked by default.'

There was that word again – 'empowering'. Reading the statement felt like violence, a weaponised rhetoric from tech giants who are all too aware of the impact they're having on young women and girls but choose to deflect the problem back to us and tell us they are giving us power.

A 2019 study found that those who use beauty filters are more likely to consider cosmetic surgery. Where offline beauty standards once dictated the creation of beauty filters, beauty filters are now fuelling changes in our IRL ideal, intensifying the level of perfection we're accustomed to seeing. Dr Tijion Esho, one of the UK's leading cosmetic doctors, coined the term 'Snapchat dysmorphia' to describe the phenomenon of patients wanting to bring a digitally augmented version of themselves to life, to redesign themselves to match their online face.

'In many of these images, people have no pores, they have pixel-perfect skin and bigger eyes. They are manipulating themselves in a way that no surgical or non-surgical treatment can do, and many of these patients don't realise that,' Dr Esho tells me. 'It concerns me because I now see fourteen-year-old girls messaging the clinic on social media asking to get work done.'

The evolution of ourselves into digital physical beings, into walking, talking, fleshy cyborg fantasies, is now also evident in the tangible beauty products that we consume. Makeup now promises to replicate filters, make us photo-ready and optimised for selfies, as beauty brands sell us ways to enhance our 3D selves for a 2D landscape, exposing an underlying acceptance that we live just as much through a digital lens as we do in real life.

We don't yet know the long-term impacts of growing up with a filtered face, of seeing a different face in the mirror to the one you present digitally, or of looking back at childhood pictures to see an augmented version of yourself staring back. We can only assume, given the immediate data, that the effect will be even more detrimental in the long run.

'I have certainly looked back at pictures I posted online and found myself getting jealous of my old self,' says Eleanor. 'I have to remind myself that that was my 280th photo, that it has been filtered 600 times and edited over and over again. It's not real. It's an insidious highlight reel, not a memory of how I actually looked.'

Multiple studies show that younger girls are largely unable to detect retouching in pictures. The internet is changing our brain function, particularly with the manipulation of images to enhance our perceived level of beauty. To assume that we, as adults or digital natives, have the ability to easily recognise an augmented image is naive, especially with the subtle tweaks available to users on apps like Facetune. I know this because the women around me do it regularly; I have done it before. Not all edits are overt, not all filters are flagged. We can nip in our waist, remove our blemishes and smooth our skin and leave no obvious trace. The augmentation of our digital selves is becoming increasingly impossible to detect and our grasp on reality is fading fast.

Even knowing that an image is edited doesn't stop your brain from engaging in comparison. With the nature of social media, our emotions can be triggered by multiple images before our brain has had a chance to process them. A study by the University of Warwick found that flagging images of models as 'enhanced' or 'manipulated' can counterintuitively increase our desire to emulate their appearance. Even when we're told a photo has been edited, the image feels more real to us than the disclaimer. We still find the content aspirational; if anything, the enhancement of the image only reinforces the standard to which we are being held, even when we know logically it cannot be achieved.

Treating our images, or ourselves, as objects to be modified can lead us to objectify ourselves and create a disconnect in our sense of identity. Author Steve Magness told *Fox News*, 'Our brain is predictive. When we put bad data in, we get bad predictions out. When the data coming in equals "everyone is flawless", that becomes our brain's predictive comparison point. These filters are a mental health disaster in the making.' If you spend an extended period of time using a filter that changes the way you look, you may begin to develop a predictive model of yourself looking like that filter. It will get to the point where you'll look in the mirror in real life and get prediction errors, which are viscerally uncomfortable dysphoric sensations.

When we objectify ourselves in this way, we literally perceive ourselves as less than human, as unfeeling, unreal beings. The result is an aestheticised but anaesthetised self, viewed constantly from an external vantage point, detached from our real selves and emotions. It also impacts how we perceive those around us. Once our brain gets used to an airbrushed beauty ideal, we find it hard not to compare others to that aspirational image. The phenomenon then extends out of the digital realm, bleeding into our wider beauty standards until a filter-enhanced aesthetic becomes the ideal for all of us, even those who aren't online.

As with most issues in our digital world, technology hasn't created the problem. Filters and editing apps weren't born within a bubble, they are the direct result of an already existing culture intent on moderating, scrutinising and 'perfecting' women's bodies; a system that benefits from us hyper-fixating on our appearance and investing time, money and energy into this pursuit. When filtering our images, we must consider what we are filtering out – often this is the features that make us individual, that make us human, whilst preferring lighter and brighter skin, and Eurocentric features. Beauty filters and editing apps reflect and compound biases that already exist within our society and reward those who already closely resemble the ideal.

*

As technology advances, we aren't only competing with airbrushed augmentations of ourselves and other women, we're also faced with the rise of virtual influencers – digital humanoid fantasies largely created as young women pursue careers in aesthetic labour, from modelling to influencing.

One of the most notable influencers of recent years is Lil Miquela, a forever-nineteen-year-old biracial effigy whose rise to online fame led to modelling jobs for brands like Burberry, Chanel and Prada, the launch of her very own brand and being named one of *TIME* magazine's '25 Most Influential People on the Internet'. But Lil Miquela does not exist outside of the digital realm. She is nothing more than a manufactured internet celebrity, digitally engineered for virtual success, the brainchild of the software media company Brud.

Lil Miquela plays on every archetype of influencer culture and behaviour to create a performance that is entirely engineered and yet somehow authentic. It is a code – her language, poses, references, outfits and personal brand mimic those of any number of young, aspiring influencers at the time. She didn't even disclose she was non-human until April 2018, letting the speculation speak for itself whilst she accrued attention (much in the same way the Kardashians deflect speculation on their physical augmentations). Lil Miquela's success challenges our very notion of what reality even means and how much we even care about it in an increasingly performative space.

The concerning aspect of the virtual female promotional bot is, firstly, that she represents a woman's body as a form of property, one that can be bought and manipulated. She, as a metaphysical being, is not ontologically bound to her body in the same way that we are. Unlike real women, Miquela will never age, never have opinions, never be too big or too small for a brand's clothing and never burn out. She will never have bad skin days, feel bloated, complain – unless manufactured to do so in a bid for so-called authenticity. Unlike Matilda Djerf's, her hair will never grow beyond its desired style. Unlike Snitchery, she doesn't have to revert to her human self. She can be anywhere and everywhere all at once and she doesn't need sleep.

Influencer culture today relies on tools such as editing, filtering and curating our digital selves to fit a constructed ideal – so how far removed is Lil Miquela from our virtual reality? Unlike Khloé, Lil Miquela doesn't need to masquerade as authentic because we know she isn't real. She is afforded the innate understanding that she will never achieve true authenticity and can therefore play in a paradoxical performance without the intense scrutiny applied to real women's bodies and behaviours. She is a literal depiction of our current culture, unreal and yet authentic.

What Lil Miquela's success suggests is that we don't care that images are manufactured as long as they are visually appealing, fit the format we are accustomed to consuming, and meet the standards of the ideal and the platform. Either that, or we are already so used to seeing digital flesh on ourselves and our friends that we don't see much difference.

What is a concerning phenomenon, however, is that the most influential virtual woman is a woman of colour and that many of our digital influencers – from Lil Miquela to virtual dark-skinned supermodel Shudu – are wrapped up in raced bodies. The notion of 'artificial diversity' online is fast becoming a talking point, as brands such as Levi's are partnering with digital agencies to supplement human models with AI generated ones in order to increase representation on their ecommerce sites.

Often, the entities that own, control and profit from these virtual women of colour are not women of colour. Instead of hiring and paying women for their work, brands are employing tech companies largely owned and operated by men to construct artificial images of women in order to present the illusion of progress. According to HypeAuditor, brands will pay more to work with Lil Miquela than they will to work with a real biracial woman, like Eleanor – regardless of follower count or levels of influence.

Ironically, whilst the virtual world preferences the commodification and ownership of raced bodies, AR filters often only work on white faces. From lightening skin to failing to match features and perpetuating racialised trends such as big lips (but only on light-skinned women), AR filters fail to deliver the same experience for women of colour.

As we are already aware, our digital realm holds so much promise for increased diversity and inclusion, but not until we eradicate the existing biases, hierarchies and structures that continue to define our current reality. Without an awareness of the harmful stereotypes and existing social privileges at play, we are only compounding and intensifying the subordination of women, women of colour and marginalised people.

It is yet to be seen how more immersive digital spaces like the Metaverse will impact our beauty ideals and sense of self – mostly still a clunky novelty, these realms are still largely removed from our day-to-day lives. Unlike with social media, we can still opt out, log off – but they do have the potential to change the way we perceive what is 'real'. According to 2022 research from Razorfish and VICE Media Group, over half of gen Z gamers reported feeling more like themselves in the Metaverse – but focus is largely on action and interaction than on aesthetics.

'I work from home so I mainly see my colleagues on Zoom and have loads of friends that I only really see on Snapchat or Instagram stories,' twenty-three-year-old Rebecca told *Style News*. 'Really, most of my generation spends the majority of our time online, so having things like cyborg filters or alien skins to customise our *Fortnite* characters, which more accurately represents what we wish we looked like (in my case at least), is epic.'

Whilst some creators are harnessing the limitless potential of virtual reality to play with identity, create surreal masterpieces and defy traditional beauty standards, that is still largely a fringe group within a still-functioning hierarchy of ideals. Needless to say, these avatars are still curated and immune to human imperfections and bodily functions. Each avatar we create is another face to fragment, another body to monitor, stylise and scrutinise.

*

In 2019, at the height of her $300,000-a-year influencing career, after she had amassed 400,000 loyal devotees, Lee from America took a break from the online world. And she cut all of her hair off.

'When I went back to Instagram, I wasn't posting pretty things, I was just posting silly videos of me and my dog, and people were like, "What the fuck is this? She's crazy. She's doing a Britney Spears."'

Of course, a woman who chooses to cut her hair short and defy pretty conventions must be insane, right? 'It was so good, though,' Lee says. 'I think I knew that was a pivotal moment in my life and once I got a taste of it, I knew I couldn't go back. I was finally able to explore all sides of myself. I was actually hanging out with people, building friendships, exploring what I like to do offline. I was more in tune with myself. I wore clothes that were comfortable, I was spending more time with my family again. I was just living life instead of living for social media. I can't go back to that level of disconnection from myself.'

Lee's withdrawal from the internet was also connected to the return of an eating disorder, one that was enabled by her brand of 'wellness'.

'During a time where I felt I had to promote the healthiest, most balanced side of myself, I was indeed the unhealthiest I've ever been: mentally, emotionally, spiritually,' she detailed in a caption on Instagram. 'I was obsessed with living the healthiest possible version of myself and had made my life small as a result. I thought I was doing something good for myself. I was fixated on "good" foods, was extremely inflexible and constantly worried about my physical health. My eating disorder had returned in the form of the "wellness diet". Who am I without wellness? Who am I without all these "healthy" diets and wellness products?'

As part of her break from the digital world, Lee admitted herself to an eating disorder recovery centre. In getting better, she lost a huge portion of her followers and her income, but she wouldn't trade it in for the world.

'It's so much better,' she gushes when I ask about her relationship to beauty now she's largely offline. 'Mainly because I'm not looking at my body. And I'm also using my body in a different way – my body is not attached to my business anymore. My body is my body. Unfortunately, women's bodies sell a lot of stuff. By not posting my body, I'm not making a lot of money, but that's fine.'

Lee is now a proud ex-influencer, who supports others who wish to come offline in creating their CVs and honing their transferable digital skills. She is well and truly back in the mortal realm, revelling in the rhythm of nine-to-five and the ease with which she can log off. She does, however, have to post on Instagram to promote her business. It seems there are still barriers to completely opting out.

Eleanor feels a similar disconnect – she realised years into her career as Snitchery that beauty was not the space for her salvation but continues to use her shapeshifting skills for cosplay and character creation. She's still deified, a darling of the algorithm – and she still feels consumed by the paradox of her existence: how might she make her career without contributing to a culture she knows is harmful?

In this digital age, the boundaries between heaven and hell continue to blur, and the question remains: in whom, or what, do we truly place our faith?

How can we create a more beautiful future for women and girls?

'I think we need to keep pushing for more real content. I have been guilty of it over the years. I look back at some of my Instagram photos and everything was just picture perfect and glossy. Now, I am really glad that I am moving towards a real, stripped-back version of myself. I'm trying to show that you can accept yourself and be happy without all of that.'

Lottie Tomlinson,
influencer and founder of Tanologist

8

Bite the Hand That Starves You

I hadn't known Chloe for long but I loved her straight away. She was magnetic and messy, haunting and hilarious. Chloe was beautiful in a sharp and dark way – in a 'parties after fashion week, tailored trousers at the art gallery, cigarettes in holders between chipped nail polish' kind of way. I imagined her eating burrata with caviar, her dark hair intertwining with the black smudges around her eyes. Her voice was low and rumbling – sardonic and sweet – like a whisky sour on the rocks. Despite her being six years my junior, I admired how fully she embodied her character. A teen Tumblr fantasy, all fishnets and cigarettes and nonchalant cool. Only sometimes could you see a flicker of chaos behind her eyes.

The first time we went out together, two older men sent champagne to our table. This had never happened to me before but I imagined it happening to Chloe all of the time. We got drunk in their company, meeting in the women's toilets to scream and stamp our feet and say 'slay queen' ironically unironically, giddy at the fact that they saw us for what we truly were: shiny, bright young things. Jewels they should treasure. Gifted girls worthy of shrines and sacrifices and champagne kisses. With Chloe, everything felt like a movie. Golden light smeared across our evening and we held each other up in the glittering haze. Look at us, everyone, over-achieving.

Chloe had patterns that were familiar to me. When we met for dinner she told me at length about the really big lunch she'd not long finished and I watched as her eyes lingered over the menu, now marked with calories. I could see her mind at work – a mind once called gifted and talented at school, one that wrote poetry she'd never share, one hardwired to buzz for a metallic sticker saying 'good job' – busy with arithmetic, managing deficits and surplus, making choices to quell a different kind of hunger that felt much deeper than her belly. If X = Y+750 then what must we subtract in order to stay sane? Mac and cheese equals how many reps of the 12:3:30? How many minutes could she spend in the bathroom before I got suspicious? Apparently, if you get good enough at maths the numbers become invisible, abstract and infinite. I hadn't reached that point yet. Chloe hadn't either.

Chloe had also grown up with an online obsession – lusting over deified digital girls.

'They had the kind of lifestyle I wanted,' she told me across the dinner table. 'They were these gorgeous creatives living in London with their boyfriends. They were just really funny and cool. And they were skinny as well. I screenshotted all their photos on my camera roll, made moodboards. I mean, physically made moodboards in a scrapbook. Pasted pictures of them on my walls. And then I'd do exactly what they were doing, act exactly how they did. Alexa Chung, Kate Moss, Tumblr famous girls, that was what I was trying to chase.'

Long before the term 'influencer' was coined, my friends and I were also buying into everything our favourite Tumblr girls promoted. Their outfits, their holidays, their makeup routine, their poses, their meals. Most girls our age have spent time down the rabbit hole. In one way or another, we were all mad here – screaming and shouting about the walls that were too tight, the houses that didn't fit the way they should, the constriction we felt. For a few months, one of our favourite bloggers embarked on a 'mono diet' – a regime in which you eat only one food per meal. Just pears. Just chicken. There was that one YouTuber who only ate bananas. So we did the same, eating portions of pineapple until we felt sick. By the time we were sixteen, all of my friends were engaging in unhealthy behaviours with food. Obsessive workout routines in our childhood bedrooms, weight-loss smoothies, no carbs before 12pm. We tried all of the potions, the lollipops, the tea, the tablets, the milkshakes, the gummy sweets, the injections and the meal plans. But still our games consoles told us that we were obese at eight years old and the adults poked at our puppy fat promising one day it would shed.

Our mums spent hours cooking dinners only to push the food around their plates, protesting that they ate so much during the prep that they couldn't possibly stomach any more, whilst our dads sat pot-bellied at the table. Our aunties ate cereal for two meals a day to fit into their red swimsuits, TV shows gave prizes to whoever lost the most pounds, our sisters read magazines with red circles around 'beached whales' and we did the 30-Day Shred and BeachBody workouts after school, using cans of beans instead of weights. We reblogged thigh gap tips, ate far too much grapefruit and relished in the feeling of hunger. We still grin smugly in our sickbeds, overcome with a bittersweet buzz because we know we will emerge smaller, deserving of praise.

We feigned pride and confidence to one another then, becoming almost competitive in our habits. I wish we had realised how much we were hurting ourselves, and one another. I wish we'd known how much our dream girls had been hurting too.

'It was just constant, people were picking at the way my body looked and sending me the cruellest messages,' one of my Tumblr idols confided in me when we finally met IRL, almost a decade after I had first discovered her online. Now twenty-eight, she is largely withdrawn from the internet. 'I suffered from an eating disorder because of it,' she tells me 'My periods stopped for three years. I tried so many diets and my relationship with food became obsessive, and it's only because of Tumblr that I became like that. I couldn't separate their comments from real life.'

I was reminded of Lee from America, who had said of influencing, 'I really did find a career that celebrated me having an eating disorder,' before she quit the internet to aid her recovery.

Like the majority of women, I have never been diagnosed with an eating disorder but many of these disordered habits have stayed with me; there have been too many years of my life spent logging calories obsessively into MyFitnessPal, my mind foggy in that liminal brain space caused by self-starvation. Now, at twenty-eight, I still repeatedly hear my colleagues, friends and mentors discussing food groups they need to cut out, the latest diet trend or detox they need to finish. I still struggle with relapsing into these practices. I could tell Chloe was relapsing too.

I knew Chloe was falling down a rabbit hole. Spiralling down, the world closing in around her. Her heart twitching, her brain swelling until it was forcing its way out of her skull and her eyes no longer knew what was real. She screamed to tell them that the walls were closing in on her but they couldn't see it. Your house is perfectly fine, they'd say. Look! Eat this! Drink this! But Chloe wasn't falling for that again, her eyes wild and feral as she pushed them away. And that's when she stopped eating. Anything that crossed her lips was soon forced out again. In and then out. In and out. There was no room in this house for anything else. Chloe could already feel her bones being crushed, her mouth bitter and her body sore. The walls only seemed to get tighter. She has been stuck in that room ever since.

'I grew up in the US and my family is Danish. So we were already not part of the norm,' she tells me a few months after we first met for dinner. 'I realised what the beauty standard was when this girl pinched me and said, "You have really big arms." Then at a doctor's appointment, they turned to my mum and said, "Your daughter's becoming overweight." The beauty standard was being skinny and blonde, a lot of the girls that I knew at school, the popular girls, looked like that with athletic builds. Even at fourteen years old, I knew that was the standard. I got this sick desire to show them – "Well, look how skinny I can become." That was success to me.'

Chloe was diagnosed with an eating disorder in 2017, after years of suffering in secret.

Despite our supposed progress in recent decades, we are still facing an epidemic of starving girls. The prevalence of eating disorders across the world more than doubled from 3.5 per cent for the 2000–2006 period to 7.8 per cent for the 2013–2018 period. Eating disorders recorded in primary care are nearly eleven times more common in women than men, with 40 per cent of newly diagnosed cases in girls aged fifteen to nineteen years old. According to the 2023 Girlguiding report, 68% of eleven- to twenty-one-year-olds would like to lose weight, and 48% sometimes skip meals in a bid to be thinner, a 15% increase since 2018. Over half of teenage girls admit to using unhealthy weight control behaviours such as fasting, smoking cigarettes, vomiting or taking laxatives.

Symptoms can occur as young as kindergarten, with nearly a third of children aged five to six in the US wanting to be thinner. By age seven, one in four children have engaged in some kind of dieting behaviour, according to a Common Sense Media report published in 2015.

Negative body image and obsession with size has become

such an inherent part of the female experience that psychologists have coined the term 'normative discontent' to describe the constant unhappiness women experience with their weight. To struggle with body image is classed as an essential element of womanhood. To be a girl is to be eternally hungry or unhappy, destined to live and die by a diet culture that punishes our bodies for taking up space.

Diet culture exists online not in a vacuum but as an extension of an already pervasive culture that's inescapable in society. It is embedded into the very code of our digital realm. The global diet industry was estimated to be worth $175.4 billion in 2022 and is projected to reach a value of $282.5 billion by 2028.

Diet culture feels like a nebulous concept but it is present in all the small pervasive ways that pressures around food, exercise and the thin ideal appear in our everyday lives, whether that's intentionally skipping meals, fearing 'bad' foods or feeling guilty after dessert.

Diet culture is a moral hierarchy of bodies that puts slimness at the top of the pyramid. It means pursuing this ideal at the cost of all else. It is sacrificing time, energy, your health, stability, social events and relationships in the name of thinness. Diet culture is ignoring your body's hunger cues. It is 'nothing tastes as good as skinny feels'. It means equating weight to health, size to value, and thinness with morality; the glorification of a harmful beauty ideal over the welfare of those pressured into pursuing it. It is a lifelong project, one that likely will never be completed.

Diet culture is when Eliza came back from Thailand after losing a significant amount of weight from shitting herself for the last two weeks of her trip, and we all cooed over her new, smaller body, as if to say 'OMG you just shit yourself smaller?! AMAZING!! Wish I could shit myself for a week! I'm so jealous!'

Diet culture is TV shows hosted and owned by fat men, debating whether fat women should be allowed to appear in media created for women.

Diet culture is a form of surveillance that pushes us to turn on ourselves. It has never been about weight loss but rather an insidious form of control over women's bodies, in which we self-police ourselves into subordination. If men are to be big and strong, then women must stay small and weak to maintain the status quo – to keep everybody comfortable, except themselves.

Diet culture, as Naomi Wolf wrote in *The Beauty Myth*, is a 'potent political sedative' designed to silence us. It is everywhere, and it is women and girls who are most at risk.

The cruellest part is that this is a sickness that often plagues the girls with the most potential. Overachievers, perfectionists, A* students with type-A personalities. WhatsApp group chat admins, Facebook event creators. The girls who loathed group projects whilst their teammates sighed with collective relief. The girls whose parents had been so proud of them, and then they grew up.

The patriarchy identified its biggest threat – and it took us down, one by one, invading our minds with cookie-cutter images with razor-sharp edges. Our psyches pierced. We're all mad here.

*

As Chloe became thinner, her popularity online started to increase. Her platform grew until she had over 80,000 followers at seventeen, with images she'd post at school on her lunch break achieving tens of thousands of likes and being shared across the world.

'I would have a schedule. I would have to post every two days and if I didn't, I'd get really stressed. It was all tied into the number-counting of my eating disorder. If I was going to take a picture, I wouldn't eat as many calories that day, so my calorie intake directly correlated to my posting schedule. When I'd taken my pictures, I would be allowed a meal. I did that for three years.'

Many of the images Chloe posted show her holding or surrounded by food. There are countless images of her looking modelesque in the aisles of the supermarket near her school, holding bread or beer bottles like babies or sacred objects.

'You know how Instagram models are like "I love burgers" and then they take one bite for a photo? That was me. Except I was taking photos in the Morrison's meat aisle.' We both laugh because the whole thing is absurd now, scrolling through images of a teenage Chloe posing over produce. 'I have so many pictures of me holding food like it's holy, or me holding a baguette like a baby, because for some reason I thought that was super indie and cool. Actually, I fucking hated bread at that point,' she shakes her head and cackles. 'Babe, it's fake bread!'

By the time she was sixteen, Chloe's images had gone viral multiple times, but it became harder and harder to disconnect the validation she received from strangers online from her disorder and continual weight loss. It became obvious to Chloe that her thinness had currency, and the further she pushed her body, the more likes she could achieve.

'At the time, I was just really excited about going viral, because you have 30,000 people who liked your photo. In real life, I wasn't even liked by four people growing up, and most of them just took pictures of me. And then you think, yeah, I have gotten this far, I can keep going. You get addicted to the likes and you start competing not just with other girls but with yourself. You start saying, "Oh, well, that one got so many likes because I'm skinny and I look like I have blow-job eyes." I was sixteen and I had mastered the talent of "blow-job eyes" already. You end up thinking, let me push it, let me see how many likes I could actually get, let me see how many times this picture has been viewed. How many comments? How interesting can I be to these random people online? That's all that mattered.'

Eating disorders have complex origins which differ from individual to individual. Neither socialisation nor digital media are sole *causes* of these conditions, but they are factors that both mediate and exasperate the normalisation of this behaviour in women and girls, and the pervasive thin ideal. Whilst social media platforms are not solely responsible for causing eating disorders, they amplify them, and harmful content, amongst wider audiences.

'More people are definitely talking about eating disorders now, which means more people are coming forward, and that is obviously increasing our stats and our referrals,' says NHS eating disorder therapist Olivia Rowe. 'But I do feel that people being on their phones and being bombarded with those messages is wrapped up in their self-esteem and self-worth being placed on body image, weight and shape.'

Various studies have documented widespread body and weight dissatisfaction amongst girls and women, and social media has been found to be a significant catalyst for these appearance concerns. Social media present innumerable idealised images of thin, lean, beautiful, edited, curated women, and the 'thin ideal' and 'athletic ideal' are displayed as a normal, desirable and attainable body type for every woman. We then internalise these unrealistic ideals and feel ashamed when we are unable to achieve them.

'Social media assessments have now become such a huge part of treatment,' Olivia tells me. 'It's mandatory for people within the age bracket of sixteen to twenty-five that you ask about their social media use, what type of people they are following and how they feel after they have been on social media.'

Studies have found that frequent exposure to the internet and social networking platforms results in high levels of weight dissatisfaction, drive for thinness and body surveillance in young women. In the mid-1990s, surveys suggested that 83 per cent of adolescent girls read fashion magazines for an average of 4.3 hours per week and that *Seventeen* magazine had an estimated readership of 11 million. Several studies reported a positive association between exposure to beauty and fashion magazines and an increased level of weight concerns or eating disorder symptoms in girls. One study found that the importance of thinness and trying to look like women on television, in movies or in magazines were predictive of young girls (nine to fourteen years old) beginning to purge at least monthly.

If we compare the readership of *Seventeen* to the following of the Kardashians alone (who have promoted a number of diet products), the numbers pale in comparison. Instead of a monthly or weekly thirty-page issue, we can consume the equivalent content in a single hour. Women and girls often spend more than 4.3 hours a day on their phones – my screentime is often in the double digits. We are living in a constant, never-ending issue of a woman's magazine, intent on promoting unrealistic beauty images, selling us diet products, workout plans and surgical procedures to achieve the look. One study found that appearance comparison via social media made women more vulnerable to thinking about diet and exercise than traditional media and in-person comparison. In 2023, 34% of girls aged eleven to twenty-one had tried a diet after hearing about a celebrity or influencer using it, compared to 22% in 2016.

Whilst the body positivity movement tries to fight back by celebrating a variety of shapes and sizes online, eating disorder statistics have worsened since the 1990s, when ultra-thin supermodels reigned supreme. The recent years spent in lockdowns have had an even more detrimental effect, as lack of routine and control, along with increased time spent online, have caused eating disorder cases to rise further. Women and girls are just as at risk as they have ever been, with the methods for indoctrinating them into a restrictive body image ever more covert and insidious.

Unlike traditional media consumers, we are now both audience and content creators. The constant monitoring of our appearance, inherent in self-objectification, has been likened to the concept of body-checking, an established maintaining factor for disordered eating. Body-checking is a compulsive behaviour in which you constantly seek information about your own body – checking yourself in the mirror, videoing your body from various angles or obsessively weighing yourself. It's a sliding scale that can quickly become extreme. Whether we're taking selfies, watching ourselves on a video call, being photographed with friends or filming online content, we're constantly exposed to the potential for self-surveillance and over-analysis. We're constantly reminded of what our body looks like in direct comparison to the ideal.

On top of that, social media companies often intensify our exposure to potentially harmful posts, providing us with personalised content that is often more extreme in order to capture our attention and keep us engaged for as long as possible.

In 2021, it was revealed that an Instagram account ostensibly belonging to a thirteen-year-old girl who had previously expressed interest in weight loss and dieting received promotions from Instagram accounts titled 'I have to be thin', 'Eternally starved' and 'I want to be perfect'. The Instagram account had been set up by Connecticut senator Richard Blumenthal's staff, who had registered it as a thirteen-year-old girl's and proceeded to follow various dieting and pro-eating disorder accounts, which are supposedly banned from the platform. Very quickly, Instagram's algorithm began almost exclusively recommending the young teenage account should follow more and more extreme dieting accounts, the senator told CNN: 'Big tech's exploiting of these powerful algorithms and design features is reckless and heedless, and needs to change. They seize on the insecurities of children, including eating disorders, simply to make more money.'

CNN followed up with their own investigation, also following some extreme dieting and pro-eating disorder accounts. Within days, Instagram promoted accounts with names like 'Sweet Skinny', 'Prettily Skinny', and 'Wanna Be Skinny' to the account that was registered as belonging to a thirteen-year-old girl.

In 2021, Facebook whistleblower Frances Haugen testified that the tech monolith puts 'astronomical profits before people', adding that Facebook knows its systems lead teenagers to pro-eating disorder content, and intentionally targets teenagers and children under thirteen. Haugen told senators that an algorithm 'led children from very innocuous topics like healthy recipes . . . all the way to anorexia-promoting content over a very short period of time', adding that women would be walking around with brittle bones in sixty years because of the anorexia-related content they found on Facebook's platforms.

Internal research Haugen shared with the *Wall Street Journal* had found the platform sends some girls on a 'downward spiral' into a rabbit hole of harmful content – creating an increasingly vicious loop that becomes very difficult for young people to escape.

'Once you look at one video, the algorithm takes off and they don't stop coming – it's like dominoes falling,' Neveen Radwan told the *Guardian* in 2021, after social media played a 'humongous role' in her seventeen-year-old daughter's eating disorder. 'It is horrific, and there is nothing we can do about it.'

When the business model of these tech monopolies is built on holding our attention for as long as possible, when our engagement leads to profit and when there is a lack of women in the room to advocate for our experiences, change feels futile. Haugen, in her testimony, suggested Facebook return to a chronological timeline, rather than one driven more intensely by the algorithm's recommendations, to reduce the spread of harmful content.

Facebook has said it works to minimise such content by restricting hashtags that promote it. However, a report released in 2021 by the advocacy group SumOfUs found twenty-two different hashtags promoting eating disorders still existed on Instagram at the time, and were linked to more than 45 million eating disorder-related posts. The report found 86.7 per cent of the eating disorder posts analysed were promoting unapproved appetite suppressants and 52.9 per cent directly promoted eating disorders.

Compounding the problem is the difficulty in finding available and affordable care for young women. The rate of eating disorders has risen sharply in recent years and waiting lists in the UK for emergency therapy sessions can be up to six months. The longer a girl waits for treatment, the closer she gets to death.

*

Do you know what happens when you starve a brain? You become obsessive, detail oriented. Your concentration is compromised. You stop being able to listen to other people's opinions. You hyper-fixate. You become unable to see the bigger picture. You lose the ability to be spontaneous, creative and flexible. Your memory worsens. You struggle to remember details about your daily life. You lose weight in all parts of your body. Parts of your organs start to die. Your brain starts to shrink.

Since learning that, I haven't stopped thinking about how much of myself I lost due to starvation. Which of my quirks are part and parcel of being hungry for a sustained period of time. How many girls are missing percentages of themselves, lost particles and potential. How many of us have been eaten away by the hunger to be beautiful, to be the best.

'The brain is such a hungry organ, it needs about four hundred to five hundred calories a day just for itself,' therapist Olivia Rowe tells me. 'Your brain becomes very lazy if it doesn't have the nutrients it needs. It finds it very difficult to zoom out and problem solve. That's just too much energy. It becomes very rigid as well, so the moment that you impose a rule about eating on a starved brain, it will stick. It doesn't want to create new neural processes. When you have a starved mind, you are also viewing things differently. It's a perceptual abnormality that's happening because you are sort of hallucinating slightly when you are looking at yourself in the mirror. It's the starved mind that then perpetuates eating disorders so much more. And you are working with a starved mind in therapy as well, which can be really tough. After three years of creating these pathways, it becomes very difficult to change the behaviour. That's when the rigidity really sets in.'

I'm reminded of Chloe's three years of starving on a schedule and posting her content. I think about my own experiences and realise three years is nothing. That's not even the entirety of high school; it's a fraction of the time women spend restricting their diets – often habits that last a lifetime and, once started, can change the course of a young girl's life.

'I do think now about what I actually could have been if I hadn't gone down this path,' Chloe tells me. 'I wanted to be an aeroengineer for a long time. If I had never realised that I was a sexual being when I was young, would I have actually gone into STEM? Because I loved maths. I was so good at maths. But I kind of gave up, I didn't really care once I realised this was an easier way to get a thrill.'

Every moment for Chloe was an image to be captured, to be analysed and reframed. The audience outside those ever-tighter walls were waiting to photograph her through the windows. Every frame was an opportunity to be beautiful. Nothing was real unless it was observed, and Chloe was clinging on to reality. To be seen. To be admired. To be aesthetic at all costs.

'I can't get out of my head,' she says. 'I always feel watched. I have these delusions, almost, of an audience watching me and I think that is so intrinsically tied to feeling like I have to perform constantly, even in the most intimate situations. Am I actually me? Or am I just performing sponsorship for a social post? Am I acting this emotion out or am I really feeling it? Throughout my eating disorder, I could convince myself I had made it all up. I'm not actually ill, I'm just doing a bit, it's just a character I play online. I don't feel any relation to the girl I was when I was sixteen to eighteen. I only feel sadness for her. I didn't get the chance to experience that age outside of the internet. I never got to sleep without thinking about getting content for tomorrow.'

It looked glamorous in the black and white photos, in the Tumblr edits and the typewriter poetry, but the reality was cold and deadly. The mortality rate for individuals with anorexia is greater than any other mental disorder and has been shown to be as high as 15 per cent. In 2004, the parents of a bulimic nineteen-year-old who had passed away from her illness released her case notes from the autopsy report as a way of raising awareness and combating the romanticised images of the disease. The notes were published in 2005 as part of a paper in *Forensic Science International.* Please read on with caution.

She was 19 and had anorexia and bulimia for five years. She died at 5'1' (155cm) and 94lbs (43kg) when her stomach ripped after eating 5.6 litres of food. She was found in full rigor mortis – which is present from 12–72 hours – naked, with her head and arms over a lavatory. If you look really closely at her stomach, you can see a greenish tint, which is a typical sign of her internal organs decaying. The bruises called for the autopsy. Because of her position when her stomach exploded, it spilled all its contents into her body cavity. When they did the autopsy, they found that her stomach had been extended from where your ribs meet each other all the way to her pubic bone, right behind that pad of fat above the genitals. Her stomach had a large rip in it. Her heart was small and displayed typical characteristics of a starving heart – destroyed muscles and dead immune cells. Her brain had swelled and had started to squeeze out of her skull before she died. Like a typical binger, her stomach was dying before it ripped. When the stomach exploded, her body responded with a typical immune reaction. It dilated her blood vessels, her blood pressure dropped, she blacked out and her heart slowed down and stopped.

It didn't seem to matter what you looked like or who you were, we were all victims of this culture. Its traps became increasingly complex and sophisticated. Even if we stopped going out in public, they caught us in our private moments. In our bedrooms. In the bath. In the changing rooms. On our phones.

It was a life spent dancing with death and only just making it out alive each time. The duels are constant and all-consuming, the obsession with winning harder to define. To be the best is to get as close to the edge as you can, as close to the other side before it takes you forever. The rabbit hole beckoning us below.

*

For as long as the internet has existed, pro-eating disorder content has proliferated online. As early as 2001, Yahoo took down 113 pro-anorexia websites from its servers. In 2012, after a *Huffington Post* exposé on 'thinspiration' blogs on Tumblr, the platform took measures to ban explicitly pro-eating disorder blogs. Despite decades passing since this issue first emerged, social media platforms still grapple with the same challenge. In recent years, all major platforms have faced criticism for failing to effectively deal with pro-eating disorder content and the ways in which their algorithms support the spread of harmful information, despite explicitly stating in their terms and conditions that users should not promote behaviours of self-harm, including content that could encourage eating disorders. Advertising policies on the majority of platforms have either banned or placed restrictions on weight-loss adverts, and any attempt to search for harmful pro-eating disorder content leads users to a 'need help' page with resources, helplines and support.

However, some social media platforms, such as TikTok, tend to rabbit-hole users into harmful echo chambers quickly, often populated with increasingly extreme content, as the algorithm learns what users are willing to view for longer in an attempt to keep them hooked. Eighty per cent of over 1,000 TikTok users surveyed by broadcaster ITV in 2022 said the app hindered their ED recovery and 93 per cent said TikTok doesn't do enough to protect against harmful content. Only 6 of 100 posts flagged to TikTok by ITV for violating community guidelines were removed by the platform; it claimed 92 of the videos didn't in fact violate their terms, and reporters had to go to the press office to get the remaining two videos removed. Which begs the question – what are the guidelines if the app says content doesn't breach the conditions but the press office agrees they do?

That young girls under the age limits imposed by platforms aren't accessing the content is unrealistic. Researching this book, I've met a number of girls under eight years old who regularly use social media platforms such as TikTok, YouTube and Instagram. Despite age limit policies, these systems are easily bypassed. Anyone can create an account with a fake age. In fact, a 2020 article in the *New York Times* speculates that a third of TikTok users may be under the age of fourteen.

It was Chloe who told me about Eating Disorder Twitter, the place a lot of girls migrated to after censorship bans on other platforms. The content was still on the other platforms of course, but harder to find. With 'free speech' a core tenet of Twitter's new leadership, the rabbit hole led to a wonderland that was thriving.

'Don't go there if you don't have to,' Chloe warned. 'But I can tell you how to get in.'

She had an account under a different name, a different character, but she wanted nothing to do with my research from here on out. To this day, I don't know who she was in that other world.

Before I entered, I protected myself as much as possible. I wrapped myself up in affirmations, in the taste of buttered toast and the warmth of my belly, and I made my way down the rabbit hole again. What I found was nothing short of horrifying. Endless posts of sharp, white bodies, inspiration threads of incredibly ill girls, invitations to group chats to keep yourself accountable (600 calories max, if you gain 5lbs you get kicked out), talk of suicide, images of self-harm, graphic depictions of bodies being sliced smaller, guides to eating 100 calories or less, threads on how to hide an eating disorder from your parents, current weight and ultimate goal weights – all in pounds and all in double digits, largely in girls under twenty, some as young as thirteen.

There was a vengeful tone underlying the entire world, anger at the unrealistic standards they were subjected to directed at themselves and others – 'put the chips down', 'you'll never be as beautiful as them', 'I ate too much today and I hate myself for it'. There were threads made entirely of content from other internet creators, used to set an example of what happens when you gain too much weight, tagging the content as 'fatspo' to shame the women in the videos. One tweet says 'this weight gain is crazy' next to two near-identical looking images of an innocent TikToker, who can't have gone up more than a dress size.

This is where I met nineteen-year-old Wish. She hosted virtual tea parties multiple times a week, posting lavish images of delicacies for the eyes only. She would post food polls to the platform, asking other users to vote on which dish they'd most like to eat. The images were delicious – pistachio ice creams, flaky pastries and pastel-coloured macarons filled my screen in a delicatessen dreamscape.

'It's like a fascination with something you can't have,' she tells me when we talk on the phone. 'But I have nightmares about eating and not being able to stop. I have nightmares of giant tables with food all over them and I am eating everything and I can't stop eating. And then I wake up in a panic because I think I would rather die than eat like a pig. If somebody held a gun to my head and said, "Eat this whole cake," I would say, "Shoot. Go for it. "'

Wish first discovered eating disorder content on Instagram when she was twelve – accounts populated with pictures of very thin girls that she instantly felt jealous of. She thought creating her own would help to hold her accountable in her weight loss.

'They can tell me how bad I look so I can fix it, that's motivation. So, I would post body checks and then what I would eat in a day on that account, and I had a few years until somebody from my real life found one and threatened to show my parents. In the past year and a half, I've needed accountability again. I checked Instagram and everything was censored, so I made a separate Twitter account instead.'

Wish eats one meal a day, which she then immediately burns off on the treadmill. She then does another workout in the afternoon and will go on the treadmill again in the evenings.

'It structures my whole day, and I've been doing that for a year and a half. My goal weight is a couple pounds lower than the lowest I ever was. In my case, I will probably only be happy with my weight when I am dead.'

Wish tells me that she doesn't sleep because she's too hungry. She wakes up every two or three hours, her body desperate to eat. She can't focus. Her vision is cloudy. She tells me her knees have started to hurt on the treadmill. The longer she goes without eating, she says, the more her entire body starts to hurt. She gets dizzy often and is prone to passing out, but her main worry isn't concussion or death, it's chipping a tooth and ruining her smile.

Wish cites some of her main inspirations as K-pop idols, the global emergence of which has had a notable effect on the eating disorder community. On regulated eating disorder forums, posts mentioning K-pop are as common as posts mentioning common terms such as 'food' or 'purge'. Many cite K-pop idols as their thinspiration, or as triggers for their illness.

A product of intense boot camps where young girls compete for a place in the next big pop group, K-pop stars in training are weighed every morning and every night, and are subject to rigorous workout schedules and controlled meal plans. Their bodies are sculpted to the ideal as a product, and there are countless videos of idols collapsing in public or on stage. With the average Korean woman already smaller than the average Western woman, our globalised beauty culture is repopularising the ultra-thin ideal.

'All these actresses, K-pop stars, and singers openly starve themselves, like it's a trophy,' Wish tells me. 'They act like it's something to be proud of. I see it affecting really young girls nowadays, and it affects me too. You want to measure up to somebody that you look up to. If they can do it, why can't I?'

As we spoke, it became increasingly clear that Wish is an intelligent, self-aware and deeply empathetic young woman. She knew she was sick but had resigned herself to her fate. She hated the perception that all of the girls posting this pro-ED content were bitchy or mean or vindictive, when in reality they were human beings struggling with debilitating mental illnesses. Her interview was one of the hardest I did for this entire project. She was a beautiful soul completely consumed with self-hatred and vengeance. She spoke about herself in such negative terms, I found myself struggling to know how to respond, holding back tears as she spoke so candidly about death. But she didn't harbour any judgement or resentment of anyone else; if anything, she struggled to balance her own issues with the responsibility she felt for her community.

'I feel really guilty,' she says. 'I don't want anybody else, especially girls younger than me, to make these decisions based upon what I do. That's why I really only post the food polls, and I use that account now to look at thinspo and mealspo. We are afraid we are influencing those younger than us but we are also struggling with our own disorders. It's like a give and take. You have to decide if it's worth the guilt and the pain that you feel triggering yourself to have a community around you.'

Even without affirming pro-ED resistance so directly, there is some evidence suggesting that pro-ED online communities cannot be dismissed out of hand as purely pathological. Users can receive important psychological support from the community. The problem is that it becomes impossible to find recovery support without stumbling into a world of warped mirrors and triggering posts. Tweets that seem to be genuinely looking for help fall in close proximity to self-punishment, deadly weight loss advice and graphic imagery.

'Social media platforms must urgently identify and remove harmful eating disorder content, increase the transparency of their algorithms and work closely with eating disorder experts to protect those who suffer,' Tom Quinn from the UK's leading eating disorder charity, Beat, tells me. 'It's important to remember that many users who create pro-eating disorder content are unwell themselves and they must not be punished. It is the responsibility of social media platforms to protect their users, and they must always direct people to eating disorder support rather than penalising them for their content.'

Recovering from an eating disorder can be a torturous process, one that's often full of setbacks, relapses and a profound sense of isolation. Those in recovery shouldn't have to constantly fight for safety on a public platform like Twitter, where anyone can poison community-building. The current policies for content removal have their limitations. As is the case with many other challenges in content moderation, individuals and organisations sharing and promoting such content have found ways to bypass AI systems. They use misspelt variations of banned search terms and hashtags, post untagged images and videos, and develop code words to evade existing detection systems.

The answer lies in specially created communities run and moderated by experts. Recovery won't happen until an individual chooses to get better but, in the meantime, they need safe spaces in which to express their illness without facing ostracisation. Mainstream social media platforms are not the solution.

'As much harm as they can do, these spaces can also save somebody's life,' Wish tells me. 'In my everyday life, I am very alone. I have nobody in the whole world. I don't tell people about this shit because they would think I'm crazy. I want to be looked at as somebody who has her shit together and who is normal.'

*

It's not crazy for a young woman to obsess over a desire to be thin. Far from it. We are socialised at almost every turn to believe that we should take up less space – to keep our bodies small and inoffensive. This – like oppressive beauty practices – has broader implications for our freedoms in society. Our bodies have become a site of immense struggle, at the mercy of a matrix we can barely decipher, let alone resist.

Studies have shown that behaviours that enhance a woman's physical attractiveness include intuitive gestures like smiling, to more insidious actions such as eating smaller meals. The ideal woman is obedient, restrained and self-disciplined – not only in her career and in the home but also in the maintenance of her body. Self-starvation is a continuation of the self-sacrifices expected of women in all other aspects of life – it is to accommodate others at the expense of the self, it is self-denial as a form of duty. It is being afforded the most vital of virtues only when you are shown to be suffering. It is self-policing on behalf of the patriarchy. It is to render yourself 'less than' in order to have value. As Sabrina Strings argues in *Fearing the Black Body*, fatphobia is also compounded by other forces of oppression and stems from a historical demonisation of the curvier Black body, in preference of a slim white ideal. Failure to adhere, or overt flouting of the standard, results in real consequences, with long-term impacts.

'At school everyone was like, "Oh! She's plus-size and dark-skinned." And so, for the next five years, I was bullied relentlessly by a group of boys in my year,' fat-acceptance blogger Stephanie Yeboah tells me. 'These boys were constantly telling me that I was ugly, I was worthless, I was too fat, I had to lose weight. Online, all I was seeing were images of thin white women, the diets that they were doing and their exercise routines. I started following the Insanity workouts religiously and I actually made a blog specific to weight loss. The algorithm glorified images of slim white women and it really made me realise that I wasn't even visible, and it made me feel terrible about myself. I just felt like my beauty wasn't worthy of being seen.'

Often, without the ultra-thin body signalling illness, people struggle to acknowledge restriction, obsessive exercise and disordered eating for what it is. Instead, we shower sudden weight loss with praise and encouragement.

'From the age of sixteen, I did every diet under the sun,' Stephanie says. 'I was doing the waterfall diet, which is literally just drinking water. I did the Cambridge diet. I did the Lighter Life diet, I did the famous Beyoncé diet, where you drink lemon juice, cayenne pepper and some other stuff. I have done the Atkins diet, and I would often starve myself for long periods of time and exercise as much as possible. I was abusing laxatives. I took illegal diet pills. I have done everything, everything that I thought could make me small. Because I am fat, people didn't see it as an eating disorder. They saw it as "Oh! You are doing really well. Keep going with whatever you are doing." I was very blind to the fact that it was a disorder. I just thought I was doing what everybody wanted me to do.'

*

During the mid-2010s, the body positivity movement reached the mainstream consciousness, with the goal of amplifying plus-size visibility and encouraging women to reject the thin ideal in favour of self-love at any size. The movement originally began as the 1960s fat-acceptance feminist movement when the National Association to Advance Fat Americans

(NAAFA) supported the concept of fatness as an illness. This context is important, as the movement began as a fight against discrimination of fat people and, often, people of colour.

Eventually, Tumblr became the space where Stephanie found the body positivity and fat-acceptance communities, at the time a small hashtag group on the platform.

'It was very nerve-wracking for me to be so vulnerable online in public, especially as a Black woman, where in our community vulnerability is frowned upon. I just needed an outlet. I always had issues with stretch marks on my arms and my back and I would always try to hide them, but by showing these parts of myself online, I could just be free.'

As the movement gained popularity on social media, it became increasingly co-opted by white women and generally conforming bodies. Large-scale media campaigns such as Aerie's #aerieREAL marked the peak commodification of the movement. Of course, the goal here was for us to purchase yet more products.

The body positivity movement began to eclipse grassroots fat activism. The message got watered down and depoliticised as it was used by large-scale companies who then sell our empowerment back to us, for a price. Much like wider empowerment discourse, the messaging promoted by the online body positivity movement is focused on an individual, commercial level. Media and marketing messages that instruct us to love ourselves and our bodies encourage individualised acts of empowerment – for example, posting a photograph on social media with the #bodypositive or buying a shirt that says 'self-love'. Instead of looking at the bigger picture and fighting for structural change, we're encouraged to identify ourselves as the problem to be fixed and improved, to compete against others instead of working in collaboration. We place blame and assign punishment to ourselves and others, whilst smiling in a selfie, purchasing diet plans, pills and programmes to 'glow up' instead of holding the system that makes us feel worthless to account. In diluting the message of fat activism, we weaken its power to abolish social injustice and limit our ability to drive tangible change for the most marginalised bodies.

'It's really frustrating. It feels as if we have done all of this work in the body positivity and fat communities over the last decade for nothing,' Stephanie tells me. 'The body positivity movement was a movement that was mostly led by Black plus-size women and larger plus-size women, and to have that safe space be completely taken over by bodies that are more privileged has been really difficult. It makes me feel sad, ultimately, because it just feels like we are undoing all of the work that so many activists, advocates and influencers have been doing. It feels like we're doing it in vain now, because everyone's like, "The fat thing was cute for a while. But let's go back to being small again."'

Growing alongside the body positivity movement was a new beauty ideal emerging from the 'slim thicc' or 'BBL' body type, except this one was built in the gym. It wasn't a holistic fitness ideal but one that focused almost exclusively on growing the glutes with minimal gain to the waist or thighs.

Pretty soon, fitspiration was everywhere, whether you sought it out or not. With the core messaging designed to build a 'strong and empowered body' through gym workouts and healthy eating, taking part often felt like a relapse into diet culture. Instead of group chats or Twitter communities to hold you accountable, apps invited you to share your progress pictures on message boards and feeds (another form of body-checking) to win prizes. Messages of 'just do what you can' were pushed alongside challenges and 'inspiring' before and after pictures. Fitspiration content often normalises compulsive exercise and spending excessive amounts of time preparing food.

Although we know we should reject the thin ideal, we often still aspire to be thin in secret, and feel shame and guilt for doing so. However, it is perfectly acceptable to express dissatisfaction at muscle tone, size and shape; to discuss a desire to 'tone up' or 'get fit' in the name of bodily transformation.

Fitness influencers began to sell packages to achieve bodies they were genetically predisposed to having and I bought them all. Despite my narrow hips and ass closer to a pancake than a peach, I squatted obsessively for weeks before feeling more pathetic than ever. We all screamed 'I'm doing this for ME!' from our sweat-covered faces, secretly hoping that 'me' would swiftly evolve into a Victoria's Secret model; else what was the point? Me, in the meantime, was avoiding eye contact with gym bros and giving myself a wedgie with my leggings in the hope of becoming more alluring. Much like the crash diets of old, it was rare for these 'fitness journeys' or 'clean routines' to last more than a few weeks. Instead of signing up to a monthly Weight Watchers subscription, I was purchasing countless workout plans, recipe guides and app subscriptions, only to torture myself for a short time and give up. Instead of plastering my walls with images of my favourite Tumblr girls, my lockscreen became a rotation of fitness imagery to 'inspire' me to get in good shape for summer. I joined communities of other girls united by a desire to become a 'better' body 'in the interest of health'. This pursuit of health, however, required constant consumption and became increasingly unhealthy the more I purchased. As part of these communities, we share images of our bodies in environments where messages of self-care and self-control are intensely intertwined. Still, our bodies remain subject to scrutiny by ourselves and others.

Strikingly, in studies, women with a positive body image seemed to be protected from the harmful effects of thinspiration but they were not protected from fitness content in the same way. This would suggest that fitness inspiration is just as harmful, if not more so, in a culture that has an awareness of the dangers of the thin ideal but doesn't process fitspiration through the same critical lens. In any case, the two operate in tandem; adding tone and strength to the already pervasive thin ideal accumulates to provide women with more ways in which to feel inadequate.

What's more, the majority of women in these communities – using the hashtags and sharing their progress – all seemed to exhibit largely the same body type: a slim and toned ideal that required huge amounts of labour to maintain. You weren't only paying for the workout plans themselves, but a gym membership, protein powders, booty bands, foam pads, body-shaping activewear, supplements and meal plans – and that's just the economic output, not including the hours spent exercising, preparing food and consuming the content itself.

Many of fitspiration's attempts to inspire women towards health and fitness focus on how much better you will feel when your body finally conforms, with quotes like 'Suck it up now and you won't have to suck it in later' and 'Summer bodies are made in winter'. Studies show that when people exercise mainly for how they look, rather than for health or enjoyment, it tends to be linked to a more negative body image, often making us feel worse about ourselves. Even those that don't use explicit messaging use dramatic before and after images which tend to reinforce feelings of shame (before) and pride (after). The ultimate result is to get closer to the beauty ideal. The very fact that fitspiration imagery is considered inspirational rather than potentially harmful makes its negative effect on body image all the more serious and insidious.

Many of these fitness influencer's pages are filled with images of other women's 'flawed' before images contrasted with their more toned, slim and fit after images, achieved through the use of their product or 'wellness' plan. These transformation posts sit within a feed of content showcasing the influencer's own sculpted body, creating a strategic sales device that subtly creates feelings of motivation through shame and self comparison. Despite the body type being naturally attributed to and fetishised on Black and Latina women, the majority of women profiting from these workout plans are white and privileged.

Just like the makeover paradigm, in which aesthetic doctors and influencers are the experts to whom we now look to guide our transformation, within the 'wellness' space, micro-celebrities and fitness influencers have become the vanguards of the aesthetic. The issue is, anyone can create this content, even those who are unqualified to give health advice. Influencers, without formal training or qualifications, can reach a vast audience making claims about diet, health and wellness, spreading harmful misinformation that can fuel obsessions and damage relationships to food, fitness and self-esteem. An extension of the halo effect, we are more likely to trust these influencers because they are beautiful. In meeting the beauty standard and advertising on image-based platforms, they become instantly more believable, virtuous and respectful.

Like a wolf in sheep's clothing, fitness inspiration may at first glance appear to be promoting a healthy lifestyle, but in fact it is as harmful as, and potentially more harmful than, thinspiration. Whereas thinspiration is, at least, largely restricted on social media platforms, fitspiration is not regulated in any way. A study comparing thinspiration and fitspiration sites indicated that they were similar in their messages intended to induce guilt or shame about body weight or shape, stigmatise being overweight, objectify women and promote dieting and restraint. Both communities objectify and fragment the body – enforcing hyper-fixation on specific body parts to be broken down, assessed and transformed into something new. Now, narratives around food restriction are masked under terms like 'clean eating', which turns diet culture into a form of self-care and social status. It is a phenomenon dominated by privileged groups, sold as a way to minimise caloric intake under the guise of a middle-class lifestyle pursuit.

We cannot be fooled into thinking that we have seen the end of diet culture in favour of a future founded on female empowerment and self-acceptance. Companies still look to profit from the cultural desire to make our bodies smaller, they're just doing it in more covert ways. Instead of overt fat-phobia and body-shaming, they now smile as they offer you a detox tea that will make you shit yourself in the name of self-care. They'll give you an inspirational quote in exchange for a monthly subscription and they'll be sure to remind you that you're doing this for YOU, whilst profiting from your low self-esteem.

*

Recovery isn't linear or straightforward, especially when the obstacles and pressures young women face are so omnipresent and consuming. In our visual digital world, the currency placed on the beauty ideal is impossible to ignore. The allure of wonderland is sometimes too strong to resist.

'I realised I didn't want to be an internet creator anymore,' Chloe tells me of her recovery. 'We were on the way to look at universities. I was at an incredibly low BMI and on the train there, my dad started crying. He was holding me and telling me he didn't think I'd make it to university, that he didn't see the point in us even looking. It felt like he could touch every single bone in my body, that was how thin I was. I knew I didn't want to just be on the internet and skinny, I actually wanted to do something. You don't really go into recovery unless you choose recovery. You can't be forced into it. At that point, I just thought, "Thank God, it's over." Like, it's over now. I couldn't lie anymore. I couldn't do it anymore. I was just exhausted.'

The exhaustion is apparent in every woman I speak to. We are all tired. We are all fed up. Whether we're fighting to take up space and to be visible as we are, or fighting for our lives in order to be desirable, we are treading water. We are exhausted. But still, we fight.

'I want to tell young girls that you are fine the way you are,' says Wish, when I ask her about her future ambitions. 'I'm not sure how much longer I'll be here, but I want to have a voice to show people that they don't have to live like this, because it's too late for me now but it's not too late for them.'

I tell her it's not too late, that she is young and beautiful and kind and sick. That her illness does not define her character and we do care, that I care. But I realise how silly it sounds and I understand she likely won't believe me. I tell her that I hope one day we get to meet properly, that I'll be looking for her at my book signings in her city, and that I hope one day she surprises me with an appearance. Just hang on for the next year, I say.

The next time I see Chloe, I am filled with a newfound appreciation for what she has survived. In the social experiment that was our upbringing online, she lived both the dream and the nightmare of internet fame. Now twenty, she is in her second year of university. I won't lie to you and say she's completely cured, but she drinks dirty martinis and makes amazing blinis and is writing her thesis on incel culture.

'I think social media is terrible now, it's getting even worse,' she says when I ask her if things are getting better for young girls. 'The entire time I have been a woman, I have had people watching. I really wish I had never experienced internet fame. What has it done for me? Free dresses? A cool party story? I could've carried on until I got half a million followers, but psychologically, it wasn't worth it. I still want the likes, because no matter what, you are always going to think about the time you got 30,000, or that you used to get sent free things, or when you got reposted and someone said #skinnygirl #goals on Tumblr and it was you. That's kind of the dream. I became the influencer that girls had stuck up on their walls and that was full circle for me. Now, I still post, I still curate, because 30,000 of my followers are people who followed me from the beginning. I think I'm better at posting what I want to post. I would hope so at least, but also I don't know how much of it is genuine.'

'Why don't you delete the account?' I ask. 'Just start afresh?'

Chloe pauses.

'That part of me has been tied up with so much success and fame and cool shit like that. I don't really want it to go away because it's the last part of that hope that remains in me. If I fully recover, I might lose that version of me completely. If I lose it, what do I have to show for it? All this shit that's happened to me, all this pain I have been through, all of that terrible bullying, the comments online, the sexualisation. What do I have to show for all of that? If I am not desirable now?'

'You would have a healthy, lovely you,' I reply.

'What do I do with that?' she asks, holding my gaze across the table. 'What currency does that hold?'

How can we create a more beautiful future for women and girls?

'To me, a more beautiful future for women and girls would mean more honest and realistic expectations of what's fulfilling and nourishing in life. Seeing a wider range of lifestyle choices portrayed in the media would empower women to make choices based on what they actually desire, rather than what they think is necessary to "win" at life. Perpetuating the idea that overachieving and being all things to all people is what a woman is needs to be looked at and flipped upside down, because, ultimately, it's forcing many of us to feel like failures, despite putting in excessive amounts of energy into being effortlessly perfect.'

Estée Lalonde,

influencer and founder of MIRROR WATER

9

The Fetishisation of Youth

Isabelle Lux posts giggling in front of a birthday cake marked with the number twenty-three. She claps her hands like a small child full of glee, until a hand comes in to rearrange the digits to her actual age – thirty-two. She pouts, frowns and bursts into tears.

Isabelle is the internet's local thirty-something who has gone viral for her anti-ageing content. She is objectively youthful and plays into it, bouncing around in her videos with glowy filters and pigtails, plaits and perfect skin. She has hundreds of thousands of followers, and most of them are obsessed with the fact that she looks far younger than she actually is.

It's not just Isabelle. There are countless girls crying on their birthdays. They scream and they shout but the cake is brought out nonetheless. The numbers accelerate nonetheless. They howl and they weep, saltwater tears on tiers of frosting, puddles of sugar sobs pooling at their feet. Pink and lilac and red run like rivers in a saccharine massacre. Each year, they make the cakes bigger – more tiers, more piping, more sprinkles, more candles – and each year they howl harder and they melt away the same as the last. At the end of the song that nobody starts on key, the cakes are half washed away and they close their eyes wet with mascara, take a deep breath, blow out the candles on the candied carcass and wish never to grow up.

There are hundreds and thousands of girls crying on their birthdays. Hundreds and thousands of birthday cakes smeared with tears. Hundreds and thousands of girls terrified of that one extra candle. Terrified of the passage of time.

'I'm already dreading my seventeenth birthday because of this. I feel like I'm wasting time,' one girl says.

'It's so painful – there's nothing to do but watch your desirability slip through your fingers,' chimes another.

'I cried when I blew the candles out on my seventeenth birthday because of this exact reason. It's so hard to think that I'm ageing without ever having the beautiful teenage girl experience.'

Isabelle is like a digi fairy godmother – teaching girls how to immortalise themselves, to stay young for all eternity. She shares tips on her routine – how to train your face muscles not to move, how to use an anti-wrinkle straw, how to hide smile lines, to *never* spray perfume on your chest and to always hold your tongue to the roof of your mouth when you're not talking. Her viral nighttime routine includes a satin bonnet for her hair, an anti-wrinkle pillow to keep her flat on her back and prevent lines on her face and chest, an eye mask, silicon facial patches and tape over her mouth. She drinks three cups of water before bed and makes sure that she sleeps a good eight and a half hours every single night.

'I think I help people because my life has been so much better since starting this,' she tells me. 'My life is literally better because I've been able to tune and craft every hour of my day to ensure that I create an image that is pleasing to everyone else, that is aspirational to some, that men enjoy and that all these people like. It's crazy but it actually does improve your relationships. People trust you more when you look a certain way.'

Isabelle is sat perfectly illuminated on our video call, her skin glowing, her cosy clothes falling effortlessly off her shoulders. Her hair is braided back, her eyes are big and blue, and, all of a sudden, I feel very self-conscious about the way my face creases when I move.

Ten minutes in and she pauses the interview to take her supplements. 'I'll admit the wedding pressures are coming up. The girls at Vera Wang told me I had to lose five pounds in three weeks. They didn't say it explicitly like that but they made my dress a little tighter because "most people drop three-to-five pounds" by their second fitting. And I was like, okay, that's three weeks away. I still have to maintain my face, though. So it's very specific, it's like a pound of balance. One less and I start to look older, which is already happening right now.'

She sips her water and starts placing capsules into her mouth.

'That's berberine, also known as nature's Ozempic; it makes you feel full all day. This is pro-collagen, for my skin. I'll take that in a few minutes, though. I want the berberine to settle first.'

I ask if she's seen the girls crying about their birthdays, the teenagers terrified of ageing.

'It's awful,' she says. 'Sometimes people will say, "Do you feel terrible about what you're doing to young girls?" But I feel like the pressure is inescapable. It's inevitable, so you might as well win. I can help people feel better and, in my case, I do feel better. I get so many comments that are like, "You've helped me so much." I went to Miami two days ago and this girl in college who was on her summer break came over and said, "You've changed my whole life, I take such good care of myself now." There are things that everyone can do and maybe people just don't know. Some of them are really easy, like eating two carrots a day. It literally will help your skin so much, and your eyes and your brain. You have to eat them with olive oil though; olive oil helps your body open up the beta carotene. Don't eat them dry. Simple things that are legendarily life-changing.'

I had been talking to Isabelle for fifteen minutes and already none of this felt easy or simple. I couldn't remember the last time I ate a carrot but it was clearly working for her. She was beautiful, youthful, successful – thirty and thriving. I had creases in my forehead.

'When I first started making videos, I was just doing thirst traps and I had 70,000 men watching me. Honestly, I think a lot of them thought I was seventeen and I used to play up to it. I did the full pigtails thing, wide eyes, giggling and bouncing around in cute bikinis, but I started to get comments from women asking about my skincare routine, and I was like, oh my god, this is how I can do social media. The goal was always social media and the hook was skincare. I feel like, honestly, I'm doing people a service. I feel like we're all in it together in a way.'

Anti-ageing rituals have, of course, always existed. Women have historically gone to great lengths to retain their youth: Cleopatra bathed in donkey milk and Elizabethan women covered their faces in slices of raw meat. What's different now is the growing pressure put on women, and increasingly younger women, to pre-empt, prevent and correct any physical signs of ageing with increasingly invasive regimes.

In the digital age, the texture of skin has been replaced by the gloss of screens. As an extension of our increasingly cyborg, technological selves, we must eradicate any evidence of humanity left on our faces and bodies. Skin must be clear, shiny and even, with no pores, texture, lines, wrinkles – no evidence of life. As Dr Asalet had told me, young girls are growing up having their images filtered from the earliest years of childhood. As we transform ourselves into unreal beings, the reality of human womanhood becomes alien, something to be scared of and avoided at all costs.

In 2012, fewer than 20 per cent of US women between eighteen and twenty-four years old considered anti-ageing skincare to be important, according to a survey by market research company NPD Group. By 2018, however, another US-focused study by beauty consumer analysts the Benchmarking Company found that more than 50 per cent of eighteen- to twenty-four-year-old women said they wanted to add wrinkle-defying products into their routine.

The message is prolific. On TikTok, a video went viral of a young girl. It opens with: 'Here's some things I do to slow down the ageing process as a fourteen-year-old. I started doing most of these things at twelve.' Her routine includes taking two apple cider vinegar tablets a day, using two face masks a day and applying retinol twice a day. She pays attention to the skin on her neck as 'that's one of the main things that ages'. Her lengthy regimen also includes 'three fingers' worth' of sunscreen and green tea with honey to tackle inflammation. She adds that on long road trips, she tapes construction paper to her parents' car window to block UV rays.

As I scroll, Sasha appears on my TikTok feed miming to a trending sound: 'That's the difference between me and you, because whilst you were sitting around waiting, doing nish, I was out, making moves.' The caption she has placed over the screen reads: 'When you start getting baby Botox in your 20s to prevent further wrinkles.'

I swipe again to see a thirty-year-old cosmetic doctor sharing a treatment breakdown of how she has 'aged backwards in a natural-looking way'. This extensive list includes a series of injectables in the cheeks, forehead, lips, chin and jaw, plus chemical peels, acids and microneedling with radioactivity. She started Botox injections at twenty-four. The two-part video series has almost a quarter of a million views.

On my feed, Kim Kardashian's face is dripping in blood. Her wide eyes are smiling out from skin dotted in red, like a Lichtenstein left out in the rain. Her own blood had been drawn from her arm into vials and processed in a centrifuge to extract the platelet-rich plasma. Her face was then punctured by a hundred tiny needles before the extracted red platelets were smeared over her wounded skin and injected into her face.

The 'vampire facial' is said to help boost collagen production for tighter, younger-looking skin. Dr Nick Milojević, a leading Harley Street practitioner, recommends this procedure to women in their twenties to combat signs of ageing. The science behind it is contested. Kim Kardashian later said, 'If you told me that I literally had to eat poop every single day and I would look younger, I might.'

A few years later, Kim's daughter North posted her skincare routine online, aged nine.

*

'In 2014–15, the average person that would come in looking for anti-ageing treatments, such as injectables, was an older patient, somebody in their mid-to-late forties, early fifties,' says Dr Anjali Mahto, a Harley Street medical and cosmetic consultant dermatologist. 'It's fascinating how in less than a decade, the people who are coming in wanting treatments are so much younger than they have ever been. I personally would never inject somebody below the age of eighteen, but the average age of people showing an interest in preventing ageing is very young. We're talking about people that are in their early twenties.'

Dr Mahto tells me one encounter has stuck in her mind. During a medical acne consultation with a fourteen-year-old girl, she ended the appointment by asking if the young patient had any extra questions or concerns.

'I'm just really worried that I've got loads of wrinkles around my eyes and I'm starting to look old,' the girl had said.

As a doctor, Anjali has perfected her poker face but inside her stomach dropped. The lines by the girl's eyes only appeared when she smiled; far from making her look older, they were a necessary function in her expression of joy.

'This pressure is feeding into young women at a much, much younger age. Yes, I'm seeing the twenty-year-olds, but what's happening is actually starting at eight, nine, ten years old. With all this information and digital accessibility, we're supposed to be moving forwards. We're not, we're moving backwards.'

I remember the girls I met at the charity beauty salon in London, the ten-year-olds who told me about their skincare routines, their baby faces beaming at me, boasting about being blemish free. My internal monologue screaming 'because you're ten!' like a siren, an alarm.

'The problem is that the industry is so poorly regulated, a lot of people are quite happy to inject twenty-year-olds that have literally no lines,' says Dr Mahto. 'There is nothing to inject but these people will now keep coming back every three months for their Botox top-ups. I don't think friendship circles help either. There's so much shame if you're the person who "can't be bothered" to "look after yourself", that if you're not doing these things, it's seen as a reflection that you don't care about life in general.'

The ubiquitous anti-ageing rhetoric and pressure to hold onto a youthful appearance forever is a further extension of the commodification of our bodies under capitalism and the impossible beauty standards women shouldn't have to adhere to. The beauty industrial complex has successfully and methodically infiltrated mainstream culture – celebrities proudly disclose their use of Botox as part of their self-care routines. 'Self-care' in this context means to spend a significant portion of your salary on painful procedures to ensure you don't 'let yourself go', i.e., have the audacity to reject and resist the beauty ideal and embrace the passage of time.

'When I was in my twenties, I had no money, so I would have gone and gotten a botched job,' says Charlotte Palermino, licensed aesthetician and founder of Dieux Skin. 'Your forehead can collapse if you get bad Botox or too much Botox. And we need to think about who can afford it. Young girls are booking these anti-ageing injections they don't need on Groupon to get a cheap deal.'

In 2021, the global anti-ageing market was estimated to be worth about $62.6 billion and it's projected to reach over $93 billion in sales by 2027. Costing £200–800 per session, 'preventative' Botox is an expense many also can't afford and further adds to the economic vulnerability of women. These treatments breed dependence. Once you start, the need never really ends; in order to maintain the effects, you have to get injected every few months, especially once your muscles get accustomed to the toxin. Repeated use can lead to permanent atrophy. This can cause your skin to become thinner and looser, and discoloured or crepe-y.

Doctors have started to speak out against the rise in DIY anti-ageing injectable kits that cost as little as 10 per cent of the price of professional administration. By injecting their faces at home, or inserting threads designed to boost collagen themselves, patients are experiencing serious complications, including blocked arteries, abscesses, sepsis, tissue necrosis and permanent scarring.

'We've got no long-term safety data on the impacts of these anti-ageing treatments,' says Dr Mahto. 'But my suspicion is that we will suddenly have a generation of people who get to midlife and their forehead has completely flattened, so you can see all the fine lines, all the blood vessels underneath, because you've been weakening the muscle for so many years. We are just going to create yet another need for some other kind of cosmetic procedure to correct that.'

The immobilisation of certain muscles can also mean other parts of the face are recruited when you inevitably make a facial expression. As these other muscles get a workout, *they* may start to wrinkle, resulting in 'bunny lines' around the nose and creases beneath the eyes. With repeated use, you can also develop immunity to injectables like Botox. Between 1 and 3 per cent of patients who take a break from their injections won't get the same results when they start back up again. Once it's worn off, it's worn off.

'Preventative Botox doesn't exist, it's just Botox, and it's wildly misleading,' says Charlotte. 'Even if you get Botox your entire life, as soon as you stop, you'd start frowning again, and the lines would start showing. And that isn't a fucking bad thing! We need to really be careful about how we're promoting things, particularly to young people. Stop scaring them. Instead of preaching "baby Botox", the name of which is just fucking weird, we should be giving people the reassurance to let those lines form and see if they even bother you.'

The more of us that conform, the worse it is going to get. We're stuck in a vicious cycle of self-comparison, struggling to stay visible in a culture intent on shutting us out. As the pressure mounts, and young women start getting treatments ever earlier, we're further exacerbating the beauty class divide, with a population who can afford not to visibly age and a population who can't. The result is an immeasurable discrepancy in social status, treatment and opportunity, and a very visible aesthetic divide between the affluent and the vulnerable. It becomes a matter of who can continue to exist and who is shunned to the shadows.

Faces have dynamic lines – our skin is designed to crease, fold and move in line with our expressions. Our faces are meant to be malleable, soft and supple, to have light and shadow. It is totally normal for your face to have lines when it moves, and to have those lines settle as you age. Botox is only really beneficial when you start to see the lines caused by dynamic movement at *rest*, and even then, your face is not in need of fixing.

*

Isabelle is telling me about her anti-ageing routine.

'Okay, so I wake up every morning at five, no matter what. I'll drink a cup and a half of water with lemon, and I will make my half-caffeine (never full caffeine) latte because it's better for your skin. Then I will wash my face. I wait at least thirty seconds in between skincare steps, but my morning skincare routine does not take long. I cleanse, then I will go straight in with a water essence. I wait thirty seconds, I apply my serum, I wait thirty seconds, I put down my moisturiser and my eye cream, then I'll wait half an hour before putting on SPF. That's regimented, I will never put SPF on before that half an hour is up.'

All of a sudden, the image changes. Everything loses its glow.

'Oh! Light just went out!' Isabelle looks around, panicked, and I realise she's done the entire call so far with studio lights set up in front of her face.

'It's okay,' I reassure her. She looks exactly the same, just less HD and visibly more anxious. 'I think you had just applied your SPF.'

'Yep, so you always wait another half an hour after applying your SPF before putting on makeup. That's literally my morning skincare routine. Sometimes I'll use my LED mask, sometimes I will do a full facial massage, or a gua sha neck-lifting routine, sometimes I'll massage my scalp, but honestly, for the most part, that's what I do in the morning. Then I film content all day, or I think about content, or I stress about content. I'm in front of my computer or in front of one of these big lights for five or six hours. I drink lots of water during the day and I fill at least one with electrolytes, which is what this is here,' she gestures to her glass. 'I'll always go for an afternoon walk, no matter what. Usually it's about an hour, but I will put sunscreen over my whole entire body, and I will sometimes put on a face shield or reflective visor. I will not go outside in the sun between 11am and 4pm. Unless I have to go to a meeting, I'm not leaving my house, and if I do, I stay inside my car. If someone wants to eat lunch outside, I ask if we can eat inside. Would I like to have fun on the beach and in the ocean? Yeah, but saltwater is bad for your skin and it ruins your hair, and the sun is damaging. So I don't do those things. It's a sacrifice, and it is sad because those are experiences that I'm avoiding, but I tell myself that I'm the one winning because I don't have salt-aged skin. In person, people are literally constantly like, holy shit, I thought you were twenty-two. I'm like, I'm thirty-two. That's the reward for me.'

'And that's really worth it?' I ask.

'I know. I know.' She pauses. 'I think that's the question that is really important right now.'

I let the silence hang in the air.

'I think the answer is no. It's not worth it at all because we're all going to get old,' she says after a while. 'Even if you look three years younger, it's not worth it. I am trying to challenge myself in a way, and be more accepting of life and where I am. But I'm scared. I'm so scared.'

'Of what happens if you stop it all?'

'No, it's not necessarily that. I see people now who are nineteen and they're so hot,' she laughs to herself. 'For so long, I was 100 per cent punching their weight, even when I was twenty-eight. And then, suddenly, it's like hitting a brick wall. It's not the case anymore, and I'm getting less desirable every day. From what I heard, from what I've read, from what I see, from what I read in the comments, women just feel like they have nothing, no one values them, and then they get cheated on, and usually it's with someone younger. So how is someone still going to love me? I literally asked my fiancé that and I'm not trying to be stupid. Will he still love me? I literally don't know. What's going to happen when people don't look at me anymore?'

Isabelle is crying into her sleeves. Something has unravelled, shifted from the woman I met an hour before. Isabelle isn't the first woman to tell me, in one way or another, that our digital beauty culture has flattened their world, leaving them at the mercy of the judgement of others – to be liked and unliked, shared or ignored. Fuelled them with fire emojis and engagement into a point of no return. I think about Chloe and her love of maths and I think about all of these women steered into subservience by algorithms that wanted them to be pretty and nothing else. Even that wouldn't last.

'It's my only self-worth,' she says. 'It literally feels like my only value. Which is actually horrible. At least when I had my jewellery company, it's not like I was hugely successful, it wasn't even close, but I loved it and suddenly it's all gone. The only thing I care about is beauty and I can't even hold onto that.'

*

A study published in 2018 analysed thousands of messages between more than 186,000 straight men and women on a popular free dating service in the USA. They found that whilst men's desirability peaks at fifty, women's desirability starts high at age eighteen and falls continuously throughout their lifespan.

A similar study from Chris Rudder's *Dataclsym* asked men and women to state the age they find the opposite sex most attractive. The results showed that women are most attracted to men within a few years of their own age range, but the results for men were much more concerning. Both twenty-year-old and forty-nine-year-old men cited women aged twenty to be the most attractive. The age of a woman men find most attractive never made it above twenty-four. It is also important to note that twenty was the lowest age they were allowed to choose.

In pop culture, the fetishisation of very young women is rife. In 2017, a twenty-year-old Kylie Jenner released three blushers, named 'Barely Legal', 'Virginity' and 'X-Rated' to her young female consumer base. She had reportedly been introduced to her then-boyfriend Tyga when she was fourteen and he was twenty-one. According to Kylie's mother, Kris Jenner, their relationship did not start until several years later.

In 2013, when twenty-three-year-old Machine Gun Kelly did an interview with *Fuse*, he raved about his celebrity crush, seventeen-year-old Kendall Jenner. When the interviewer asked if he was counting down the days until she was eighteen (the legal age of consent), MGK responded, 'I'm not waiting till she's eighteen, I'll go now . . . Robert Plant, who is one of the greatest lead singers ever . . . dated a girl that was fourteen. Axl Rose, who is one of the biggest badasses ever, dated a girl that was sixteen.'

Many of us grew up with the infamous image of Britney Spears in her 'Teen Dream' *Rolling Stone* cover in 1999, immortalising the world's twisted obsession with 'jailbait'. Britney was a minor at the time and the shoot played up to it – she's clutching a Teletubby on satin sheets, wearing hotpants and a bra.

I vividly remember listening to the radio as a child as adult male DJs counted down the days until singer Charlotte Church's sixteenth birthday – when she would reach the age of consent in the UK. Chris Moyles told listeners on his BBC

Radio One afternoon show that he wanted to take fifteen-year-old Charlotte's virginity when she came of age and the country laughed along. That might've been two decades ago but things clearly haven't really changed. Online forums were set up to count down to Millie Bobby Brown's eighteenth birthday; they gained thousands of followers before being taken down. Kylie Jenner was reportedly offered $10 million to create a sex tape when she turned eighteen, after viewers had watched her grow up in the spotlight from the age of nine. Female celebrities, including the Olsen twins, Natalie Portman, Emma Watson and Mara Wilson, who played Matilda in the original movie, found themselves heavily sexualised from childhood.

'Even before I was out of middle school, I had been featured on foot fetish websites, photoshopped into child porn and received all kinds of letters and messages online from grown men,' Mara told *Elle* magazine in 2017. 'What's really at play here [is] the creepy, inappropriate public inclination to sexualise young girls in the media.'

Now we're adults, we notice that the catcalls have largely stopped. We look back and realise we got the most attention walking home in our school uniform. 'Pigtail theory' started trending online as women servers began to notice their tips at work increase, sometimes up to 400 per cent, when they adopted the child-like hairstyle. On Reddit, a user asked, 'How old were you when you first noticed men looking at you sexually?' Below, 260 answers are displayed on a graph. Starting at seven years old, the numbers reach a crescendo at eleven and twelve before flatlining after fifteen.

It's an intensely dark and disturbing form of violence on the female psyche. It is symbolic sexual abuse – and it happens to all of us from an ever-earlier age. Our modern beauty standards value women's bodies the most when their minds are at their most malleable and naive. So much of our current beauty ideals prize the prepubescent – we must be hairless, smooth, submissive and small, taking up as little space as possible and cosplaying inexperience. Desirability is filtered through an ageist, patriarchal lens, intent on sexualising and pedestalling very young girls.

On OnlyFans, reality TV personality and former *Geordie Shore* cast member Sarah Goodhart makes herself look younger in order to make more money online: 'On FaceApp, there's an age filter that makes you look instantly younger,' she says. 'So I just put it on at level one for all of my OnlyFans content. It makes your eyes wider, your skin a bit brighter and it makes your cheeks chubbier. You can put it all the way up but even on level two you just look like a child.'

'And you only use it for sexual content?' I asked.

'Yeah – it's fucked up when you think about it. I feel guilty – like, am I perpetuating the problem? But I have to make money and I know that's what's trending.'

Sarah is only twenty-nine and admits to already looking younger than she is. And yet, she feels filters are necessary for her visibility and success.

'People will say it's so ridiculous that young girls are doing things like Botox and editing, but no, we make women feel like this,' says Charlotte Palermino. 'We completely erase older women from the media.' Our beauty culture turns women into products with a best before date. Once the possibility of fertility is no longer apparent, women become invisible, or are branded hags, crones, spinsters, battleaxes or cougars. 'Giving up power has been what aging traditionally felt like for most women,' writes bell hooks in *Communion*. In a form of cultural gaslighting, society tells us that our power is diminishing, when we know the opposite is true.

'These stereotypes of older women take a huge toll on how adults view themselves,' says Dr Candace Konnert, a clinical psychologist who specialises in ageing. 'If people buy into those stereotypes, you'll see an impact on their cognitive ability, you'll see an impact on their health and wellbeing over time – both their physical and mental health. They're very damaging.'

'The Age of Beauty' research project, in collaboration with the Diversity Standards Collective, revealed that 74 per cent of respondents said the beauty industry still doesn't offer positive or empowering representations of their age. According to the research, older men are portrayed as 'handsome' and 'positive' by the industry and aren't subjected to the same pressures to 'defy' ageing as women.

This gender imbalance may not be surprising, considering more than 70 per cent of the top-level executive roles in the beauty sector are held by white, middle-aged men, a demographic that only gains respect with age and the knowledge, experience and wealth that comes with it. So why is our society so determined to keep women young? Why are we so afraid of women who appear old enough to have acquired knowledge, experience and wealth? Why must those women who are fortunate enough to age expend huge amounts of time, money and physical pain in order to cling on to the sill of society and remain in peripheral view?

Representation appears to be a huge issue contributing to the fear in young women. Back at the Mayfair club, I had seen girls' eyes widen as I told them my age. I've lost count of the number of times a teen has turned to me in shock and said, 'Oh my god!! You look *amazing* for twenty-eight!' I wondered what they thought happened when you dared to hit twenty-five – that your face fell off, your muscles melted, you disappeared into thin air, ceased to exist, to mean anything at all?

'I understand why people then start getting Botox, it makes a lot of sense. It's a really shitty thing to experience when somebody just completely invalidates your experience, your knowledge and your humanity, just based on something that is naturally happening to you,' says Charlotte. 'Society hates women. I honestly don't know how else to describe it because I see the standards that women are held to versus men. I think that for women, any way that we can keep any form of power is going to feel impossible to resist.'

Like much of the power we derive from beauty, what we stand to gain by staying young is a trade fraught with paradoxes. It's a nebulous power that is never truly ours, one we never truly own. The idea of exchanging our time, money and energy for a few extra years of respect feels much like the illusion of 'beauty investments'. In the short term, it seems like a no-brainer. But in the long term, the facade starts to fall. We're still held on that same tightrope – if our beauty work is too overt, our efforts too obvious, we face ostracisation once again. Capitalism grooms women from a young age into the consumption and promotion of these anti-ageing practices, weakening us physically, emotionally and financially, so that the patriarchy can retain its control.

'I spend around $1,500 a month – between what I would be spending on skincare, makeup, anti-ageing and beauty treatments,' says Isabelle. 'Which is what? $18,000 a year.'

One of Isabelle's videos shows the $7,000 three-month beauty schedule she's following to get ready for her wedding. Whilst we aren't all spending to that extreme, the expectation that we will have to invest in maintaining our youth was palpable in the conversations I had with women across the globe, only adding to the beauty tax women experience, as anti-ageing becomes an inherent part of future financial planning.

When I spoke to Mira about her desire to get an eyelift for the chapter 'Build a Body', she also cited the pressure to immortalise her youth. 'I want a breast lift and a mini face lift once I'm over forty,' she said. 'I spend a lot of time thinking about these procedures. The more cosmetic procedure content I consume the more I feel like I need to start preparing to get things done to ensure that I age gracefully, as if ageing is a sin. I do feel increasingly self-conscious about the way I look in a different way to how I felt five or so years ago. Before it was a "God, I hope I look good" anxiety and now it's "I hope I don't look old and ugly". Which is sad but a shift I've been working hard to shake.'

It ties into our political freedoms. After all, silly young girls need to be told what to do. They have nothing to say and can't make decisions for themselves. Silly young girls shouldn't be believed, shouldn't be in politics. Silly young girls should just be pretty and cute. The fetishisation of youth is a tool to infantilise us and strip us of our autonomy. The more of our precious resources we pour into maintaining our youth and beauty, the more products we buy, the longer our visibility lasts. But, in doing so, the less time, energy and money we have to put into changing things, to challenging the status quo.

I thought about a conversation I had had with Venus in the beauty salon: 'Particularly in the last five to ten years, the intersection of ageing and filters as a new standard has become really hard,' she said. 'I did the thing I thought I would never do – I started to question how much space I could take up because I didn't want to interrupt people's perception of me. I wanted to keep that version of me that they thought was beautiful. And yeah, I didn't want to get older, and I didn't necessarily have the capacity to commit to a filtered version of myself. So I just quieted my presence and went into hiding. I feel like I've been doing that for the last five years or so.'

'As a way to preserve that younger version of you?' I asked.

'Totally – yes.'

The pressure to remain youthful, static, heavenly beings no longer falls just on the influential, it's extending out to any woman who wants to be visible in our hyper-visual culture. You must either conform via surgery and injectable procedures or succumb via editing and filters. The alternative is to stop participating in the digital realm. To remain frozen – a silent and static image that stays forever young.

'I put the skin smoothing filter on every single time I post,' says Isabelle. 'It's a numbers game. If I look even two years older, I'm going to get less views in the first twenty minutes and the entire video is going to tank. These videos have to perform. And a filter performs. Every ounce of lighting, the filter to make you look more tanned, the bright light which makes your eyes bluer, it all counts.'

'Why do the videos have to perform?' I ask. Isabelle had already mentioned that she doesn't depend on the money made from her content.

'Because my entire self-worth now revolves around my views, right? It's a numbers thing. You actually get a dopamine hit. And when you go down, it's like you're crashing off drugs. And all you need is that hit again. I'm getting so much pressure to lean back into hardcore anti-ageing because of the financial opportunity. But it's literally the only thing I care about. I wake up in the morning and I check it, check it, check it, and you do everything to keep it up. You respond to every comment, you do everything you can to improve, it's all-encompassing. Somewhere between the fact that my entire self-worth revolves around stupid numbers on a screen and my beauty, which every day is waning, I feel like I have nothing. I have no idea who I am anymore.'

What Isabelle describes feels eerily similar to the feverish obsessions and compulsions of an eating disorder – the counting, the numbers, the routine, the control, the fear of failure, the desire to be the best.

'I actually recovered from an eating disorder at twenty-five,' she tells me when I point this out. 'Everyone asks, "When did your anti-ageing journey begin?" It started at twenty-five. It's not as obsessive in the way that when you have an eating disorder, if something goes wrong, you freak out and the whole world crumbles into a black hole. This is not like that. If I went away for two days and I didn't have any of my skincare or supplements or even enough water . . .' She pauses to reflect. 'I don't . . . *think* I would have that same anxiety, so I don't think it's a direct replacement. But it does stem from the same competitive idea that if I keep doing this thing, I'll literally go up, up, up, and I can figure out ways to win this game. Which is crazy because, clearly, nobody wins.'

The cruellest part of this slice of the beauty standard is that everybody ages. It's the one form of oppression that is inevitable, unavoidable and it affects us all. The paradoxes continue to plague us – as girls, we want so badly to be seen as women. We try to make ourselves look older with makeup, padded bras and sexy outfits, whilst simultaneously paralysed with panic about our diminishing desirability. We mistake objectification for admiration, fetishisation for respect. In the attention economy, we are rich and so we learn to suppress that sickly feeling in our stomachs. Once we become women, we're left desperately trying to cling onto girlhood, hoping to be objectified because at least then we'd be seen. Perhaps for a fleeting moment, we achieve the ideal in both our body and mind. For a few seconds, we achieve the nebulous perfect age, before the target moves once more and we are left longing again.

The fixation young women and girls as young as eight have with their appearance in our hyper-visual digital culture is causing teenagers to adopt the routines, fears and concerns previously reserved for those in their mid-life and beyond. Convincing teenage girls and young women that they must expend valuable energy and resources into *stopping the passage of time* is a genius move on behalf of a patriarchy that wants to keep us hopelessly occupied, physically and psychologically, for evermore. Whilst we're all fighting to immortalise our faces in their teen image, what we're actually facing is the death of teenage girlhood, as the bridge between childhood and adulthood gets shorter and shorter. With the increasing fixation on appearance and the fetishisation of youth, many young women and girls are being robbed of a time meant for experience, freedom and experimentation. Instead of pushing boundaries, taking risks, learning who we are and what we like, what we're capable of and what we demand, we're learning how much acid will burn our skin and how many millilitres of poison we can safely inject into our heads.

So much of our disgust for women's bodies is tied to their natural function, whether that's body hair, stretch marks, menstruation or weight fluctuation – all key markers of puberty and the ascent into womanhood. To go through puberty whilst growing up online, in this glossy, beautiful space, is to face a horrifying discovery, as you watch your body deviate from the standard in real time. We grow up surrounded by these images of ideal beauty and we believe it is our birthright to transform. Kylie Jenner – who got a breast augmentation at nineteen – spent years telling her young fans her enhanced figure was a result of puberty and her periods. Instead, young girls experience a bodily betrayal that feels so at odds to the perfect promise of womanhood. No wonder so many girls are terrified, alienated from themselves. From the minute we leave childhood, we are pushed into an obsessive, all-consuming conformity that requires a rigorous set of rituals and routine.

These collective realisations happen again and again, generation after generation. A fresh wave of fear sets in, and we are still unprepared and unarmed. It is not enough to have us fighting to exist in 2D, to be visible, or 3D, to take up space – now we must fight to exist in 4D, for the right to evolve in *time*.

'I think the skin space, the fitness space, the food space, the nutrition space, they all have exactly the same issues,' Dr

Anjali Mahto says. 'There's so much overlap within those areas and how they relate to self-esteem and control.'

Anjali recalls a young patient she was treating for her skin. Her mother was a baker and every year would make her the most beautiful, elaborate birthday cakes, each one better than the last. As the years went on, the patient became more and more restrictive with her food, refusing to consume anything she feared would accelerate the ageing process. By the time the young woman reached her twentieth birthday, her mother, in despair, served the only thing she knew her daughter would eat – a carrot lit with a single candle. The sugar, the girl feared, was too bad for her skin.

Childhoods are stolen, psyches are damaged and birthday parties are ruined. By twenty-five, your brain has only just finished developing. You're not ageing, you're *growing*. These pressures are psychologically damaging, robbing us of years that are meant to be spent *living*, not focusing on freezing our features.

With evermore girls going viral or achieving online fame before they turn eighteen, our digital culture has flattened our perception of timelines. Influencers, friends, celebrities and strangers are all on one feed promoting their highlight reel, announcing milestones and achievements, which is fuelled by an algorithm that preferences a youthful, filtered beauty ideal. This all makes it so easy to compare ourselves to someone much more affluent, 'beautiful' or #sponsored. Our life experiences accelerate and expectations inflate.

The women we deify as influencers online are overwhelmingly in their late teens or early twenties. The digital realm is itself a fountain of youth – there are always young, fresh people to follow online, elevated by the algorithm and pushed to visibility. In a mirror image of our physical realm, women find themselves increasingly pushed out as they age, pressured into intensive beauty regimes in a bid to stay visible, as it becomes harder to make a living online. SevenSix Agency discovered a 153.6 per cent pay gap between influencers aged eighteen to thirty and those aged thirty to forty-five. We're left with a generational divide which inhibits the spread of wisdom, representation and reassurance – younger girls are duped into believing that older women have nothing of value to offer them, whilst older women are taunted into resenting youth. When we turn on each other, we lose the community, networks and intergenerational insights that are essential to shatter the illusions presented by the patriarchy.

'The truth is that young-old is a very happy time of life,' Dr Konnert tells me. 'Survey after survey shows that people are very satisfied with their lives – they're happy, often happier than younger generations. This stereotype of the old, depressed person is simply not the case. That just doesn't happen for most people.'

Overlaid with the caption 'I don't want to be younger', influencer Dannielle Norman's video says: 'I don't want to be younger versions of myself. There is nothing I would trade for the connection and the understanding and the depth of knowledge that I have within myself now.'

Dannielle refuses to share her age online, despite mounting comments.

'You could not pay me to do my twenties again, you could not pay me to think that the centre of my universe has to be my desirability. I didn't have a personality, I had a response, I was so reactive. Ultimately, there will always be someone with longer legs or bigger tits, but you have to invest in who you are, as a person, not as a performance piece.'

The bittersweet sentiment seems to be that much of this fear dissipates with age – that women in their mid-thirties arrive reborn into the world after the labour that is their teens and twenties. It's a cruel paradox that so many young women and girls waste over a decade of their life paralysed by a fear that, once confronted, births a fresh sense of self-assurance. The number of times older women have told me that no amount of money would see them return to their twenties is both soothing and heartbreaking. If the meaning of life, ultimately, is to enjoy the passage of time then why are we wasting so much of it in fear or resentment?

How can we create a more beautiful future for women and girls?

'The concrete thing that comes to mind is delaying social media exposure – letting young girls be who they are outside of the algorithm for as long as possible. For me, it's more protected space for a longer period of time.'

Dr Debby Herbenick,
author and sexual health professor

10

(M)otherhood

The first apartment I lived in as a 'working woman' was ordinary and rough around the edges, but we went out of our way to make it nice. There were plants, posters, tote bags, candles, coffee table books that had never been read. Items of beauty and pride, mostly mismatched – a symbol of our separate-together lives. We were not initially friends but had developed the strange kind of connection only formed in a flatshare of two. Monica was a third-culture kid; she had moved around a lot as a child and was never afraid of introducing herself. We had met online, brought together by a shared need to find a home. We had decided that of all the weirdos we could possibly live with in this city, we were each other's safest bet. Despite being in our mid-twenties, we existed in that liminal state between women and girls. We would resent being called girls but sometimes ate Lunchables for dinner.

We sat there, on our two-seater couch one Thursday evening, our legs intertwined, both mindlessly on our phones or laptops. Scrolling, typing, half reading, mindlessly checking – each of us clutching a pregnancy test.

'This one still says pregnant,' Monica said, looking down at the pregnancy test in her hand, and then back up at me.

I glanced down at mine to reread the word written on the little digital screen. 'Yep . . . same.'

'I don't know why I keep thinking it's going to go away.'

'I just thought there might be something going on with the moon.'

'The moon has been weird lately,' Monica nodded. 'Do you wanna swap?'

We exchanged pregnancy tests and continued to stare at our devices. Monica half on her laptop, half on her phone, me looking at nothing at all, just staring into the void and biting the inside of my cheek.

'I can't believe you're actually pregnant, Ellen. Like full-on preggo.' Of course, Monica had to break the silence. 'You didn't even finish peeing and it was like "PREGNANT". You probably didn't need to waste your money on the second one.'

I shot her an eye roll.

When I had bought the pregnancy tests, I had walked down every aisle in the small convenience store, grabbing at random snacks and dropping them distractedly into a basket. I didn't need three packs of Hula Hoops, Cherry Bakewells or mouthwash, but despite being a grown adult woman, I felt the need to make it a 'balanced shop', not an emergency run to the nearest supermarket because oh my fucking god my period is two weeks late and I only met this man two months ago.

And yet I had felt oddly calm as I walked around the store. I knew I had options, I assumed they'd be easy to access and I had all the privilege of living in a city that allowed me autonomy over my body and reproductive rights. Still, I had to tell Store Manager Steve, with as much dignity as I had left at this point, that yes, I did want a bag for my many packets of Hula Hoops but that I would also need him to unlock the pregnancy tests from the cigarette cupboard. It might as well have had chains clamping it shut and the words WHORE emblazoned on the front. As is often the case when you're dying inside, Steve didn't hear me the first time.

'You need a what, sorry?'

'I need, erm, a pregnancy test, please,' I craned my head to keep my voice soft but audible, until I was practically in the till.

'I've only got a double pack of the DIGITAL PREGNANCY TESTS,' Steve shouted from the cupboard, just a metre away from me. He might as well have added 'SO YOU CAN BE DOUBLE SURE THAT YOU'RE AN ABSOLUTE SLAG.'

'Yep, yep, thanks, that'll do,' I hushed back, smiling in a way that said 'I hate you Steve' whilst practically ripping the test out of his hands and turning to speed-walk out of the shop, through the rather long queue that had now started to form behind me.

*

In my bedroom that night, I lay in the dark as I scrolled, my face lit by the glow of my phone. An American voiceover started to play.

'If a foetus is a baby, we should be able to take life insurance out on it. So if a woman has a miscarriage, she's entitled to a life insurance policy.

'If a foetus is a baby, men should start paying child support the second the pregnancy is confirmed.

'If a foetus is a baby, low-income women should get more food stamps and more welfare for the baby whilst she's pregnant with them.

'If a foetus is a baby, we should be able to claim them on our income taxes for that year.

'If a foetus is a baby, every single state should have a law that makes assaulting a pregnant women also child abuse.

'But no. Because a foetus isn't a baby, you just want to control a woman's reproductive rights.'

I switched apps, apparently keen to torture myself. A high-pitched squeal bled through my phone.

'Hey cupcakes! Welcome back to my channel! You are six weeks pregnant – congratulations! You probably peed on loads of pregnancy tests and the news is finally starting to sink in, you're going to be a mum! We are all sending you a big squeeze! At this stage, your baby is the size of a pea but if you consider that, last week, they were just the size of a sesame seed, that is some serious growing! Now, if you're anything like I was, you're already imagining the future and what this little baby is going to look like. Admittedly, they're a bit alien-like right now, but their little ears are starting to come through and they already have tiny fingers starting to form. You'll be holding those hands in years to come . . .'

I buried my face into my pillow and sobbed myself to sleep.

*

The next morning, I walked into the kitchen to find Monica cooking a healthy breakfast from one of her latest workout plans. It had protein powder and blueberries and some kind of batter, and she was making a mess.

'Morning! How's the baby?'

I ignored her as we wove around each other in the kitchen – like threads braiding into a friendship bracelet. It was a synchronised dance we both knew off by heart.

'You know, I've always known I wanted kids, ever since I was little. It's probably the only thing I've ever consistently wanted,' I told her. 'I think it's because my mum had to go back to work straight away when I was a baby, so I was always in nursery or after-school clubs, right up until I was a teenager. There's always been little kids around me. Plus, that baby smell is just . . .'

I took a deep breath in, heart emojis covering my eyes.

'You can't have a kid just because you want to smell them, Ellen,' she laughed. 'I hate kids. I'd be terrified of getting fat and then no one would fancy me anymore. And if this is your way of telling me that I need to find a new flatmate, then fine, but I'm not moving out for at least six months because I just renewed my gym membership.'

'I'm being serious, Mon. Can you take this seriously?'

'Sorry! Fuck, I'm sorry! It's just that sometimes you say it's a thing and sometimes you pretend it's not a thing and I'm not really sure how to talk about it. Like, is it a baby? Is it not a baby? I don't know what to say. They didn't cover this in Life Skills! And I know there's no perfect time, but there's *definitely* better times and . . .' She realised she was very much not helping and realigned herself. 'When do you think it happened?'

'Pretty sure it was the eleventh.'

Monica started typing on her phone and scrolled, wide-eyed. 'OMG, you'd be having a Libra baby! October is a pretty good birthday month – they'd be one of the oldest in school. Oooh birthstone is an opal, that's so cute.'

'That is pretty cute.' I smiled to myself. 'They could have Halloween-themed birthday parties.'

'With little costumes.' Monica stuck her bottom lip out. 'You know, if we rearranged the flat a bit, we could fit a crib in here. We could move the table, I could put my desk in my room?'

'I thought you hated kids?'

'Yeah, but this would be your kid, so it'd be at least fifty per cent decent. And I'm a pretty heavy sleeper so I probably wouldn't even wake up in the night when it cried. So . . . are you gonna tell him?'

'Who?'

'Oh, c'mon, Ellen. It takes two to tango and, no offence, but I doubt you're the highest on God's list for the next immaculate conception.'

I shot her a glance.

'But seriously though, you need to tell him.'

'At some point, yeah . . . I need to sit with it for a bit. I want to be sure in my decision before I put it on him. You know?'

'Yeah, I guess, it just seems a bit unfair, making yourself go through all this on your own.'

'I'm not on my own. I've got you, haven't I?'

Monica smiled at me.

'And anyway, I know for a fact he doesn't want kids right now. He'd support me in whatever I wanted to do, which is nice I guess, but it sort of just feels like a lot of extra pressure with his eyes on me. What if I do want to keep it and he doesn't but he goes along with it anyway because it's what I want and he wants me to be happy and feels bad because of all the hormones and shit, and I'll be crying every five minutes and he won't have the heart to tell me he actually hates babies and really wanted to travel a bit more before he settled down because he is super-lovely and wants to be supportive but a year or two down the line all that pent-up resentment comes flowing out and then he leaves me for a barely legal Instagram model with no baby belly and no screaming child?'

Monica didn't know what to say but now that I'd started I couldn't stop.

'And even if he did want to keep it, then that's a whole load of extra pressure. Am I really going to deny a man his child? How could I possibly have that conversation? But what about me? What about my body and what I want? What if I can't do that? And even then, I could carry his baby and get all fat and have that wrinkly stomach skin and he could still decide to leave me afterwards and I'd be left with the child that he said he wanted when he said he wanted me but now he's decided he needs a gap year because it's all "getting a bit much". What will I do then?'

'Hmm,' Monica replies. 'I just hate how men always seem to get the easy way out. It's always like "hormones make women so crazy . . . OMG you're being so dramatic." And then they literally go to war.'

*

Part of the reason I didn't tell anyone but Monica was because I already knew how it felt for your body to become an empty shell for other people to project their wants, hopes and dreams onto. To accommodate and submit, to lose yourself in the process. This (m)otherhood felt objectifying in an entirely new way. I feared that in telling those I loved, especially my family and his, that they would lay claim to something they assumed was theirs, regardless of my wants or needs. I felt I would relinquish control of myself and instead become the vessel for *their* grandchild, *their* cousin, *their* niece or nephew. The decision, instead of being about what I wanted to do with my body, would become about what *I* would be doing with *their* baby. I couldn't bring myself to do it.

I was twenty-five but at that moment I felt like it might as well have been a teen pregnancy. I still felt alone, I still felt like a disappointment, I still felt like my experience of motherhood had been taken away from me, dulled down from something magic and rendered scary and logistical.

Women had told me about their bodies becoming public property during pregnancy, with family, friends and strangers touching their stomachs, commenting on their appearance, giving unsolicited advice about their behaviour, invading their personal space as if the body 'mother' had been rendered invisible but for a bump housing a baby. They would walk around as 'baby-carrying vessel', with people shooting judgmental looks at the bar whilst they sipped their tonic water, asking if they'd gained enough weight or commenting on how high they were carrying. The pregnant body felt out of control, an experience happening *to* me not *with* me.

I always knew in my heart of hearts I wouldn't keep the

baby – the timing was wrong, I was living in a flatshare with a girl I hadn't long met and had been dating the guy I'd had sex with for even less time. I had recently gone freelance, had just started a masters programme, had no formal full-time employment and a list as long as my arm of things I still wanted to do and achieve before I became a mum – this book being one of them.

Under neo-liberal feminism, I should aspire to have it all, to achieve balance between my work, social and family life as the ideal. I should also be a high-earner who dresses impeccably, doesn't age and has a perfect blowout. I might've escaped the expectation to be a mother and only a mother, but now I felt like I had to not only one day be the perfect mother, but also be the most perfect, successful version of myself in every iteration. I knew, as I lay in my bed alone, that no matter how my partner reacted, how many people said they would support me, that the responsibility would always fall on me. I would either have to succeed at everything simultaneously or be seen as a failure. A mother who neglected her child to go to work, a mother who threw away her career to *just* look after a baby all day, a mother who was obsessed with her looks and couldn't possibly be healthy, a mother who had let herself go, a mother who had chosen the wrong father for her child, a mother who was a father and a teacher and a cleaner and a beautician and a model and a chef and a nurse and a carer and a hostess and a businesswoman and a photographer and a friend and a sister and a niece and a grandchild and a creative and a partner. I wasn't ready to do it alone. I knew that I couldn't have it all.

Over the next few weeks, I gained weight. I felt bloated all of the time but I stopped wanting to eat food. I started to get nauseous in the shower and brushing my teeth became its own kind of torture. I wore baggy clothes and felt anxious that my body would never return to its pre-pregnancy state. My body felt haunted – shared and invaded. I became intensely aware of the space I was occupying. I felt resentment that this had happened to me when so many other women prayed for it. Despite my ardent feminist views, I still felt a huge amount of shame. I chastised my former self for ever thinking this would be a quick and easy 'fix'. I resented the ideology of 'for' and 'against' because all of a sudden, none of it spoke to me. I sat in the centre of the debate whilst the world, like angry parents, screamed over the top of my head.

*

Each night. I would lie in the dark, phone light illuminating my face, my spare hand on my stomach, looking for answers.

A Twitter thread:

Abortion does not make you unpregnant. It makes you the parent of a dead child.

This is factually inaccurate – get some brain cells incel.

They're not humans, they're slaves! 1860

They're not humans, they're Jews! 1938

They're not humans, they're cells! 2020

Feel free to scoop up that ball of cells, pop it in a stroller and walk around the park cooing at it dementedly. It still won't make it a baby. Also, not your body – none of your damn business.

There's nothing to be proud of. Killing people isn't good, you are a human in the womb. Even if you're just developing slowly from a fertilised egg to a little human.

Exactly. I lost a brother to abortion. The fact that ppl are taking pride in taking away someone's life just disgusts me.

I had 2 abortions, one when I was 18 and one when I was 30. I don't regret either one of them, neither of them were traumatic or sad at all.

Just call yourself abortionists. When was the last time a so-called pro-choice advocated for giving mothers other options than straight-up abortions? Never heard a pro-choice advocate for adoption.

Abortion just bcos someone doesnt want a baby is cold-blooded murder and u know it.

Why should women's bodies bear the weight of your religious beliefs? I'll do what I wish with my body, uterus, face, hair. I don't care what you do with your bodies, leave me the fuck alone.

I threw my phone across the room and screamed.

*

The next day, I had a work meeting I couldn't cancel. A video call I would have to sit through, despite the fact that my brain could think of nothing other than what my body was doing against my will. Before I had a chance to figure out how I could get through this, Jane's face filled the screen.

Jane was a light, the kind of boss you dream of having when you're a teenage girl fantasising about a job in media. In the *Ugly Betty* or *Devil Wears Prada* spin-off that became my life, she was the antithesis of Wilhemina Slater and Miranda Priestly. She was warm and approachable, supportive and strong-willed; she knew how to balance just the right amount of office gossip with feedback that was firm and fair. She had hired me for commissions throughout my career and sat in that beautifully messy space between colleague and friend. Months before I found out I was pregnant, Jane had miscarried. I knew she'd been trying to get pregnant ever since.

'How are you, angel?'

And that's when time stopped. And I couldn't breathe. And my mouth wanted to say, 'Yeah, I'm all good!' and beam like the sun, but my face couldn't lie and I could feel my eyes starting to sting. I willed them to stop because I was at *work* and how dare my body betray me like this. I put my head in my hands to hide my face and once I started I couldn't stop.

'Oh honey, what's happened?'

'It's okay, it's okay,' I said, desperately trying to pull myself together. 'I just got some news recently and it's a lot. I'm sorry I'm such a mess. I found out recently that, erm, well, I'm pregnant. And I don't know what to do. I'm so sorry but I'm not ready and I feel so guilty and I know this is so unprofessional, I just can't think of much else right now and I keep thinking I'm fine but clearly I'm not. I'm pretty sure I'm going to get an abortion but I wanted the first time I took a pregnancy test to mean something and not in this way and I don't know what's going to happen and I just feel . . .'

Jane told me that she'd had an abortion in her early twenties too. She explained the process to me she told me what I could expect – what I might find helpful and what I should avoid doing. She signed me off for the rest of the week. She told me I was important and strong and that I could text her whenever I needed. She spoke to me calmly and patiently, her voice full of love in a way only women have mastered. She was so gracious with me, despite her previous loss. She held the space for me to bare my soul to her and she looked after me.

'All of your feelings are totally valid,' she said. 'I'm proud of you for coming to this decision for yourself, and I know that the children you do have in future will be so appreciative of the full woman you are, of the woman who had the time and space to achieve her dreams.'

But there was something else happening, an intuition sparking in my brain. I could sense there was something she hadn't told me.

'Wait, Jane . . . are you pregnant too?'

Her eyes widened. I squealed. All of a sudden, she became the most important person in the world and I forgot myself. 'I knew it! I could tell!!'

I sat with my mouth wide open, kicking my feet under my desk, because I knew she wanted this more than anything in the world.

'I'm nine weeks but you cannot tell a soul,' Jane hushed me through a giddy smile. 'No one knows but this is too spooky. I knew I couldn't hide it from you.'

We talked for the rest of the meeting about Jane's baby and Jane's pregnancy, which were real in a totally different way to mine. We started thinking about names and how she would tell her family and our team at work. I made space for her in the way she had made space for me. And there we sat, both pregnant, both making our own choices, both holding each other across the void.

*

The abortion process was a fairly straightforward one. I called a number, scheduled an appointment over the phone, spoke to a lovely doctor who was kind and gentle, answered some questions and was referred to a second doctor. In the UK, all abortions must be signed off by two doctors before treatment can be administered. I had the choice of going in for a simple surgery or receiving medication at home. Terrified of hospitals, I opted for the latter, and they walked me through the process and told me to expect my treatment medication in the post.

During this in-between stage, I returned to my phone to watch the world fall apart. When Donald Trump had been elected president, he said people who had abortions should be punished and he promised to appoint Supreme Court justices to 'automatically' overturn Roe v Wade – the landmark 1973 Supreme Court case that guaranteed the right to an abortion in the United States. Trump confirmed three justices to the court during his term in office – giving conservatives a six-to-three super-majority.

During the pandemic, hospitals and clinics across the US attempted to restrict abortion as a 'non-essential' service. We had not long lost Justice Ruth Bader Ginsburg, and she was replaced by staunch conservative and anti-abortionist Amy Coney-Barrett. The fear was starting to set in. I didn't live in the US but I had friends and family who did. The world still looked up to the supposed Land of the Free and we worried what was coming next.

Only two years later, the Supreme Court would overturn Roe v Wade in a watershed decision to repeal women's rights all over the country. State by state, women's bodies were dictated to, dissected and discussed. Women like me were left with no choices, women whose pregnancies put their lives at risk were left with no choices, women who had been raped were left with no choices, young girls who had been abused were left with no choices, women who were being abused were left with no choices, women who simply didn't want a baby were left with no choices.

I sat looking at my phone, filled with anger and guilt, knowing that just because I happened to exist here in my two-bedroom flatshare in London, that I would be okay. Thousands of other women did not have the same choice. Women across the world were being shown that they were second-class citizens – that once impregnated, they lost their right to autonomy and their right to life.

The choice over bodily autonomy should work in every direction. A long-term friend of mine, Sarah, has known she doesn't want children since she was a child herself. At thirty-three, she's still sure about her decision. Despite her steadfastness, she still finds herself having to fight her corner until she's blue in the face – with strangers, family members and medical professionals.

'In my twenties, I was always told I was too young to be sterilised, that there was a "high chance" I would change my mind and I should wait until my thirties. When I turned thirty, I was still being told the same thing, with the added bonus of, "Well, do you have a partner? What do they think? Do they not want kids?" Erm, hello? It's my body! When does it end?!'

Sarah tells me that she feels like she's never taken seriously in her desire to have autonomy over her own body, treated like a 'silly little girl who doesn't know what she wants'. She says it's exhausting and makes her feel defective for not wanting to be a mother, for living her life for herself, and for considering her partner and dog enough of a family. The dictatorship over women's bodies extends across every angle of (m)otherhood – from choosing not to have children, to the abortion debates, restrictions around birth control, and the birth itself.

*

Forty-two-year-old Stefani from Seattle had had multiple complications when her first child was born – the umbilical cord was wrapped around her daughter's neck, she was stuck in the birth canal and wasn't breathing properly. Despite the pain she was in, all of Stefani's focus was on her baby girl. The doctor who supported her during the birth announced he'd had to perform an episiotomy, a cut between the vagina and perineum to deliver the baby safely. He hadn't asked, he just told, but Stefani didn't care what he said, she just wanted her baby to be okay.

In the moments after delivery, after stitching Stefani up, the doctor stood up, took his gloves off and said: 'I had to do a couple of stitches and I put an extra stitch in for your husband.'

Stefani heard what he said but the words didn't really register. 'There was so much other stuff going on,' she told me. 'I didn't know at the time what a "husband stitch" was, why he did it or what it even meant. I was just so focused on my baby girl and whether or not she was going to be okay.'

The 'husband stitch' is an extra stitch made during the repair process after a vaginal birth, supposedly to tighten the vagina for increased pleasure of a male sexual partner.

It wasn't until her daughter was a few months old, when she started trying to have sex again, that Stefani realised something was really wrong. 'It was impossibly painful,' she said. 'I started looking into what the procedure had been and I realised what he had done. I just sat with it for a while because I didn't know I had any right to be mad. I wrote it off as something I would have to deal with forever but it made sex impossible for the best part of a decade, it was so incredibly painful.'

Objectified and robbed of their humanity, after literally just creating life, many women have had this additional stitch without their consent, often with the approval of their male partners, sometimes causing them needless pain and long-term complications.

'I wish I had understood ahead of time what it meant – there are so many things you have to prepare for before you have a baby and I thought I knew it all, but I didn't know how to advocate for myself against this. I don't want other people to go through it – as small and insignificant as it seems, it had a huge impact on my life for a long time.'

Listening to Stefani made me angry – angry about how often we downplay our trauma, the objectification of our bodies and the ways in which they are stripped of their dignity and humanity. At twenty-nine, Stefani had felt she had no right to be angry about what had happened to her – no recourse when a professional whose job it was to help her through one of the most vulnerable moments of her life abused her body and reduced her to an object designed to please.

When I speak to Dr Hillary McBride, a therapist, author and researcher who specialises in women's embodiment, I tell her how angry it makes me that we have created a society that does not revere mothers, these women who create and nurture a brand-new life. How have we created a world that refuses to put these women on a pedestal? That insists on punishing them the moment their bodies are no longer child-bearing vessels?

'The story that we're told about what makes a woman valuable is that you must become an object that can be sexualised and is desirable,' she responds. 'Then there is an adjacent narrative, that your body as a woman, if not for sexual purposes, is valuable for maternal purposes. Your body is always defined by the value it can hold for somebody else, either for the purposes of sexual gratification or for the purposes of bearing life. Instead of saying how your body deserves to be revered because it created life, what we should say is that your body deserves to be revered because it *is* life.'

This floored me. I had felt so confident in my belief that women's bodies – as mothers and creators – should be celebrated for the awe-inspiring things they can do. They should be, but what I had failed to see was that I was playing into the virgin/whore dichotomy yet again – into the idea that the value of women's bodies should be at the mercy of external factors. Some women can't get pregnant, some don't have periods and some can't carry a baby to term – that doesn't make their bodies any less worthy of womanhood or deserving of respect. We all deserve to be revered, to feel confident, desirable and safe. We are worthy, simply because we exist.

*

I didn't see Jane for a while but we texted back and forth. She checked in to see how I was and I responded with baby name ideas inspired by her Welsh heritage and her love for cute abbreviations.

Months passed and things looked more and more promising, but one day Jane didn't show up to a photoshoot and I heard that she was in hospital. Jane's baby was deemed 'incompatible with life' after being diagnosed with multiple conditions in the womb. She had to make the decision to have doctors terminate and deliver her pregnancy in the hospital or risk carrying to term and watch her baby struggle to survive its first few months of life. She lost her baby at nineteen weeks and five days.

'I was going through all the symptoms of pregnancy, there were weeks where I didn't know if my baby was going to be okay or not, and I remember lying in the bath one day and looking at my tummy and saying, "I love you so much but please don't kick me, please don't kick me." I never felt anything and I'm so grateful for that. I wouldn't have been able to bear it,' she told me.

She never told anyone how she felt, never said where her mind went when the bleeding had stopped. But she tells me now, in the safe space we have created together. She tells me that looking down at her body, the one that had grown to accommodate what was once her future child, now rippled with scars and stretch marks, she thought, 'All of this damage for nothing.'

'I didn't moisturise, I didn't look at my belly in the shower, I didn't look in a mirror, I didn't want to touch my body. There was no connection at all – I didn't touch my stomach for a really long time.'

Despite her high-powered job and incredibly busy life, six months after her loss, she tells me that the hardest part of her day is getting dressed in the morning.

Pregnancy loss is sadly very common. According to *Goop*, one in four known pregnancies end in miscarriage, one in one hundred result in stillbirth, still more are terminated because they are medically risky to either the mother or the baby – and yet most people who lose a baby mourn in silence. In many countries, Jane would have been forced to carry to full term. The enforced secrecy around early-stage pregnancy, when the risk of loss is higher, serves to make everyone else more comfortable, whilst leaving those who are pregnant alone to suffer in silence. For those who experience loss, the pain and grief are compounded unnecessarily by secrecy, shame and societal expectations.

'The result is that women often experience these things alone because they're trying to keep their experience private,' says Hillary. 'We hide and I think that that can make for an extra-complicated experience with loss. When I was pregnant, in the first trimester, it was bizarre to me that that was the time when I felt the worst, but I had the fewest people around me, scaffolding me in that experience. In the literature, we often call perinatal loss disenfranchised grief because it's grief in secret. I think grief is always an embodied and relational process, and in addition to the changing body you experience through miscarriage, the feelings about the loss often are invisible.'

The trinity of silence, stigma and shame that shroud the topic of pregnancy loss prevent access to open conversation, emotional support and community. It's a shame that ripples out across all areas of women's health – like the way we hide tampons up our sleeves on the way to the bathroom or the needless pressure we feel to shave before a smear test. Left alone to internalise their emotions, women can often feel guilty, ashamed and to blame for their loss. On top of the emotional turmoil, women are often left with a lot of the physical symptoms of pregnancy after a miscarriage, creating a sense of alienation from their bodies. It can feel like a betrayal. In speaking to women as part of the research for this book, I often heard how a compounding part of the trauma is the sudden perception that their supposedly fertile and healthy bodies have failed, broken their biological promise and become 'defective'.

'Why can't my body do what everyone else is finding so easy?' was the question that plagued Jane. 'Every time I did anything, all I saw were mums and pregnant people. I just felt like they were all goddesses and I was this lower being that just couldn't do it.'

For those who do not identify as the gender they were assigned at birth, or who struggle with body dysmorphia or dysphoria as it relates to their identity, that sense of bodily betrayal is heightened. Whether it's trying to conceive, being misgendered by medical staff, or dealing with the conflicting physical signs and symptoms of pregnancy, the relationship with the body becomes a site of struggle.

*

Under a patriarchal, capitalist society, women's bodies will never be regarded with the value, autonomy or respect they deserve. The idea is still perpetuated by our digital media, in celebrity culture and the pressure we put on new mothers to 'bounce back' after birth. Whilst 'dad bods' are accepted, even celebrated, the body that created, housed, birthed and nursed human life is immediately put under intense scrutiny.

During pregnancy and postpartum, women face huge changes to the look, feel and function of their body. The common portrayal of pregnancy often showcases a woman at her 'most beautiful' – her hair thick and luscious, her skin radiant with a pregnancy glow, her long, strong nails caressing a perfectly shaped baby bump. However, this is not the reality for most expectant mothers. Pregnancy can take a huge physical and mental toll, with expectations and pressures constantly levelled at an expecting mum. It's understandable that not every woman is able to view the changes in her body purely through the prism of creating life and – due to the pressures levelled against her her entire life – can't help but focus on weight gain or on becoming an unattractive or undesirable woman.

'We are exposed to a narrative of the pre-pregnancy body as being the standard against which women postpartum should compare themselves to, and that this should be an infantilised, youthful, undefiled, fertile body without the markings of motherhood,' Hillary tells me. 'The ideal in Western societies, particularly in a white supremacist, androcentric, patriarchal culture, is that women's bodies are youthful and that they retain purity in a way that connotes a body that is an object to be desired. So often, what that means is losing weight, shifting body size, managing stretch marks and breast changes, even the way hair grows postpartum. These things are all really normal and meaningful changes in the life of a woman postpartum, but they need to be eradicated as a means of securing social value through proximity to this youthful, prepubescent body.'

In this way, objectification and anti-ageing rhetoric compound body image issues during (m)otherhood, as well as the pressures of diet culture. Women often report difficulty in the first trimester, when physical symptoms of pregnancy – from nausea to fatigue – are high but the pregnancy itself is still shrouded in secrecy. We speak of this 'in-between phase', when you just look bloated and swollen, with no 'excuse' for having a larger body. The fatphobia and thin ideal that permeate our existence translate directly into our experience of pregnancy and postpartum, when you're no longer perceived as having any excuse to carry the extra weight.

In some cases, we are able to suspend judgement, allowing our body to take up space, safe in the knowledge that it is doing so *for* someone else. We give ourselves permission to eat and grow to nurture another being, in ways many of us cannot do for ourselves. Whilst pregnancy weight gain is allowed, fatness is not, and any pregnancy weight gain in areas other than the bump (on the arms, legs or ankles) can result in feelings of inadequacy and shame. Pregnancy can provide some respite from pressure to stay small and slim, but any temporary relief is likely replaced with compounded pressures after the birth.

The World Health Organization describes the postpartum period as the most critical and yet most neglected time in the lives of mothers. Studies consistently suggest an increase in body image concerns after birth. Mothers with young children are especially vulnerable to low self-esteem and worry about their appearance, which can lead to significant psychological suffering, symptoms of postpartum depression and disordered eating. I have met women at every stage of life who have been impacted by this cruel extension of modern beauty standards, which shames women's bodies for their most natural and awe-inspiring functions and robs them of what should be some of the most joyous moments in life.

One young mother, Sophie, explains how the perfection portrayed on social media made her experience of motherhood more difficult: 'Postpartum for me was really hard,' she says. 'I had my son at the same time Emily Ratajkowski had hers – I saw her body after she'd given birth, and I saw so many other women's bodies on social media after birth, and they looked nothing like mine. I'd gained eighty pounds and two years later I'm still not at my pre-pregnancy weight. I'm covered in stretch marks, I had a C-section so my stomach hangs over my scar and my belly will never be flat now unless I get a tummy tuck. I used to feel so guilty about not being able to lose the weight. People would say, "When the baby sleeps, just do exercise." But I was so tired. I felt so bad because it felt like all these women were just snapping back, having these great bodies and getting back in their clothes, and I just couldn't do it.'

The idealised images of parenthood on social media didn't just affect Sophie's relationship with her body – they took away from her ability to bond with her son.

'I did feel a bit resentful towards my son, which feels awful to admit, but for a few months I found it really hard because I didn't really recognise myself. And then I felt guilty about feeling resentful. Being a mum is wonderful but it is hard. What makes it harder is the constant comparison to everyone online – they're all perfect and unreal. I think without that, we'd probably think we were doing a pretty good job.'

There is a distinct lack of research around the impact that social media is having on women at all stages of (m)otherhood, despite the fact that women of reproductive age are amongst the highest users of social media, with new mums engaging with social media over 10 per cent more than the general population of young women. The studies that do exist point to digital platforms playing a significant role in women suffering from poor postpartum body image. Time spent alone, up late at night, feeding a newborn and scrolling on social media compounds the image of perfection we are already so used to seeing. New mothers compare themselves to both perfect images of postpartum and perfect images of women without children.

'I had to block quite a lot of people. I did block Emily Ratajkowski in the end,' Sophie says. 'Especially nowadays, where you've got the fillers and the cosmetic surgery and the diet culture and all these women with beautiful faces, I found it so hard. I just look tired. I don't have enough money to do those things and I don't have the time. I do everything I can to not see these posts because I know they will affect me, but they pop up on your feed even if you're not following anything like that. I try to remind myself that it's their job to look perfect, but a lot of us women think that's something we have to be like and it's completely unattainable.'

A 2022 Australian study examined 600 Instagram images with the hashtag #postpartumbody and found that only 5 per cent showed bodies bearing stretch marks, cellulite, sagging breasts or scars. Looking at images from the 'recent' and 'top' posts categories, 91 per cent of images portrayed lean or average-weight women, often dressed in activewear. These images were also likely to be digitally enhanced and carefully curated by those who uploaded them.

Lead researcher on the study, Dr Megan Gow, a dietician and senior lecturer at University of Sydney and Westmead Children's Hospital, told the *Guardian*, 'The overwhelming thing we felt when we were looking at these images is that they weren't really representative of your typical woman during the early postpartum period. They're thinking about feeding their infant, they're probably sleep-deprived . . . And then on top of that they look at Instagram and think: "I also need to be super-fit, I need to be thin."'

'When you're pregnant, everyone tells you how beautiful you are and how important it is for you to eat, and then as soon as you have the baby, it's like, "So when you're gonna lose weight? When are you going to do some exercise?"' Sophie tells me. 'There's no care for the fact that I nearly died during my labour, I got maternal sepsis and my body took a long time to recover. But people would come up to me and just comment on my body or my weight.'

Research has identified an emerging phenomenon called pregorexia, in which a woman suffers from an eating disorder during pregnancy and after childbirth. Much like a typical eating disorder, the behaviour becomes all-consuming and competitive, and largely focuses on keeping body weight as low as possible throughout pregnancy and postpartum. Those who struggle with pregorexia may use self-starvation, very low caloric intake, vomiting or intense exercise to gain the minimum amount of weight and 'bounce back' to their pre-pregnancy body as soon as possible after birth. In Sophie's case, she just didn't eat.

'There's something really significant about how much time we're spending looking at images that reflect the ideal,' says

Hillary. 'We are seeing only the most desirable, only the most valued images that seem to create this narrow feedback loop about who we need to be, what is valuable, what is ideal. There is a counter narrative emerging on social media, where people are also posting unedited photos of the struggles that they have, but there is still huge pressure to present our experience of motherhood – both our bodily experience of motherhood and the relational experiences of motherhood – in an idealised way, which then reinforces back to us and to the people in our communities who we think we're supposed to be.'

Whether it's the Pinterest mom with her perfect blowdry during her morning feeds or the influencer who is back in her pre-pregnancy clothes within a few weeks, it's easy to feel surrounded by perfected, romanticised images of motherhood as you scroll. Maternity photoshoots are an increasingly popular part of the pregnancy experience, especially in a world of online pregnancy announcements, gender reveals and baby showers, but once the baby is born, the focus tends to shift to the newborn and we see far fewer photos of the postpartum body in its raw, unedited, uncurated state. What we do see, overwhelmingly, is images of celebrity mothers who re-emerge six weeks postpartum looking tiny, tight and toned.

When Hillary was four days postpartum, she asked her doula, who was also a photographer, to come and take photographs of her in her home. Not just of the baby, but of her body. The doula replied that she had tears in her eyes, that she was shocked, 'not because that's wrong, but because most of the time, when I take postpartum photos for women, they ask me to hide their bodies. We spend most of the time during the photoshoot arranging clothing, kids and props in front of their belly to hide that they still have what appears to be a pregnant body.'

'It felt really important for me to capture what my body looked like then,' says Hillary. 'I wanted to capture what it was like to feel the most powerful I've ever felt, to feel the most soft, strong, wise and vulnerable, the most fierce and wild and animal and transcendent and interconnected and spiritual that I've ever felt. It felt so important for me to remember what I knew to be most true about myself at that moment.

'I had this sense of reverence. But not just because of the baby, because of myself. I wish that there were ways of posting images like that on social media without becoming sexually objectified. I would love to disrupt the narrative that so many of us are handed that your body needs to disappear or needs to be thin or needs to be back to how it was pre-pregnancy. I think that the way that we do that is we share more images that reflect with accuracy what our bodies actually look like and we celebrate them. It doesn't need to be about love necessarily, but respect, appreciation.'

*

I developed a para-social relationship with a few mothers online but the first was Anna Saccone. I had discovered Anna's YouTube channel at fifteen, when she was in her early twenties, reviewing makeup online. It was the first time I had seen a beauty channel on YouTube and it kicked off a lifelong obsession – my blog, my social media channels, my life online, my career and this book. I have been a loyal follower ever since, watching as Anna got her dogs, moved house, got married and had her children.

Anna was one of the first content creators to post pregnancy vlogs online in the 2010s. The birth of her first child was the first to be documented on YouTube – the video edited and posted from the hospital suite. Millions have watched Anna give birth (four times now), share her pregnancy journeys and document the day-to-day life of motherhood.

When I first found out Anna was pregnant, I was shocked. By 2011, I had known her online for years and she had always said that she didn't want children, posting candidly about her fear of pregnancy. It wasn't until years later that Anna opened up to her audience about the eating disorder that had plagued her for her entire adult life, making her petrified to gain weight, to get pregnant, of her body changing. Her first pregnancy did provide some respite from the symptoms of her bulimia, but during postpartum, with the intense scrutiny of a public life online, all those feelings came back with a vengeance.

'With my first, I didn't allow myself to gain that much weight,' she tells me. 'It's so messed up but I remember challenging myself to lose all of the baby weight by the time I had my six-week check up with my OBGYN. It shouldn't have even been on my radar but that was at the forefront of my mind. And I did it. Nobody knew at the time that I was suffering. I obviously wasn't documenting that, and I wouldn't wish it on anyone because it really was horrific. Even when I did get to my pre-pregnancy weight, I still felt miserable because I was making myself sick all the time. It's not the win that you think it's going to be if you do it in an unhealthy way. After my fourth baby, I got really skinny and everybody online was saying I was "goals". Behind the curtains, I just felt like death. I was miserable and I didn't enjoy it at all. It completely robbed me of that time in my life.'

Popular gossip sites would upload images of Anna postpartum, circling her stomach in red. Fans commented, with no intended malice, that they couldn't wait for her to get back to her pre-pregnancy body and be a super-fit mum who looked amazing with her four children. The cycle was vicious and drove Anna further into her disorder.

Just like the female body generally is under neoliberalism, the postpartum body is portrayed as a project to be worked on, to get under control and restore to pre-pregnancy state. The expectations held by most women of their postpartum bodies are incredibly high and most times unrealistic, especially to achieve in a safe and healthy way. Across multiple studies, women reported experiencing a tension in priorities between caring for their new baby and pressures to regain control of their body image, and 'bounce back'. That the two can even be considered of parallel importance, that being attractive and meeting the beauty ideal is as important as caring for yourself and your child, speaks to how deeply ingrained this form of symbolic violence is in women's psyches. The paradox of needing to nurture and nourish yourself whilst you recover, but also feeling pressured to punish and purge your body into submission, is the cruel reality many new mothers face.

Despite the pressure for us to have it all, many women find that the role of 'mother' is incompatible with being themselves, being sexually desirable or being a working woman. Women, like Monica and I, worry about being unattractive to our partners postpartum, becoming invisible and losing our identity as women to our identity as mothers. I feel ashamed for the number of times I have said that I want to have children after I get married, purely because I want to look the best I ever have in my wedding dress. And by 'best', I mean slim, tight and toned.

Peanut, the social media app for new mothers, tells me that they witness women talking about their struggles with body image 'every day' – thousands of posts from women detailing their worries about no longer feeling desirable or like they recognise their bodies:

I feel so ugly. I can't believe how much I've changed. I didn't 100 per cent love my body before but this is so much harder than I thought it'd be . . . my stomach stretch marks feel so embarrassing. I don't even feel like I'm the same person.

I'm hungry all the time, and I know that it's giving my baby girl the nutrients she needs, but it's really taking a toll on my self-esteem. I'm almost five months postpartum – how can I lose weight without affecting my supply?

I feel awful saying it because I know how lucky I am to be pregnant but if I'm honest I completely hate my pregnancy body. I feel massive and disgusting. It's really getting me down . . . I just hate what I see in the mirror.

'What's really sad is that, when I started posting online, I really wanted to do good,' Anna tells me. 'I didn't want to be toxic in any way, I didn't want to trigger anyone, but I know I invariably did, because that was just the unhealthy space that I was in.'

When her fourth child turned one, Anna started on her recovery journey, and she did so publicly, with millions of people watching as she told her story, sharing the truth behind the seemingly perfect family life she had cultivated online and allowing her weight to fluctuate as her body found its balance. It was one of the first times I had seen an influencer shed the perfectly filtered facade and show the reality of modern womanhood.

With her youngest almost five, Anna is now proud to say she is fully recovered. 'I really do care less,' she says. 'I'm not going to say that I don't have wobbles now and then, everybody does, but I have respect for what my body has been through and I won't let body shaming stop me from doing anything.'

Still, Anna hasn't ruled out the possibility of cosmetic surgery in future.

'I've spoken about this publicly, and I knew I was going to get so much shit for it, but I think it's important to be honest. I feel so let down by people I follow who don't disclose when they've had work done, so I'm not saying that I will never have a tummy tuck or get my boobs done. I'm under no illusion that it will change my life, I know it is purely for vanity, but I don't think that makes me less body positive.'

A week after I spoke to Anna, she uploaded a video showing her first consultation for a tummy tuck. By the time I came to edit her interview, she'd had the operation done. In her videos as she recovered from surgery, she explained that she wanted to do something for herself after sacrificing so much for her children.

*

Recent years have seen the rise of the 'mummy makeover' – multiple cosmetic procedures performed in one operation, usually consisting of a tummy tuck, breast augmentation, breast lift, liposuction and vaginal rejuvenation surgery – designed to help women 'regain' a pre-pregnancy body. Of course it was a male surgeon, Dr Grant Stevens, who originally developed and popularised the concept of performing these multiple surgeries on mothers. It is a largely male medical establishment that has pathologised the changes in a woman's body post-partum, reframing them not as natural signs of a healthy and successful pregnancy to be respected and revered but instead as medical 'problems' to be fixed.

The website amommymakeover.com, by the creators of the procedure, states: 'That beautiful "baby bump" that everyone was reaching out to feel has been replaced with a saggy imitation of your older, tighter stomach.' And, 'Nothing can bring on an aged facial appearance like the challenges of motherhood.' And, 'Doesn't it sometimes seem like you just stuck those cheese crackers or that dish of ice cream right to your thighs?'

When I think of memories from my childhood, I remember my mum's soft body with nothing but warmth – the way she held me, the way I moulded into her belly, the way she made me feel loved and safe and comforted. The marketing of the mommy makeover characterises natural symptoms of pregnancy and childbirth as disfigurements, deformities to be corrected and restored to social acceptability. The postpartum body is a condition to be cured; any embodied evidence of motherhood becomes a badge of shame. Historically, it hasn't always been this way. As *New York Times* writer Natasha Singer puts it, 'In 1970, *Our Bodies, Ourselves*, the seminal guide to women's health, described cosmetic changes that can happen during and after pregnancy simply as phenomena. But now, narrowing beauty norms are recasting the transformations of motherhood as stigma.'

These procedures, often involving multiple invasive surgeries performed at once, aren't without risk or harm. In 2023, MTV star Jacklyn Smith, known to the world as Jacky Oh, reportedly died in Miami, where she had allegedly travelled to undergo a mommy makeover. She was found unresponsive in her hotel room just a day after she had her surgery.

In a 2017 interview, Jacklyn had opened up about pregnancy, her love for her children and the pressure to snap back after having babies: 'I looked in the mirror and said, damn I need to lose some damn weight, because my stomach lookin' crazy, but ya know, it happens, I had a baby,' she said. Jacky was thirty-two and only ten months postpartum when she died, leaving behind her three children.

There are rumours circulating around Hollywood that celebrities accelerate their postpartum weight loss by getting liposuction shortly after, or even during, a C-section, adding to the bodily trauma experienced during birth. Others are opting to preserve their pre-pregnancy bodies by hiring another woman's womb in a new phenomenon of 'social surrogacy' – in which women who don't want to endure the physical effects of pregnancy or take the time out of their career instead have another woman carry their baby. As more celebrities –

from the Kardashians to Tyra Banks – are normalising the use of surrogates for a variety of reasons, and as the beauty standard becomes ever more restrictive and pressure for women to 'have it all' mounts, an increase in social surrogacy feels inevitable.

The laws around surrogacy are complex and different in every country. In the UK, commercial surrogacy is illegal. In the US, surrogacy is legal but rules vary by state and costs are high. As a result, surrogacy hotspots have started popping up across the global south, with British people as the top 'consumers' of the Indian surrogacy market.

When I spoke to Dr Herjeet Marway, founding chairperson of the Surrogacy UK Ethics Committee, she compared this overseas 'labour' to 'sweatshops'. Whilst commercial surrogacy in the USA often costs into the six figures, an Indian surrogate can cost as little as $5,000. Whilst I knew people were travelling overseas for cheaper cosmetic surgery, I didn't realise they are also travelling overseas for cheaper deals on wombs. Regardless of how you view the labour of pregnancy and birth, there is undoubtedly huge room for exploitation, and the further commodification and exploitation of women's – particularly vulnerable women's – bodies.

*

The bath was a salve. It was run in panic, water splashing over the plastic, as the blood continued to pour. It wasn't what I had imagined for the death of my child that was not yet a child. The daylight felt obscene. Too cold. Too white. The sun had continued to move across the sky like it did every day, but the room was drained of saturation. Dust hung in webs across the window and the sink was crammed with cleansers and razors, toothpaste and floss. It was all inane, glowless. How dare this be the place my child is both born and dies. I exited my body to view the scene from above. There was no pink hue, no soft glow blurring the horrors of my reality. The floor was strewn with my debris; the collateral of death. Red watercolour dropped into the shallow pool; butterfly prints marked my thighs. It was barely past my ankles when I stepped into the warmth, but I needed the relief from my own body. I felt feral. I screamed because that is what I'd seen them do in the movies. I cried even though I could barely bring myself to. My body purged, pushing out what I wished, in another universe, it would hold onto tight.

And then I saw it. Red and foamy, clusters of sinew carried by the waves and swirling before they dissolved down the drain. It was disgusting and beautiful and then it was gone.

I looked down at my still-swollen stomach. I thought of Jane and I felt guilty, and I thought of all the girls who wouldn't have this autonomy over their own futures and I felt ungrateful, and I thought about my future and I felt an intense relief. I was me again, changed and unchanged, and I was free.

*

In 2022, after one medical termination and two miscarriages, Jane gave birth to her baby girl, Evie. A strong and beautiful rainbow baby carried to full term with no complications.

'I've never been so happy in my life,' she tells me when we meet for coffee. 'I want to give you all the cheesy clichés in the world – everything gives me goosebumps. I could kiss the grass, or that tree.' She points and we both laugh.

'You know what, it's so good when you wait until the right time.' she continues. 'You have to be ready to deal with so much. I think I needed every day of life up until the moment I had her to be okay.'

Jane keeps the scan of the baby she lost next to pictures of Evie and she whispers, 'I love you so much,' every night before going to bed.

'And how does it feel to be a girl-mum?' I ask.

'If anything's going to make me cry, that will make me cry, because it's such an important job. I feel like I constantly want to set a good example for her,' Jane says. 'I've been through so much and I've done a lot of work on myself, and even now she holds me accountable. I'm so conscious of how I behave and how I talk to myself – my best friend and I have promised to never, ever body shame ourselves anymore, and I genuinely feel like I am embodying that. It's all because of her.'

'Maybe that's what we all need,' I say. 'To act like Evie is watching.'

'Always watching!' Jane jokes, smushing Evie's cheeks.

I look over at Evie in all her perfection – her chunky legs and chubby cheeks, her dimpled skin and gummy smile – and I watch as she absorbs the world, wide-eyed and wondrous, taking it in, in all its beauty.

How can we create a more beautiful future for women and girls?

'As a mother, I want my daughter and all girls to know they are beautiful inside and out so they can live by their own standards and not conform to others. Every day, we have the opportunity to empower people to love their unique qualities and embrace their authenticity. By taking that chance, we build a more beautiful future for everyone.'

Huda Kattan,
founder of HUDA Beauty

11

The Witches of Cyberspace

I once met a man who called me an attention-seeking whore for posting bikini photos on my social media. I once met a man who demanded nude images of me and didn't stop hounding me even after I said no. I once met a man who said he'd never hurt me, whilst looking at the bruises he left on my arm. I once met a man who videoed me during sex without my consent. I once met a man who pinned my body down and had sex with me even whilst I repeatedly said no. I once met a man who made me so unsafe in my own home I had no choice but to leave. I once met a man who told me I couldn't wear low-cut tops. I once met a man who called me an 'ugly bitch' and followed me in his car because I refused to give him my number. I once met a man who screamed at me for interrupting him. I once met a man who smashed my phone against a wall because he was angry. I once met a man who told me to smile more. I once met a man who told me to lose weight. I once met a man.

When my friend Willow was a teenager, she met a man who harassed her and touched her against her will. She was later masturbated over whilst on her journey home from school. Willow doesn't identify as a victim of sexual assault but she's become obsessed with watching true crime videos on YouTube – studying male violence as a way to get ahead.

A *Sunday Times* headline in October 2021 quoted actress Emily Atack on her experience of online abuse: 'They put their daughters to bed, then go online and send me rape threats.' Emily receives hundreds of messages a day on Instagram in which her physical appearance is attacked and men describe how they would assault her, defiling her pictures and using her Instagram posts to further personalise the attack. The obscene messages that flooded her inbox were daily reminders that her body was not her own. It belonged to men on the internet.

In 2015, Leslie Jones, an actress in the all-female reboot of *Ghostbusters,* and the only woman of colour among the female leads, was forced to leave Twitter due to the online harassment she endured. By the summer of 2016, her personal website had been hacked and filled with photos of the gorilla, Harambe, her driver's licence and passport, as well as explicit photographs, stolen from her iCloud account. One of her abusers, alt-right journalist Milo Yiannopoulos, tweeted that the cast of *Ghostbusters* were fat and ugly, adding that 'mainstream' discourses of body positivity had 'started to marginalise traditional beauty standards'. When confronted about the tweet by CNN, he brushed it off, shrugging and saying, 'This is a bitchy little tweet. Who cares?'

In 2016, Hillary Clinton went up against a man in the run for presidential election. Her opponent, now former president Donald Trump, stated, 'When she walked in front of me, I wasn't impressed.' Trump made it very clear that he bases his respect for women almost entirely on their appearance, but he also has a history of suggesting that women he deems unattractive are somehow incapable in other ways. 'The woman's a liar, extremely unattractive, lots of problems because of her looks,' Trump told the *Hollywood Reporter* when questioned about a *New York* magazine interview with Marie Brenner, in which he had said, 'You have to treat women like shit.' This man was elected to hold one of the most powerful political positions in the world. Throughout the election campaign, Hillary was repeatedly referred to as a witch – the hatred extended far beyond her policies, becoming vehement anger at her audacity to exist in her body and make a bid for power.

I know many witches – women who have been shunned, silenced or subjected to violence simply for existing, for daring to take up space. Every woman has a story; sadly, most have more than one. Stories of experiences in which it has been made clear, one way or another, that her body does not belong to her. Whether by groping, assault, revenge porn, pressure to send nude pictures, abuse in online comment sections, men dominating discussions on reproductive rights, slut-shaming and victim-blaming – the entitlement over women's bodies doesn't seem to have died down despite our supposed progress.

Violence against women and girls occurs in all countries of the world and remains one of the most serious unresolved problems of our time. In 2020, UN Secretary General António Guterres said that gender-based violence had reached epidemic proportions, that discrimination against women still flourishes in the modern world and that 'men are at war with women, but no one is calling for a ceasefire or imposition of sanctions'. Violence against women in all manifestations is a violation of our human rights, freedoms and autonomy.

As the world intertwined with the web, offline forms of oppression – such as harassment, flashing and stalking – were recast into online equivalents (cyber harassment, cyberflashing, cyberstalking), but the digital world also devised its own unprecedented forms of violence against women – such as revenge porn, upskirting, deepfakes, sextortion, doxxing, cyber-rape and grooming online. Women are disproportionately victims of all these types of abuse, and research shows that all forms of cyberviolence against women are increasing. Persecution online has simply become a part of the continuum of witch hunting that women and girls suffer throughout their lives. I've had many conversations with women of all ages, races, locations, vocations and gender expressions who told me the same thing: that the internet can be a scary place for women and girls.

In 2006, researchers from the University of Maryland set up a series of fake online accounts and then dispatched them into chatrooms. Accounts with feminine usernames incurred an average of 100 sexually explicit or threatening messages a day. Masculine names received only 3.7. These behaviours do not occur in a vacuum. Within tech monopolies, created in the image of a patriarchal culture, the violence that feels inherent in womanhood is amplified, fostered and normalised as part and parcel of the digital experience, and it's only getting worse. According to the 2023 Girlguiding report, 81% of girls and young women aged eleven to twenty-one have experienced some form of threatening or upsetting behaviour online, compared to 65% in 2018.

*

At a festival in 2017, whilst waiting for The Killers to start their set, Gina Martin met a group of men who insisted on talking to her. Though she asked them to leave her alone multiple times, they refused, making crude jokes and continuing to harass her. Five minutes later, Gina could hear the men sniggering behind her, their eyes burning into her flesh. She turned to see what they were laughing at and saw a photo that had been sent to one of their phones: a photograph of a woman's crotch, taken up a skirt. Gina knew instantly that it was hers. She grabbed the phone and, with tears streaming down her face, ran through the crowd with the men chasing her. Pitchforks in hand.

Eventually, Gina found a security guard who protected her whilst he called the police. When they arrived, they told her there was nothing that she could do. That yes, she should be able to go outside in the middle of summer wearing a skirt and not be violated, but because she was wearing knickers, the image was not graphic enough to be considered a sexual offence. The men were allowed to go back to the festival and Gina was left feeling empty and humiliated. A few days later, she received a call from the police. Her case had been dropped; there was nothing else they could do.

Whilst she could brush aside the countless times she'd been groped on public transport, the time a nightclub security guard grabbed her boobs to 'check if she was wearing a stab-proof vest' or the times she'd been harassed in the street, this particular incident of violence was harder to ignore. Those men still had that intimate image of her; they probably still have it now.

Not long after the festival, Gina posted a picture online of her and her sister in the crowd, a picture that just so happened to have the men in the background. Gina asked her online community to help her to identify the men in the image. But she then received a notice from Facebook to say that she had violated their guidelines. By posting the image of the men on social media, she was being punished for harassing them.

At every stage, Gina faced silencing. There was no action she could take, no recourse for justice, no recognition of the abuse she had suffered. Filled with incandescent rage, Gina knew that silence wasn't an option anymore. She started a social media campaign, she wrote editorials, ran adverts, began asking why upskirting wasn't illegal. Quickly, her DMs filled with stories from women and girls. Teachers telling her the issue was rife in schools, trans women saying they were regularly targeted, women in Japan explaining that upskirting had become such a problem that phones had been redesigned so that the camera shutter sound couldn't be turned off, so that women would be alerted to a photo being taken. Then there were the messages from children, including a number of pupils from a school in south London where a teacher had been upskirting students for months. They found thousands of images on his devices but he could not be convicted because what he had done didn't constitute an offence. That's when Gina knew she had to do something, even if that something meant changing the law.

*

Ray Bradbury once wrote that 'a witch is born out of the true hungers of her time'. Between the fifteenth and seventeenth centuries, tens of thousands of women were persecuted for being witches – a term used to define the 'evil' aspects of femininity, levelled at marginalised women, promiscuous women, queer women, self-sufficient women, single women, 'difficult' women, older women, women of waning fertility, disabled women and wise women. The persecution of these women was a means of control, a way for a God-fearing, patriarchal society to preserve its power structure at any cost, to maintain the gender hierarchy and control women's bodies.

Many of those who were tried for witchcraft were barely surviving on the fringes of society. Some, however, were iconoclasts, visionaries, midwives and healers – women who refused to be quiet, who had knowledge of the body and the reproductive system and used it to help other women. They were seen to be in possession of a power, an intuition and a divine wisdom that threatened the very fabric of patriarchal lore. As writer Elizabeth Nicholas said in an article for *W Magazine*, the line between a witch and a prophet has always been gender.

Our foremothers were ridiculed, silenced, tortured, drowned and burned alive. They became scapegoats that powerful men rounded up to distract from their failings. They were thrown into rivers – if they sank they were innocent but would inevitably drown, if they floated they were accused of witchcraft and would be sentenced to death.

In the digital age, women who dare to be visible or audible are ridiculed, silenced, taunted, hunted down and attacked too. When it comes to online abuse on social media, women are by far the most regularly targeted group. Much of this degradation focuses on women's physical appearance. That abuse doesn't stop online – turn on the news and it feels like a non-stop assault on women's safety. Whether we're walking in our neighbourhoods, in our own homes or seeking help from a police officer, there remains a fear that our bodies are at the mercy of men, both digitally and physically.

*

After more than a year of campaigning, working with legal teams and lobbying MPs, in January 2019, Gina and her family squeezed into the gallery at the House of Lords and watched as their law to make upskirting a criminal offence was passed, almost exactly as they had created it. In the eight months after the law was enacted, there was a case reported every single day. The law was catching not just 'upskirters' but pervasive sexual predators, abusers and paedophiles – 'All misogyny and sexual violence is connected,' Gina says. None of it is trivial.

In the eyes of the media, Gina became the ultimate 'girl boss'. Stories of her success were captioned with clickbait titles like 'I fought the law, and won', but that wasn't how campaigning felt. This isn't where the story ends. As soon as Gina started advocating for change, a new witch hunt against her began, this time more violent than before.

'Without the shiny feminist wrapping on it, it was the most difficult and uncomfortable period of my life,' she says. 'I will cry, but it's okay, because not crying isn't about power anymore. You can still be powerful and cry. But I received a never-ending stream of online abuse, slut shaming, rape threats, and I still get them now. Read these as if they're about someone you love . . .'

I hope you get raped you lefty fucking whore

Fucking feminist witch. Hope ur happy with your little bill getting passed fucking dirty cunt who the fuck would wanna look at your dirty fanny anyway . . . Plus, it's not gunna change fuck all people will still do it anyway hope you get fucking raped senseless

'I got these messages intensely for two years during the campaign,' Gina says. 'The majority of the abuse I got was either to do with my body, how I look, talking about me as some sort of object or just straight-up violence, trying to depict the most terrifying thing in order to stop me from continuing my work. The more I voiced opinions that weren't submissive or placating, the more I named the problem, the worse it got.'

Gina dabs at her eyes with a tissue. 'We have to stop calling them trolls because they're not. They're the men who serve you coffee, they work in your offices. They're everywhere. They're people who are so angry about a woman standing up for herself that they will threaten her with rape, and there are a lot of them.'

In 2017, a new wave of horror unleashed itself in the digital realm. As women were being deified for their beauty across platforms, mortal men wanted them brought back under control. A Reddit thread called 'deepfakes' made a list of AI augmented videos showing female celebrities' faces seamlessly imposed onto pornographic videos. The content they had meticulously created to maintain their perfect images was destroyed and defiled. The thread was eventually shut down but not before amassing almost 100,000 subscribers. Deepfakes have been banned on platforms such as Reddit, Discord and Twitter, but entire websites exist dedicated to deepfake pornography, in which people can watch 'Scarlett Johanson',

'Anne Hathaway' or 'Taylor Swift' having sex, in videos edited and published without the knowledge, far less the consent, of the women they purport to show.

It's not an issue that only affects celebrities, or those with hours and hours of video footage publicly available to manipulate. A fifteen-second Instagram story clip is enough to create a dataset of a face, which can train a machine-learning algorithm to create a deepfake of your likeness. An investigation by *Vice* found that a pornographic video can be superimposed with anyone's face for as little as \$30. Anyone with a video of you, any video of you that can be downloaded from the internet, can place your face on any other body and create content of 'you' doing whatever they wish. In most countries, this is entirely legal.

According to cybersecurity firm Sensity, deepfakes are growing exponentially, doubling every six months. As of 2019, 96 percent of deepfakes on the internet were pornography, according to analysis by AI firm DeepTrace Technologies, and virtually all pornographic deepfakes depicted women non-consensually. One investigation found that of the top thirty deepfake creators listed online from across the world, all except one were male.

The technology is advancing far quicker than lawmakers, academic researchers and medical experts can react, and the result is an ever-evolving weaponisation against the bodies of women and girls, with new levels of humiliation, objectification and degradation. Once posted, the videos can be incredibly difficult to contain and detect, and victims have few options for recourse. In the US, deepfake revenge porn is only illegal in Virginia and California, whilst in the UK, the Online Safety Bill introduced in October 2023 criminalises the sending and sharing of deepfake porn, but not the creation of the non-consensual content in the first place. In the rest of the world, no other country has banned non-consensual deepfake porn on a national level. Far from heavenly beings, we are being butchered into Frankenstein's monsters.

*

In 2020, a group of women approached the UK Revenge Porn helpline as a collective. Each one of them, they'd discovered, had had their intimate images shared online without their consent. The women all lived in the same local area and they'd all been violated on the same public board. The abuse was the result of an anonymous forum created online for their region, with the sole purpose of hunting down non-consensual images of women. Men take to the boards, with their identities hidden, and enlist the support of the community to track down and defile women's digital content. On some boards, you can't view the content unless you comment; the more you post and comment, the more community points you earn.

'One of the main boards is called Anon IBS,' Zara Ward from the Revenge Porn helpline tells me.

I look at Zara and Zara looks at me.

'Anonymous IBS?' I ask, incredulous.

'Yep.'

'Anonymous . . . irritable bowel syndrome?'

'I know, I know.' She laughs softly, both of us glad for this moment of levity. 'You can tell men made this up. Like, Jesus Christ, you guys really didn't think this through. But it's actually Anonymous Image Boards.'

On these boards, of which there are many, one man might take a creepshot of a woman he wants to hunt down in a cafe, or he might know her name, and he will ask the forum if they can find her social media accounts, her phone number, her OnlyFans content, any leaked nudes or previously shared intimate images.

'One man might say he knows her from school and offer up her social media. One man might say he dated her and share sexual images,' says Zara. 'There was one comment I saw that said, "I love seeing her boyfriend and looking him right in the eye knowing I've seen her naked." And that's stuck with me since 2020. These are people you know, who speak to your partner and speak to you. The violation is even more cutting knowing that. Because it's completely anonymous, they can say whatever they want, and it's so difficult to get content removed if you're a victim. I don't think we're that successful.'

Some of the boards have now evolved to an even more insidious level, putting the non-consensual images behind a paywall for men to subscribe to and access. There is an entire business online, like OnlyFans in reverse, of men selling non-consensual images of women's bodies for profit. And this is all on the surface-level web.

'Even if you are not a person who is actively on social media, they can hunt you down on such a local level that anyone can be at risk,' says Zara. 'Even if you've never taken sexual or nude images, once they have images or videos of your face, they can request a deepfake be made of you. As a woman, you can't win, because your body is still an object that can be traded amongst people.'

We sink and drown, or float and die.

*

Amanda once met a man in a chatroom when she was thirteen years old, much like the ones we used to play on at sleepovers. He told her she was beautiful and sexy. He convinced her to flash her breasts to the webcam, before taking a screenshot, posting the image to a porn website and threatening to send the link to all of her friends if she refused to put on a 'show'. The man continued to blackmail Amanda into performing increasingly explicit sexual acts on camera, triggering a vicious cycle of abuse. Amanda was publicly shamed, called a slut and shunned, further amplifying the violence she experienced. A few months later, Amanda committed suicide in her bedroom. The man who abused her was sentenced to thirteen years imprisonment in 2022.

The man knew what he was doing. He knew how powerful those compliments and affirmations could be in a culture that raises girls to have low self-esteem, a culture that teaches us to criticise and deconstruct our own bodies. He knew the power he'd hold in making her feel whole for a moment. Meanwhile, the same society that told Amanda her value was inherently tied to her sexuality and her ability to appease men punished her for being a sexual being and falling victim to a man's manipulations.

There are many high-profile cases in which social media is used to revictimise women and girls, blaming them for their sexual assault. In Steubenville, Ohio, a young girl was raped by two members of the high-school football team. The boys took pictures as they violated her naked body and made videos of themselves bragging about their actions. In the videos, they utterly dehumanise her, calling her a 'dead body' and laughing about how someone 'peed on her' and that she was 'so raped'. She was simply an object that existed purely for their pleasure. The assault and the boys' intentional promotion of it through social media is a clear illustration of the sexist objectification and entitlement to women's bodies. This entitlement is part of what creates an attitude accepting of horrific violence against women.

Between the fifteenth and seventeenth centuries, men devised ways to hunt witches – often through sexual humiliation or bodily degradation – and expose them in public. They would force women to sit on burning hot stools, mutilating their genitals, and cause social humiliation by stripping women's bodies and searching for the 'witch's' mark.

For Steubenville's Jane Doe, the witch hunt continued online, as students following the events on social media called her a 'whore' and egged the boys on with their comments and their laughter. She faced death threats, was consistently blamed for the violence enacted upon her and was chastised for 'ruining the promising young futures' of the boys who violated her. In the media, and in court, she was repeatedly victim-blamed. Judge Thomas Lipps, who presided over the case, told the perpetrators and the young people present 'to have discussions about how you talk to your friends, how you record things on social media' – implying that they should be more careful about how they document their crimes, rather than not violating girls in the first place.

This horrific story is not a rare occurrence sensationalised by the media. It happens more often than we think. To experience violence is to experience womanhood. To experience violence online is to exist as a woman with an internet connection. Just existing as a woman online can be enough to inspire abuse.

*

Cyberbullying has been defined as an 'emerging public health problem' for teenage girls. In one study of thirteen- to seventeen-year-olds, a quarter said they frequently observed cyberviolence against women and girls. More than a third of those who had witnessed violence said they did nothing, and whilst girls reported more active responses to help the victim, both girls and boys normalised and even justified this behaviour. The result of all of these forms of violence, both online and off, is to maintain patriarchal control.

There was a time when the promise of feminism online felt like it could be kept. That the notion of a brave new world was truly underway. In the era of #MeToo, it felt, for a moment, as if change was actually possible. But as popular feminism increased and, arguably, achieved little by way of widespread political or structural change, so did popular misogyny and the mainstreaming of sexist attitudes and behaviours. The backlash to the online feminist movement feels even worse than ever before. It feels as if we took one step forward and two steps back.

'We're seeing representations of different types of women, we're hearing the word "feminism" more often, we go on Instagram and there's countless pieces of content that are like, "Get it, girl!" On the surface, it feels like things are changing. I think that has created a false sense of progression in everyone's minds,' says Gina. 'In actuality, there wasn't legislative change or structural change behind any of that representational politics, or that narrative. The actual structural work that we need to be doing in the collective wasn't happening, whilst we're all being like, "Woo, girlboss!" online.'

As the digital era flourished and feminism gained new visibility both on and offline, the manosphere evolved – separatist men's groups that both defined and brought together incels (involuntarily celibate men). Their ideology is an internet phenomenon where views, statements and language radicalise easier and faster because they are anonymous and rarely face consequences. The incels' hatred for women stems largely from their inability to find sexual partners. They romanticise traditional gender roles and believe they should be able to control and restrict women's sexuality in order to subordinate them and alleviate their own sense of deprivation. Somewhat ironically, incels form communities around their hatred of women, whilst simultaneously feeling entitled to our bodies.

As such, incels resent feminism for its power in moving women away from traditional gender roles. Their 'rules' for women are closely tied to an androcentric beauty standard that requires a very specific display of submissive and conservative femininity. Women, according to incels, must be clean and pretty and meticulously groomed in a way men do not need to be. She must shave her legs, maintain a slim figure, halt almost all natural bodily functions and be seen to be putting effort into her appearance. Sound familiar?

It may sound innocuous, but the rise of the anti-feminist movement, incel culture and its infiltration into the mainstream through high-profile speakers such as Andrew Tate is fuelling a worrying return to a world that feels entitled to police women's bodies and impose a rigid beauty ideal intent on enforcing subjugation. Although largely existing online, incels have been associated with several terror attacks, murdering more than 100 people over the past decade. The proliferation of the discourse online has normalised a violent and hateful rhetoric towards women and their bodies. In newspaper comment sections, social networking profiles, blogs and forums, women are repeatedly subjected to harassment, insults and online abuse – usually tied to their appearance or a graphic description of what a man would or wouldn't do to her body. The rise of popular misogyny has birthed a new era of abuse by way of revenge porn, deepfakes, public sexual humiliation, the broadcasting of sexual violence, the reduction of women to biological organisms with a reproductive function, the extreme objectification of women and their general degradation and dehumanisation. What we now see is what research director at the Center for Democracy and Technology Dhanaraj Thakur describes to the *Washington Post* as 'a perverse democratisation of the ability to cause harm', whilst the current tools for identifying and combating this abuse simply can't keep up.

'I believe that social media platforms don't solve the problem of abuse against women because of the engagement they receive,' says Gina. 'They make a huge amount of money from abuse online. And then they make more money from us organising against the abuse that is happening to us online. Then, they host events about equipping us as influencers and creators against abuse, and people pay to go. They should be free every week because we're being traumatised.'

*

Part of the power of online abuse is the cultural gaslighting that occurs alongside it – the refusal to acknowledge the violence as real because it takes place in a virtual world. We're told to simply ignore the threats that confront us every day online – the violence that threatens our careers, our political involvement, our ability to speak, our psychological wellbeing and our freedom.

Authorities treat the internet like a fantasyland. Comments such as 'it's only online, it's not real', 'just ignore it' or 'just log off' are rife in response to abuse – not only minimising the experience but placing the onus on the victim to build barricades around themselves in order to avoid violence, making their world smaller whilst their aggressor faces no consequence. To stay off the internet is akin to asking someone not to see their family – our digital lives are inseparable from our physical selves. Shockingly, minors face the same response, even when they are being sexually exploited by adult men online. The police responded to appeals for help from Amanda Todd and her family with: 'If Amanda does not stay off the internet and/or take steps to protect herself online . . . there is only so much we as the police can do.'

When I tried to leave my abusive partner, he threatened to send explicit images of me to my family, agent and editors to blackmail me into staying. He would call me countless times from withheld numbers and then show up outside my house if I didn't respond. He would monitor my social media posts and rage against a bare shoulder or 'sexy' pose. He contacted my father through Instagram to slut shame me and share intimate details about my sex life. Despite the bruises on my body and the fact I had nowhere I could live, an emergency restraining order took months to pass. I felt paranoid for months, I still do. I feel watched, I feel scared writing this, I worry about this book's publication, about how he might respond. I feel stifled and I censor myself, even now.

British organisation Women's Aid found that 75 per cent of women were concerned that police don't know how to respond to online abuse, whilst 12 per cent had reported to police and hadn't been helped at all. When the majority of police officers are men, just as 85 per cent of the founders of tech start-ups are male, a lack of understanding of the level of violence women face on these platforms, and how to police them, is unsurprising.

'I've started retreating from social media in the last six months,' Gina tells me. 'It got to the point after seven years when it wasn't worth it. I can understand why women retreat because none of the safety nets that we have are working for victims and survivors. The institutions that are meant to support us, like policing, are perpetrating the issue as much as the average guy is. We can't run into the arms of people who are the ultimate cocktail of misogyny and white supremacy and expect to be held and looked after by them. No wonder we're retreating and making our worlds a little bit smaller. That's the only recourse that seems to be available to us.'

Even in our response to cyberviolence we are expected to adopt a submissive position, to retreat. Women who post about their abuse are subjected to yet more abuse. Women who respond to their abuse with the same vehemence are accused of 'bullying' or failing to take the high road. We sink and drown or float and die.

Feminist writer Jessica Valenti told Amanda Hess in 'Women Aren't Welcome Here' that she has stopped promoting her speaking events publicly, enlisted security for her public appearances, signed up for a service to periodically scrub the web of her private information, invested in a post-office box, and begun periodically culling her Facebook friends list in an attempt to filter out readers with ulterior motives. But not only is there the tangible, financial and temporal costs of the constant threat of violence, there's also the emotional trauma. 'When people say you should be raped and killed for years on end, it takes a toll on your soul,' she said. Whenever a male stranger approaches her at a public event, 'the hairs on the back of my neck stand up'.

'We interviewed 10,000 women and girls about safe spaces,' said Claire Barnett, former executive director of UN Women UK. 'One thing that stuck out to me was the extent to which we modify every little movement that we make, just trying to stay safe and survive. People were changing the way that they sneeze, or the way that they clap, constantly modulating their physical body to appear dainty and unassuming. Women with big boobs were really hunching over in order to not attract dangerous attention. Sexual harassment is a spectrum, from death-causing violence to little things every day that make you feel constantly unsafe. It makes you feel like you're on hyper-alert all the time, and that's really not good for your nervous system. You cannot have the same voice in society if you're constantly hyper-aware of your safety.'

There are multiple lenses through which we are filtered and filter ourselves – the male gaze, the Eurocentric gaze, the cosmetic gaze, the digital gaze and, finally, the self-censoring, silencing gaze we experience as a result of rampant violence. The prevalence of cyber violence only compounds the very real fear and discomfort that is felt routinely, as a result of everyday sexism – the common disrespect, shaming and discrediting of women in all areas of life. We learn to negotiate – to constantly calculate safety and visibility – to accept that there will always be a price to pay, a penalty for daring to exist publicly as a woman.

*

We had hoped that digital spaces would provide a utopia free from the violence of the old world, one in which everyone had a voice. We had hoped that our current social hierarchies based on stereotypes and outdated systems could be erased, that the witch hunts would end. That did not happen. The inequalities that have structured our corporeal life for centuries followed us online. Beauty standards heightened and technology became a new weapon with which to subjugate women and minorities.

A study from the Center for Democracy and Technology revealed that women of colour who run for office in the USA are over five times more likely to be targeted with 'violent abuse' than their white counterparts. Research director Dhanaraj Thakur told the *Washington Post* that this abuse is part of the reason government institutions continue to uphold the 'unrepresentative status quo'.

Black UK MP Diane Abbott said of the abuse she faced in 2017: 'I've had death threats, I've had people tweeting that I should be hung if "they could find a tree big enough to take the fat bitch's weight" . . . I've had rape threats . . . and n*****, over and over and over again.'

This kind of hostility is a key pillar in maintaining patriarchal control, and the sexism, misogyny and objectification that comes alongside it. For women of colour, the vitriol is compounded by racist abuse. For disabled women, the violence is compounded by ableism. Asian women who are outspoken are often targeted for not fitting into the stereotype of a 'submissive Asian woman', and Black women are particularly vulnerable to cyberflashing and racialised slurs.

You don't need to experience violence to feel its effects. In a culture of violence against women, all women suffer. The attacks against prominent or hyper-visible women are aimed at disciplining all of us, just as the witch trials demonised divergent women in order to strike fear into every woman and girl. In this culture of gendered violence, we are all at risk. When one woman is attacked, we all are attacked. That is how control functions – you don't have to experience violent repercussions, you just have to think that you might.

Over a century after women won the right to vote, our participation in public life is being threatened again. There is a valid fear that the increasing levels of online abuse against female politicians, particularly women of colour, creates a deterrent, a hostile environment, for those who wish to forge a career in public service. The result is an attack on democracy, one that is also causing female journalists to self-censor according to a survey by UNESCO, which showed that Black, Indigenous, Jewish, Arab and lesbian women journalists experienced both the highest rates and most severe impacts of online violence. This not only poses a potential long-term threat to the representation of women in the sectors that control our day-to-day lives but also continues to deepen societal inequality between genders.

'I think the online abuse I get makes younger women of colour very hesitant about entering the public debate and going into politics. And, after all, why should you have to pay that price for being in the public space?' Diane Abbott said in an Amnesty International interview.

One study noted that offensive comments aimed at women online often 'displayed a preoccupation with physical appearance and suggested that a woman's worth and value lies in her sexual appeal to men'. The hostile, sexist abuse is strategic in nature. It is violence designed to enforce traditional feminine beauty ideals and stereotypes, and shame women who fall short. The implicit message, therefore, is that women should align themselves with traditional images of beauty in order to be safe, heard and respected, or be forced into silence and subjugation. To show yourself as non-compliant, as unwilling to adhere to the norms – or to fail as a result of race, disability or age – makes you defective, sub-human, a witch.

Whilst the medium is new, the message sits within a far older tradition – one which insists that women are inferior, that our primary value relates to our appearance or our sexuality, that we do not belong in the public sphere, and that those women who dare to speak up should be put back in their place or reprimanded in public.

'From 2015 to now, I've had stalking cases with the police,' says Gina. 'This is why I started to retreat, because as a result of having a public platform, I now have multiple live police cases. There hasn't really been a period of time for longer than maybe three months for the last eight years in which I haven't had a guy trying to terrify me through stalking or harassment.'

It isn't only well-known or influential women who are experiencing enough online abuse to consider quitting social media entirely. A YouGov poll commissioned by the dating app Bumble showed almost half of women aged eighteen to twenty-four received unsolicited sexual images within the last year. In gaming communities, commentators have argued that the 'misogynist backlash' is so virulent it constitutes a form of terrorism. A 2023 survey of 2,000 British women by social media app Communia found that over a third of women had experienced online abuse, 47 per cent of women aged sixteen to twenty-four had been victims of cyberflashing, and 40 per cent of gen Z and millennial women are turning away from mainstream social platforms in fear of their safety and well-being.

The tactics used by trolls, incels and misogynists online can be viewed as 'silencing strategies', designed to remove visible or audible women from a conversation or debate, or discourage them from engaging in public spaces altogether. As a result of inaction and lack of hope in the systems designed to protect them, it often works, with many women reducing their online interactions, leaving platforms, or going offline completely. Pew found that from 2000 to 2005, the percentage of internet users who participated in online chats and discussion groups dropped from 28 percent to 17 percent, 'entirely because of women's fall off in participation'. But for many of us, staying offline isn't an option. The digital realm is essential in modern life – in finding communities, making a living and connecting with loved ones. If drastic steps aren't taken to address our cyber safety soon, many women will go permanently offline to avoid online abuse, the social impact of which would be catastrophic, not only due to the effects of social isolation but also the impact on our democracy.

'While witch hunts were used to violently and systematically coerce women to conform with the requirements of the emerging industrial capitalism, online misogyny is using digital violence to prohibit women from participating in building the forthcoming technological future,' Professor Eugenia Siapera writes in *Online Misogyny as Witch Hunt: Primitive Accumulation in the Age of Techno-capitalism.* 'Any resolution of the digital violence to which women are subjected is likely to necessitate radical ways of redistributing power and resources rather than mere policy changes by social media corporations.'

'The issue of cyberviolence against women is prevalent and it's urgent, but it's not being recognised as such because it would change everything if they recognised it for the problem that it actually is,' agrees Gina. 'If women felt safe in the online space, there would be a complete sea change in the way that the collective mobilisation of communities happens and I think they know that. Women are phenomenal at organising and phenomenal at bearing witness to each other, affirming each other and creating things that we need. You can't retain a patriarchal space that reflects all the horrendous systems we have in society if you solve the problem of women being abused online, because then we'd actually have the safety, tools and freedom to create change.'

Just as women have historically been banished from public spaces because of their gender, and just as many women still face restrictions across the physical realm, they now face censorship, ostracisation, harassment and violence online.

*

We know the stories of Gina, Amanda and of Jane Doe in Steubenville because their experiences led them to take action in court, or to take their own lives. We know what happened to Leslie Jones because it happened on a world stage. I know what happened to Willow because she was brave enough to open up to me for the benefit of this project. But many women and girls around us who experience this type of violence feel unable to confide in someone – their stories are hidden.

We must also acknowledge that many of the high-profile media cases surrounding abuse depict young, white, middle-class and assumed to be straight and cis-gendered victims. This emphasises a certain archetype of woman who is viewed as the closest approximation to the 'perfect' victim but sidelines the stories of the most marginalised and most vulnerable.

I was lucky in my experience of abuse that my family, my editors and my agent were understanding and supportive. They went above and beyond to show up for me, to tell me that it wasn't my fault and that they thought no less of me because of what that man had tried to do. I was fortunate that I didn't have compounding factors contributing to the threat I faced.

'We've had people come to our helpline fearful of the ramifications of their intimate images being leaked or shared,' says Zara. 'Women fear physical violence, cultural shaming or ostracisation from their homes and communities. Intimate image abuse is a horrific experience for anyone, but if you're part of the LGBTQ community and you haven't come out to your family yet, or if you face particular cultural or religious shame, this content could really jeopardise somebody's life. We've seen teachers whose careers have been ruined, foster parents who have had their foster children taken away from them, all because someone else has decided to violate their consent.'

Our entire notion of a 'perfect' victim is inherently intertwined with our beauty standard – of beauty's affiliation with virtues such as purity and truth, and its association with wealth and respectability. Beauty, ultimately, defines who gets to be seen, who gets to be heard, who gets to be believed and who gets to be human.

*

Our beauty culture in and of itself is a form of coercion, a form of violence. Our value is directly linked to our ability to obey, to master our appearance and constrict ourselves into a narrow ideal. The paradox of being raised under a sexualised male gaze whilst experiencing male sexual violence creates a psychological trap in which crucial thoughts around safety and self-protection sit almost in parallel priority to appearing attractive at all times. When jogging down a street in the evening, I'll often find myself fearful of the man behind me before wondering if my ass looks good from his angle. Should I cross the street to avoid him? How can I subtly reach for my keys? Does my face look red and sweaty? Are my hips swaying in a way that turns him on?

The beauty standard and entitlement to women's bodies is a form of violence and psychological warfare that is harming women and girls every day. We are pressured into taking pride in our appearance and then blamed when we are harassed or assaulted. Sexual agency around beauty politics and image sharing are enmeshed in rape culture. 'What were you wearing? Did you have your hair in a ponytail? You know that makes you easier to grab? Why did you post that photo if you didn't want attention? You can't have it both ways, you know.'

For the first century and a half, witchcraft was seen as a collective practice, something that women did when they met in groups, when they formed networks and bonds. Up until the witch hunts, the word gossip was akin to 'godparent' - and it was the name given to the woman who helped a new mother through birth. The name, a noun at the time, was given to acknowledge the powerful bond shared in that intimate space between women, between new mothers and early modern healers and midwives. But the patriarchy began to fear this power. They began to fear the wisdom that was passed through these networks, the bodily autonomy and awareness that could be understood from centuries of intuition and herbal medicine. They began to fear the power of the bonds between women, of the networks they could create and the communities they could corral. Gossip, the noun and verb, which had come to stand for female friendship and affection, was demonised. Witchcraft, in Western contexts, became about the elimination of female power in the face of the patriarchy. Laws were made against women who gossiped or held meetings between other women in public or private spaces, women were kept captive in their homes, and breaking the rules put them at risk of being accused of being a witch. In a cruel twist of the knife, they were then pressured to snitch on their sisters, friends, mothers and daughters. The male power system had succeeded in turning something beautiful into something evil. Centuries later, we are still pitted against one another. Those bonds, once fractured, have still not healed. We are still trapped, psychologically, financially, subconsciously. Gossip and the sharing of women's bodily truths, are still shamed into silence.

'In our research on safe spaces, we spoke to a lot of older women who were really struggling to empathise with younger women's experiences. Obviously, this is entirely convenient because it fragments that movement, and allows patriarchy to flourish,' says Claire Barnett. 'You'll get young women saying they are sick and tired of being catcalled, and older women saying, "Oh, well, you don't know how lucky you are." When we asked more questions, it was that actually their social value was linked to being objectified in the eyes of men. They were saying that as they got older, they felt quite worthless in society. We are told that adhering to the beauty standard is part of you staying safe and having value, and that if you're unsafe, it's your fault, because you didn't stick to those constrictions well enough.'

As in the witch trials, women are turned against one another, young against old. We are constantly towing the line of safety, even if it means punishing ourselves and each other.

As in wider beauty culture, you either comply and end up perpetuating the ideals that harm you, or you don't adhere and you are punished for your ugliness. The beauty standard, and so many aspects of our beauty culture, operate as both tangible and symbolic forms of violence that impact women's lives across the world. There's the obvious physical violence intrinsic in the performance of beauty, through the cutting and shaving of the female body to fit social standards, but there's also the self-policing, self-surveilling violence we encounter countless times a day.

To be visible as a woman is to expect to be objectified and harrassed. To exist as a woman is to prepare for violence. Sometimes, it is to be told to enjoy it. It is to self-surveil, to self-monitor, to self-censor – not only your words and behaviours but your hairstyle, your outfit and your body shape, in an intricate balance between visibility, social value and the threat of violence. We get ready in our sexy outfits but wear something baggy over the top so we can step out of our front door. We fight for visibility and then hate the way we are perceived. We cut our bodies apart and tell ourselves it's self-care.

*

If women fear being visible, being audible and being honest in conversations and debate, our digital worlds become an all-encompassing patriarchy. We all suffer if everyone does not have a seat at the table, and not only are these platforms largely run, built, owned and operated by men – they are largely dictated by men.

Participation in digital life is necessary for participation in the workplace, in society, in our ability to create change. It can be easy to dismiss the violence that forms the background noise of our lives, to underestimate the toll that it can take. We don't deserve to have our bodies dissected, our worth devalued, our images disseminated, our freedoms dictated, our sexuality demonised, our sorority destroyed. We don't deserve to be reminded constantly that we are under threat – online or off.

When we shut our mouths, when we are silenced, we internalise the violence against us. We find ourselves crying at the news, every woman's story feeling like our own. We feel ashamed for what has happened to us. We take on the burden of the violence and our perpetrators run free. This is not an issue of individual tweets, posts or images being used against women, but an epidemic of violence that makes the internet a wholly unsafe and inequitable place.

Women who do not conform are still persecuted for their differences. Women are still routinely sexually shamed and humiliated on public platforms. Women are still demeaned and not taken seriously. Our bodies are still up for debate. Our freedoms are still not truly ours. We are still stereotyped. The glass ceiling remains intact. Gender parity has not been achieved. We are still fighting a lose/lose battle: to sink and drown or float and die.

Beauty is its own form of witchcraft – of rituals, of healing, of transformation. It was seized from our hands, poisoned and sold back to us as something devolved from what it once meant. They took the knowledge gathered about our bodies, the wisdom that went unwritten, passed down through experience and intuition, and they burned it at the source. They targeted generational bonds – turning young against old. They stopped women from talking honestly to one another, poisoning female friendship and making enemies of our sisters.

After all of that pressure and poisonous perfection, they still shun us, find a way to burn us. That our fight is over, that feminism is done, that we have progressed to the point of complacency, is part of the propaganda. Beauty is both a blessing and a curse – glory and terror. Let us not warm ourselves by the fires set to burn our bodies.

How can we create a more beautiful future for women and girls?

'It's going to be up to us to make the future more beautiful. It's going to take individuals standing up and rejecting the beauty standards, rejecting body trends, for people in positions of privilege to take a stand against airbrushing and photoshopping. It goes back to the concept of sisterhood – to make sure we are working with each other rather than against more marginalised groups. It's making sure that when we're talking about body liberation, we're talking about everybody, rather than just the liberation of a few.

It's for all for us to think critically, to act carefully, and to think about the wider purpose of why we're here. We're not here to be beautiful.'

Sophie Bellamy,
founder of Normal Bodies

Conclusion

Beyond Beauty: A New Way to See

This is my twisted fantasy:

I am a beautiful person. I no longer think about my body or the way I look, but when I see my reflection in the mirror I smile. I eat until my belly is full and sometimes I give in to cravings because I deserve to enjoy the little things. I don't feel guilty anymore. I have the energy to *live*. I read and watch and listen to things that make me think, that make me laugh and that make me feel inspired. The media loves women. I move my body for fun and I don't care who's watching. I have no idea how much I weigh and taking up space is not my concern. People compliment me on my soul and I let their words soak in. I smile a lot. I no longer see girls with their little scars in places they hope no one will notice. I have abundant opportunities coming my way. I tell my friends I love them. When the sun sets at night, I go for long walks under the stars. I feel safe. I put my phone down and I don't think about it for hours. I'm excited to get older. When I get into bed, a sense of self-loathing does not wash over me. I don't punish my body anymore. I don't lie to myself about anything.

*

Over the course of the research for this book, I interviewed over a hundred women and at the end of every single conversation, I asked the question: 'How can we create a more beautiful future for women and girls?' In other words, what is your fantasy? How can we fix the problem of our toxic beauty culture? Some of the answers have been collected and lie nestled between the chapters of this book, but a lot of the time I was met with silence.

So often it felt impossible to think of a response, of any power we have to change the system we are in, of any scope to dream of a different world, of any hope that there could ever be one. Digital beauty culture is entrenched into our skin, into our sinew, our muscles and our flesh. It feels all-encompassing, all-consuming. The more you invest into beauty, into technology, the more consumed you become. Disengaging from this culture in a capitalist, patriarchal society can feel like trying to wean yourself off of air.

When there is no precedent for a brighter, more equitable space, it can feel impossible to fathom alternatives. As Gerda Lerner wrote in *The Creation of the Patriarchy*: 'It is this feature of male hegemony which has been most damaging to women and has ensured their subordinate status for millennia . . . The picture is false . . . as we know, but women's progress through history has been marked by their struggle against this disabling distortion.'

Even our visions for the future have been filtered through a distorting lens. In the pursuit of power and material gain, our culture has blinded us to the diverse array of beauty that exists in every individual, relegating us to a sense of inadequacy and self-doubt. The goal of feminism was to create a society in which we are free from the suffocating expectations placed upon us, to simultaneously collapse and expand our experience of beauty, and to see the world with eyes anew. However, this goal has not been achieved. The feminist movement has opened up countless avenues but it has not succeeded in removing the inherent feminine obligation to conform to conventional beauty standards. We have more freedom than ever before but, according to the data, our relationship with beauty culture is only getting worse. Only recently have we started to explore alternative ideas of beauty, or even the possibility of divesting from it altogether. To exist as a woman right now feels like a constant battle – one fought inside and out. It is to fight between compliance and conformity, rejection and responsibility. It's to spend far too much time trapped in that loop, and then to feel resentful at yet another form of labour you're forced to endure.

In truth – and this is my final confession – writing this book has been one of the hardest things I have ever done. I have spent over a year and a half of my life fixated on beauty, falling ever deeper into the rabbit hole, and my self-esteem has never been lower. The more I immersed myself in the research, the more I fell into this digital realm and the more my sense of self fragmented. In immersing myself in this industry, in all of the ways in which it affects women's lives, I have felt myself picking apart my own. I became obsessive, hyper-self-aware, overly self-conscious and began to surveil myself from every possible angle. By the time it came to have my author photos taken for the inside jacket of this book, I couldn't think of anything worse than being confronted by my own image.

I set out on this mission with a list of questions, wanting to know how I might balance my feminism with my experience of beauty. I think, after the year and a half spent working on this book, and in the twenty-eight that I have now been alive, I have come to the conclusion that the more we can resist these structures – the more we can say no, the more we can embrace our natural features and functions – the better the world will be for all women. I have come so close to booking appointments, I have requested consultations I never attended and fought with myself over my desire to be beautiful. In my refusal, I have worried that I may be resigning myself to a life of ugliness, a life that is inherently more difficult, one of less visibility. But no sooner do those thoughts form in my head than I am reminded of my privilege. My refusal to participate in aspects of beauty culture will not leave me unsafe or marginalised in the same way it would for many – and perhaps that's what makes it necessary. It is not on oppressed groups to bear the burden of our collective subjugation whilst those with wealth and privilege use their cheat codes to game the system. We must, instead, use the relative power we do have to tear the system apart. To disrupt the very fabric of the code. That sounds like a near-impossible feat, I understand that. But we have too much at stake to get complacent; we can't afford for things to stay the same.

At times, I have been overwhelmed with the sense that this issue is far too great and intricate for me to untangle. I felt angry. I felt let down. But no sooner would I resign myself to these feelings than I would have another interview – another meeting with another woman who had agreed to share her story in the service of sorority. Those conversations were a lifeline. I have never felt more inspired by women and their power, intellect and passion – by their ability to show up for one another, to articulate their feelings and sit with vulnerability. I have never felt more seen, understood, inspired or energised as I have when in conversations for this book. Creating spaces for sharing and solidarity has opened up parts of myself that I never knew existed. I have laughed in these meetings, cried on Zoom, shared parts of myself with strangers that I never thought I would reveal, listened as women told stories they had kept suppressed for so long.

I opened up this book with a series of confessions and I close it with a vision for the future that seems so ludicrously simple and yet so out of reach. To be a woman is the most violent thing I will ever experience and yet I wouldn't want to be anything else. To have access to that depth of sorority is the single most beautiful thing I could imagine. I realised in those countless hours spent listening and sharing why the patriarchy has been so fixated on keeping women apart – on demonising gossip, pitching old against young, turning us against one another in competitions of beauty. It is because when we come together, we realise that we don't need beauty or technology as a new form of spirituality; we don't need to spend money or harm ourselves or starve ourselves or fixate on our features. What we need is the same as ever – each other. Touch, connection, affirmation, support. We, as a collective, have the power to create a more beautiful future for us all.

The issue is systemic and structural – and that is something we should never lose sight of. The intersecting forces of the patriarchy, capitalism, racism, ableism, ageism, classism, colourism and fatphobia are directly responsible for our experience of beauty culture and they won't be neutralised overnight. What we can contribute to is our collective wellbeing. We have immense power within our communities, both online and off.

As bell hooks insists, 'feminist ideology should not encourage (as sexism has done) women to believe they are powerless'. It should instead 'clarify for women the powers they exercise daily and show them ways these powers can be used to resist sexist domination and exploitation'.

I've tried to summarise and synthesise the lessons I've learnt from the women in this book – the teachers and the tastemakers, deities and disciples. Below are the powers I do believe we have – the ones we exercise daily to build both our physical and virtual realities. Consider this a new gospel, a hymn sheet we can all sing from to create a more beautiful future for ourselves and each other.

Centre women – sorority is self-care

The biggest and most important lesson I have learnt, the true answer to all of our questions, lies in our collective action, in our shared reckoning and response. Yes, this is a book about beauty and technology and the ways in which our lives are made more difficult by our current culture, but it is also a story of the beauty inherent in womanhood – found at sleepovers and in nightclub bathrooms, in salons and shared spaces. It's about the moments of beauty we find with each other, about connection, sorority and sisterhood.

We cannot expect a single woman to shoulder the burden of the patriarchy alone, but with our arms around each other we can make that burden lighter. Whether it's your sisters, your friends, your flatmates, your cousins, your daughters or nieces – you possess the power to change the settings for them, to render an image that's safer and more beautiful than it was before.

When Audre Lorde wrote that oft-instagrammed quote: 'Caring for myself is not self-indulgence, it is self-preservation, and that is an act of political warfare,' she didn't mean that self-care should be selfish or a form of self-flagellation, that it should be an overpriced moisturiser or a painful procedure. Self-care, in reality, is supposed to coincide with community care. It means taking time for yourself so that you can better support those around you – resting so that you can be a part of the revolution, helping other women with childcare, prepping meals for those in need or providing a voice for the voiceless. We, as women, win and lose together. Sorority is self-care.

We can't spend our way out of beauty culture, out of self-loathing or harmful algorithms. Not even billionaires can escape. What we need is to focus our collective bandwidth on something more meaningful – to care and support one another where our systems don't.

The actions can be small. Smile at other women, hold space for other women, assume they're feeling just as vulnerable and tired and in need of connection as you are. Default to allies over enemies and recreate the sisterhood of the nightclub bathroom in every interaction you have – it is vital for our survival in this world.

Make decisions with your sisters, daughters, nieces and friends in mind. Rather than acting in the interest of self, be the woman you needed to see growing up and try, as much as possible, not to add to the noise that is already so loud that says: beauty is pain; you must spend money to be pretty; you are defective by default. Act for the collective, dress for the female gaze, be the woman that a younger you would have beamed at in the street – wear colour, use glitter, have fun. Find what feels desirable to you and return beauty to the realm of self-expression once more.

'It's easy to get this feeling of, well, the system exists and everybody's a part of the system. Why should I have to be the one up on the cross?' Eleanor Barnes told me, and I understood. 'My friends seem to be happy; it doesn't seem too dangerous – that's the mindset that I fell into and that so many of my friends have fallen into. But it's that mindset that creates the entire culture we're suffering in.'

Of course, it is easier to shout empowerment from the rooftops whilst we continue to make ourselves happy at the detriment of everyone else. To say 'go girl!' instead of unpacking the feelings of discomfort in our stomachs. When the world feels like it's ending, it is natural to rely on nihilism and a dark sense of humour and say, 'We might as well be beautiful, right?' But the quest for beauty is not translating into a more beautiful future for us all. It does not bring us into increased safety, sexual agency, nourishment, happiness, mental stability, freedom or any real financial reward.

There are outliers, of course – women who have managed to tick one item off the list, but often at the expense of everything else. If those who make millions, or billions, are not free, if those deemed the most beautiful, influential and divine are not free, if those who claim to be empowered are not free – the way we are currently operating is not working. It is an illusion, a filter over the reality we survive each day.

It is easy to underestimate how much of this behaviour has been coded into us by systems put in place long before we were born. We must give ourselves grace whilst understanding that it is our responsibility to decode our internal software, to confront our privilege and to explore uncomfortable truths about our own role in perpetuating the standards that oppress us. Be mindful of intersecting forms of oppression and how they might amplify someone's experience of beauty culture. Harness your privileges and use them to the betterment of the collective – do what you can to share resources and platforms with those who may not have access. Take time to listen to other women, hear their stories and understand – find points of sorority and find areas to learn. Believe women. Believe each other. Believe in yourself.

Feminism, ultimately, is not about women making choices, it's about liberation from the patriarchy. It is radical and political and, at times, not very pretty. This is a rally cry for a true collective mindset – one that we need to live and breathe – and the creation of a bigger picture that's more beautiful than any 'quick fix' can make you feel.

If it feels too big at times, then that is when we practise self-care in its truest form. Have empathy with yourself; if you fail or stumble or relapse or break, don't quit. The path to liberation is not always linear, but I promise that if we all take even the smallest of actions, it will help to set us free.

'There's something transformative in the collective, about the idea that there are lots of different women across lots of different identity lines who have realised that they can't win, and therefore don't even try to abide by those rules and systems anymore,' says Gina Martin. 'Even though we will all get punished for it in one way or another, there's something wonderful and galvanising in the collective realisation that the entire game is rigged against us all.'

We need to combine the collectivism of second-wave feminism of the 1960s and 70s with the individual responsibility of modern movements. Instead of channelling your focus into the creation of a shrine for the self, ask how you can take action in service of others – in service of the sisterhood. This is not to return to the troubled trope of a singular female identity but a call to remember that we have more in common than we realise – that we share more suffering that we know, and that we win and lose together. There is a mythological girl reborn in all of us, who will continue to reincarnate until we create tangible change. Our inter-generational goal should always be, as bell hooks says, to 'rebirth the girl within' into a world where she is eternally worthy, not forever young.

Re-immerse yourself in reality

'I'm running out of battery,' we say, before taking that separate part of our brain and placing it down on the bedside table. The part that isn't soft. Metallic – not in the same way that blood tastes but in the way that feels cold to the touch. It isn't the precious part that keeps everything running – not quite. Rather, the part that houses all of those peripheral memories, the images you'd otherwise forget. It remembers our conversations, our best ideas and those of all humans ever to exist. Now, none of us are separate from our devices long enough to know what it feels like to just live. They mediate our existence at all times. We don't even look at anything anymore. We just take pictures.

I realise that it is not realistic to conclude that we should all delete our social media apps and throw our phones into a fountain à la Andy from *The Devil Wears Prada*. To do so would require huge amounts of privilege and would mean disengaging from vital elements of our society and culture. However, we can make a conscious effort to reject the artificial sphere and immerse ourselves back in reality – constantly reminding ourselves what it is to be and *feel* real.

Whilst we should curate our social feeds and follow accounts that better represent our reality, paying careful attention to what makes us feel good online, so much of this work needs to be done away from the digital: in our everyday interactions, thoughts and actions. Studies have shown that just three days away from social media improves girls' body image and boosts self-compassion. We don't have to opt out completely, but it is essential that we schedule in breaks in order to cultivate a life for ourselves away from the environments controlled and curtailed by companies who do not have our best interests at heart.

In re-immersing ourselves in reality, we also need to recognise that not everything has to be beautiful all of the time. Sometimes things are difficult or uncomfortable or just 'fine', and that's okay. You do not owe anyone perfect, and you don't owe anyone pretty. Remove the glossy filter that smooths out any negativity, resist the feminine urge to lighten the mood or to make others comfortable, practise radical honesty with yourself and with others, and, most importantly, don't be afraid to say no.

When I interviewed eating disorder therapist Olivia Rowe, she spoke of an activity she encourages patients to do as part of their treatment. I think it is something we could all benefit from. 'It sounds so simple, but just look out the window, look at a busy street or sit on the bus and look around you,' she said. 'Look at all the different body shapes there are. With every third person you see, notice how your body is similar or different to theirs. Often, what you're doing online is comparing your body to the same perfected images over and over again – that is not a reflection of reality. Make an effort to consciously open your eyes to all of the different body shapes and types of beauty that exist in the world around you.'

I'm reminded of the summer I spent sunbathing with Eliza and Sienna – how seeing their bodies at ease allowed me to be at ease with my own. In times of insecurity, I try to decentre myself and prioritise creating that feeling for the women around me – as much as I am able, to give them permission to be at ease in themselves by modelling comfort myself.

In these moments, I also try to reflect on the miracle that is my existence – the reality of the improbability that we exist at all, because therein lies a poetic truth. You are made of stardust. Every atom within us, every intricate strand of DNA, traces its origin to the heart of distant galaxies. We have a shared heritage with the universe – an undeniable, cosmic beauty that courses through our veins. As Annabelle said, you're an ancestor in the making as well as a representation of faces and bodies cherished over millennia. The sheer fact that you have a body and a beating heart is mystical and magical and miraculous in and of itself. I urge you to use it. Do what you can to embrace reality – go swimming, sunbathe, seek out spaces where women's bodies exist as they always have done, as they always should. Cover your digital and physical walls in images of your friends, of your loved ones, of yourself – smiling and happy – and immerse yourself in the beauty.

Relegate 'Beauty' to the background of your life

On the eve of my twenty-eighth birthday, just as I was submitting this book for publication, the age of indie sleaze had returned from its short orbit around the trend cycle. My Saturn return is pending and I have now lived long enough to see the most treasured parts of myself targeted and torn down, whilst the body I was once bullied for is back in style. There is always a new feature to fixate on, a correction to covet, but the turbulence that used to have me struggling to get off the floor is now a faint oscillation, a steady wave in the background of my life. I have learnt to let it swirl around me, to stand in the centre and look, to really look. I have started to form my own core in the eye of the storm.

That doesn't mean I'm exempt from the inevitable pressures of existing as a woman in a culture that positions beauty as ultimate value, and I won't pretend beauty is unimportant – just as I didn't with the girls on the Dollis Valley estate. But it does mean that I am making a concerted effort to reduce its prevalence in my life – to not get swept up in the cycle of self-loathing.

In order to do so, we must work collectively to relegate beauty to the background of our lives – the elevator music, not the motor that keeps us in a constant up and down. We can do this in many ways. As much as the problem may seem too immense to tackle, it has been proven that we have so much power to make a difference to one another in our everyday conversations and interactions. As friends, as mothers, as sisters, as aunts, as strangers – we are all influencers in each other's lives. The language we use to talk about ourselves and other women has a huge impact on how we go on to perceive ourselves and others. Imagine a Bechdel test: a measure of the representation of women in film that asks whether a movie features at least two named female characters who have a conversation about something other than a man. But instead, measure how often we talk about beauty or our physical appearance. It happens automatically but often, I'll find myself apologising for my hair, quipping about weight loss or greeting a friend whilst gushing about their looks, instead of how much I've missed them or how proud I am of the work they've been doing.

By constantly drawing attention to our physical appearance and the appearance of others, we're giving it power and reinforcing its importance in our lives, reminding everyone in earshot that beauty is of primary value. It echoes in the ways we talk to young girls – often commenting on their looks far more frequently than we do boys'. We may think we're being kind and, of course, balance is key, but we want to ensure that young women feel their physical appearance is the least interesting thing about them. Removing negative talk is one thing, but the aim is to withdraw our attention from our physical appearance entirely. Studies have shown the power these interactions can have on all women involved, noticeably shifting their self-perception. As we move forward, we can be more mindful about how these conversations on beauty crop up and, when they do, we can swiftly move them to the side.

Raising girls with a holistic mindset equips them with the self-protective tools needed to navigate a society determined to constrain them. A more beautiful future for them is one in which they are free from the shackles of societal expectations, where their worth is not measured by arbitrary standards but by their intelligence, creativity and the kindness they bring to the world. It is a future where they are empowered to embrace their uniqueness, be confident in their own skin and are celebrated for the remarkable individuals they are, beyond the limitations of appearance.

My hope is that we can all return to the incubator of girlhood – to a place of play and self-exploration that feels joyful and unencumbered. Make small changes and build up to bigger ones – eat the croissant, wear one less product, take off the filter, allow yourself to be comfortable, set boundaries, be disobedient, move your body for fun, tune into what gives you pleasure, spend your money on things that bring you joy, smile at other women, trust your intuition and start to create a life that feels nourishing and delicious.

In our utopia, with our endless rainbow of references, we use the technology we have to design rather than defy. Women draw stretch marks on their skin, braid their body hair, add bumps to their noses and indulge in their double chins. These procedures, and their inverse, happen simultaneously, all at once. We approach beauty with imagination. We explore and embrace every artful element of ourselves and reclaim the rituals of beauty once more. Who were you before Beauty with a capital B took hold?

Focus on action over aesthetic

Whilst it would be unrealistic to pretend that Beauty with a capital B doesn't exist, we can begin to decode our brains, to undo the programming that ties our worth to our value as aesthetic decoration. We can train our brains not to default to that mode of thinking. We can start to take its power away by actively trying to appreciate ourselves as human beings and not as commodities. Thinking and speaking about what our bodies can *do* for us has been proven to lead to a healthier mindset around beauty and body image. Next time you find yourself talking negatively about your body, or thinking negatively about how you look, try to redirect your thought pattern with phrases like 'My arms allow me to . . .' or 'I love that my body can . . .'. Psychology professor and author of *Beauty Sick*, Dr Renee Engeln, describes the responses to those sentences as 'the happiest data we've ever seen in the lab', adding that reading them was a 'balm for beauty sickness'. What's more, the women in the study who focused on those sentiments actually felt better about how they looked, creating a protective factor against future negative thoughts.

'Instead of rebuilding our fragmented bodies with surgery or corrective treatments or filters, there's another way to reconstruct ourselves that focuses on this holistic sense of embodiment, of rebuilding your body in a spiritual way, in a mindful way,' said Dr Hillary McBride when we spoke. 'Focus on aligning your mind, your body and your soul – think of yourself less as an objectified image that can be liked or unliked, shared or not shared, and return to your sense of self within your own skin.'

Transcend what simply looks 'good' and remind yourself what feels desirable to you – refuse to exist on a single plane and indulge in every dimension. What feels good? Smells good? Sounds good? Tastes good? Try to maintain a holistic approach in nurturing yourself and the girls around you – try new activities, explore your potential, dance and be silly, eat delicious food, use your voice and speak up when it matters. Remind yourself that what makes someone desirable extends far beyond the physical. You were never meant to exist in 2D – refuse to make your world smaller when there is so much joy beyond the surface.

Become builders of a better world

One of the things that Chloe said of her experiences online and being ill with an eating disorder still haunts me to this day: 'I do think now about what I actually could have been if I hadn't gone down this path. I wanted to be an aeroengineer for a long time. If I had never realised that I was a sexual being when I was young, would I have actually gone into STEM? Because I loved maths. I was so good at maths.'

To build a more beautiful future that prioritises women and girls, it is imperative that more women are involved in building the products they use daily – more women in STEM, founding tech companies, taking an active role in the regulation of these industries. We need more women in politics, more women in investment, more women in journalism and more women in research.

So much goes wrong when companies put profit over people and when there is a lack of diverse representation in the room, including women and girls of all races and genders, to advocate for our collective needs. But it's not enough to have more seats at the table, we need to go beyond inclusion to look at how the table is constructed in the first place, to interrogate the dominant structures that keep us all subjugated.

This is only possible at the highest levels when young girls are nurtured from day one, when they are nourished, when they are eating enough food to fuel their brains, when they feel safe on the internet, when they are focusing on facets of themselves other than their appearance and when they are raised with the understanding that their intelligence, talents and capabilities are their true currency. We all have the power to uphold these standards. We must insist that the systems change, we must report en masse, protest en masse and use our voices en masse. We must demand corporate policies, practices and tools that respect women's rights and prioritise their safety. We must refuse to be silenced. We must refuse to be drowned out.

*

History is lived by all of us, and I wanted to document the experiences of the women on both sides of the statistics we see in the news and the curated reality we see on our social feeds. Every woman I spoke to about this project confided a secret self-loathing in response, seemingly grateful for their suffering to be seen and understood, to not be the only one. These are the secrets that we are all choking on. We must push past patriarchal paradigms and dare to dream of a world in which we are inherently worthy, to arrive reborn into a watertight resilience against the rhetoric that keeps us oppressed. We need to work together to break the cycle of the paradoxes that paralyse us, and we need to start having these conversations out loud. *Pixel Flesh* is my way of breaking that silence and standing in solidarity.

We have a huge amount to contribute to the next generation of women – as we take increasing amounts of power on this planet, we can aim to create the spaces we needed when we were growing up, and we can start that now. Working together, we can make changes to move beyond beauty, towards a better future. I would recommend sharing this book with other women in your life and starting a healing circle – one of openness and sorority. One in which you give yourselves permission to be honest and ugly and problematic and brave. Re-immerse yourself in reality by practising radical honesty. Remove the filter, hold all of the pieces of your fragmented self and look in the mirror. Then repeat your fantasy until it becomes our reality.

'Go now and do the heart-work on the images imprisoned within you' – but remember, you don't have to do it alone. If you feel like you don't have a community to share with, you have one now. The women who appear in the pages of this book are real, all of them. These stories are about them, and about us. The thing I found most compelling when interviewing women throughout my research was how many times a conversation repeated – despite class differences, gender assigned at birth, wealth disparity, genetic fortune or social standing, the women I spoke to often echoed one another, their tales transcending traditional social barriers and arriving at a universal truth. A hum of reverberation that built into a chorus of collective voices – screaming in empathy and rage. A rally cry so loud I hope it becomes impossible to ignore.

I hope you found yourself reflected in these pages, and I hope you found solidarity amongst the discomfort. I hope it has ignited something inside of you and I hope you will add your voice, because there is still so much more to be said. These women are all of us, all at once. And we're still fighting for change.

Glossary

Abject – A state of extreme unhappiness, hopelessness and misery, or a situation that is unpleasant and degrading.

Aesthetic labour – Coined by Dennis Nickson and Chris Warhurst, aesthetic labour refers to the work that employees do in order to portray the right image within the context of their organisation and role.

Agency – The ability for an individual to choose and take an action.

Algorithm – A set of rules followed by a computer to complete a process. Colloquially it is used on social media to describe specifically the systems used by social platforms to recommend and organise the content that an individual is shown in their feed.

Androcentric – An ideology in which a masculine point of view is at the centre of all things.

Autonomy – The ability for an individual or a group to make decisions for themselves, to self-govern.

Beauty premium – The idea that more conventionally attractive individuals will receive better financial compensation for their work than their peers who might be considered less attractive and undertake the same kind of work.

Beauty work – The work that individuals undergo to meet beauty standards – such as shaving, dying one's hair or having manicured nails – often because appearing conventionally attractive can lead to both social and economic rewards.

Binary – Refers to systems in which everything fits into one of two categories: for example, the gender binary categorises every person into 'man' or 'woman'.

Blackfishing – The process of using makeup, hairstyles, filters, Photoshop and other cultural markers to present yourself as Black when you are of a different racial origin.

Capital – A term that denotes anything of value to its owner. Can refer to financial assets, physical assets, or more abstract ideas, such as cultural capital.

Catfishing – Using another person's information and often images to pretend to be them online. It has also been used to describe the process of luring someone into a relationship by pretending to be somebody else and 'catfish' is sometimes used as a derogatory term to describe people online who look significantly different to how they do in real life.

Choice feminism – A form of feminism that suggests that any decision a woman makes for herself is inherently feminist.

Collectivism – A belief system that advocates for shared ownership and responsibility.

Colonisation – The process of establishing control over other countries, often by sending people to govern and form colonies. In the process, the colonisers will often attempt to change the culture, language and nature of the country, and may try to tax the individuals living there or use the natural resources of the area for financial gain.

Colourism – Discrimination against members within a racial group with a darker skin tone.

Corporeal – Used to describe the quality of having or consisting of a physical form or a body. Often used in opposition to the term 'spiritual'.

Cyber rape – Rape that takes place in an online or digital setting. The term does not have a fixed meaning, but can refer to unwanted actions during cyber sex, or forcing unwanted sexual acts on someone in a cyber environment.

Deepfakes – Deepfakes use deep learning artificial intelligence to replace, alter or mimic someone's face in video or voice in audio.

Doxxing – The act of publishing personal and otherwise private information about an individual on the internet without their permission.

Embodied – To be representative of an idea, quality or ideal. Usually refers to humans, e.g., 'she was the embodiment of virtue'.

Eurocentric – A way of thinking that places Europe and European people at the centre of importance.

Feminism – Refers to both the belief that people of all genders should have equal rights and to the movement that seeks to achieve these rights.

Fetishisation – The process of making aspects of behaviour or a person's identity into an object of sexual desire.

Hegemony – A position of dominance of one group over another, often used to describe the dominance of a set of ideas that overrides alternative ways of thinking.

Individualism – A belief system in which freedom of actions and of thought is considered more important in a society than shared responsibility and ownership.

Misogynoir – A term coined by Moya Bailey in 2010 to describe the misogyny that Black women experience which is based both on gender and on race.

Mixed-fishing – The process of using makeup, hairstyles, filters, Photoshop and other cultural markers to present yourself as mixed race when you are of a different racial origin.

Monolithic – Used within sociology to describe systems and organisations that are rigid and reject diversity in favour of homogeneity.

Monopoly – A market within which one seller or service provider dominates and faces few or no competitors. In a pure monopoly, the company will have 100 per cent of the market share and consumers will have no alternative options for the product or service that the company provides.

Neo-liberal – A belief system that favours free-market (unregulated) capitalism and the reduction of state control and regulation.

Neo-liberal feminism – A term coined by Catherine Rottenberg to describe the rise of a form of feminism in the twenty-first century that advocates for equal rights whilst sidelining the centrality of the wider social and racial issues that may be causing inequality. Neo-liberal feminism primarily posits that women may overcome discrimination through individual rather than collective efforts.

Objectification – The process of treating or viewing an individual as an object without emotions or rights.

The panopticon effect – A term popularised by Michel Foucault to describe the self-regulation that occurs when a person believes that they are being observed. The power of the panopticon effect derives from situations in which they do not know whether or not they are being observed, thus leading them to self-regulate at all times.

Parity – The condition of being equal. Often used to refer to financial compensation, for example pay parity, or status, such as achieving gender parity in politics.

Patriarchy – A society in which men hold the majority of the power and authority. Also seen in the adjectival form 'patriarchal', which can be used to describe a society or a set of behaviours.

Post-feminism – The belief that the main goals of feminism have been achieved and that there is no longer a need for the feminist movement.

Postmodernism – An ideology that responds to modernism with scepticism. It rejects the enlightenment ideals of rationality and universal truth in favour of foregrounding a multiplicity of perspectives and an inherent instability.

Racism – Overt and implicit prejudice and discrimination against an individual or group of individuals based on their race. This can take the form of individual actions and behaviours, or it can be implied within the organisation of a society, which is known as systemic racism. Modern scholarship considers racism to be a combination of the power of one group over another alongside acts of discrimination and marginalisation by the more powerful group against the second group.

Revenge porn – Sexually explicit material shared to the internet by another party, often a former sexual partner, without the subject's consent and with the intention to cause harm. More correctly acknowledged as intimate image abuse.

Sextortion – A form of extortion whereby the perpetrator uses the threat of revealing sexually explicit information about the victim – such as photos or videos – to exploit the victim.

Shadowbanning – Refers to the partial or complete blocking of a user from an online community in such a way that it is not immediately obvious to the user that blocking has taken place. It is also used colloquially to refer to social platforms deprioritising a user's content within their algorithm.

Subjugation – The process of bringing an individual or group under control, in a way that offers them no freedom or individual rights.

Surveillance – The act of continuously watching a person or place, whether through digital or physical means.

Symbolic violence – A term coined by Pierre Bourdieu to describe the use of one's symbolic power (for example, in patriarchy, the power that a man holds in comparison to a woman) to impose a dominant social ideology on the oppressed group.

Texturism – Discrimination against members within a racial group with hair that is more textured and further from the Eurocentric ideal of straight hair.

Transcultural – Used to describe phenomena that extend across multiple cultures.

Upskirting – Taking a picture under somebody else's clothing without their permission and often with the intention of viewing intimate parts of the victim's body.

Notes and References

A full bibliography of all references can be found at https://www.pixelfleshbook.com/bibliography

Epigraphs

Virginia Woolf, 'Professions for Women', read to the Women's Service League in 1931 and published posthumously in *The Death of the Moth and Other Essays* (1942)

Rainer Maria Rilke, 'Wendung' ('Turning Point'), translated by Stephen Mitchel, 1993

Prologue

Jessa Crispin, *Why I Am Not a Feminist: A Feminist Manifesto* (Melville House Publishing: New York, 2017)

John Berger, *Ways of Seeing* (BBC and Penguin Books Ltd: London, 1972)

bell hooks, *Communion: The Female Search for Love* (William Morrow: London, 2002)

1. The Cult of Kylie Jenner

Jia Tolentino, 'The Age of Instagram Face', *New Yorker*, 2019

Kathleen Hale, 'Is Teenage Plastic Surgery a Feminist Act?', *Harper's Bazaar*, 2017 https://www.harpersbazaar.com/culture/features/a9555312/teenage-plastic-surgery-feminism/

Andrea Dworkin, *Woman Hating* (E. P. Dutton: Boston, 1974), page 113
Naomi Wolf, *The Beauty Myth: How Images of Beauty Are Used Against Women* (Chatto & Windus: London, 1990)

2. Venus and the Voyeur

Mary Richardson, as quoted in *The Times*, 11 March 1914
Unattributed quote with 'viral sensation' – attributed to Chloe, appears in Chapter 8

3. Algorithms of Desire

Kim Kardashian, essay posted on her official site, March 2016 https://www.kimkardashianwest.com/behind-the-scenes/776-kim-kardashian-nude-instagram/
Victoria Smith, 'Women in poorer countries take more sexy selfies – this is what that tells us about global female oppression', *Independent*, 29/08/2018 https://www.independent.co.uk/voices/women-sexy-selfies-patriarchy-inequality-class-sexism-a8512421.html
Stephanie V. Ng, M.D., 'Social Media and the Sexualization of Adolescent Girls', *American Journal of Psychiatry*, 10 Mar 2017 https://doi.org/10.1176/appi.ajp-rj.2016.111206

4. Coloniser Culture

Unattributed quote about 'Habbo Hotel' attributed to Stephanie Yeboah, appears in Chapter 8
Unattributed quote about lip fillers attributed to Eleanor Barnes, appears in Chapter 7

6. Build a Body

Sylvia Plath, *The Bell Jar* (Heinemann: London, 1963)
Susan Sontag, 'The Double Standard of Aging' in *On Women* (Hamish Hamilton: London, 2023), page 20

Ellen Atlanta, 'Is the BBL About to Burst?' in *The Face* 27/7/22 https://theface.com/beauty/is-the-bbl-bubble-about-to-burst-plastic-surgery-kardashian

Elizabeth Grosz, 'Notes Towards a Corporeal Feminism' in *Australian Feminist Studies* (5), 1987, page 2

7. Everything Is Content and Reality Is a Myth

Rayne Fisher-Quan, 'standing on the shoulders of complex female characters', *Internet Princess* Substack, Feb 2022 https://internetprincess.substack.com/p/standing-on-the-shoulders-of-complex

Amy Francombe, 'Flannels Thinks: Beauty in the Metaverse – What Does It All Mean?' https://www.flannels.com/stylenews/post/metaverse-beauty

8. Bite the Hand That Starves You

Sinicina, H. Pankratz, A. Büttner, G. Mall, 'Death due to neurogenic shock following gastric rupture in an anorexia nervosa patient', *Forensic Science International*, Volume 155, Issue 1, 2005, pages 7–12, https://doi.org/10.1016/j.forsciint.2004.10.021

10. (M)otherhood

Yvonne C Lam, Post-pregnancy body positivity? On Instagram, it's hard to find, *Guardian* (Oct 2022) https://www.theguardian.com/lifeandstyle/2022/oct/23/post-pregnancy-body-positivity-on-instagram-its-hard-to-find

11. The Witches of Cyberspace

'*a witch is born out of the true hungers of her time*', Ray Bradbury, *Long After Midnight* (Earthlight: London, 1976)

Elizabeth Nicholas, 'Recasting Witchcraft as the Ultimate Act of Feminist Rebellion', *W Magazine*, January 6 2022 https://www.wmagazine.com/culture/taschen-book-witchcraft-library-esoterica-photos

Gina Martin, 'They told me to change my clothes. I changed the law instead', TEDxWarwick (2021) https://www.youtube.com/watch?v=_K_n-x-W7pY

Conclusion

bell hooks, *Communion: The Female Search for Love* (William Morrow: London, 2002)

Acknowledgements

Writing acknowledgements as a debut author feels like a monumental task – to thank the people who have contributed to the person I am, to this project and to the pages of *Pixel Flesh*; to do their love and support justice feels impossible, but I shall try my very best.

Firstly, to Livvi. I can't tell you how many times I wished you were here during the writing of this book. Thank you for passing on the torch. I promise to always remember your light.

This book only exists because of the women within its pages – those who are quoted directly, those who are named and unnamed, those whose stories didn't make it in but who inspired and informed me nonetheless. Your generosity, candour and raw honesty in the service of sorority was the greatest gift and one I never took for granted. The conversations I had with you all were a lifeline. To write your stories was a huge honour, and I hope you know how incredibly proud I am to have met you.

Most of all, to my parents. This book is a testament to you. There aren't enough words to describe how much I love you, and how grateful I am to have a family who will love and support me no matter what. To my Mum – you are so beautiful and I don't tell you enough. Thank you for never saying no to a book, thank you for telling me stories and for always nurturing my dreams. You made me feel limitless. To my Dad, thank you for championing every page of this book, and for being there every step of the way. To Andrea – for showing me strength and self-worth and beauty inside and out. I can't imagine this was the easiest read, but I am the woman I am today because of all of you.

To my Grandma Jackie – you are the most generous person I have ever met. Thank you for always believing in me and reminding me that my best is good enough. I hope Grandad would be proud.

To my brothers – Wilder and Orin – for when you eventually read this. I hope I have embarrassed you just the right amount. I love you both infinitely, let this be a reminder that you can do anything you set your mind to. Follow what sets your heart alight, and I promise I'll always be here to cheer you on.

To Max Edwards – thank you for showing me how it should be done. You are everything I needed in an agent. Thank you for advocating for me at every turn – for holding my hand through a very dark time and for somehow always knowing when to tell me to keep going and when I should stop. Thank you for hearing the things I didn't say, and for looking after me when I didn't know how to. I will always be grateful for your support and guidance, and I'm so proud to call you my friend.

To my incredible editors Bianca and Hannah – thank you for championing this book and for being my biggest cheerleaders. I couldn't have done it without you. To get one editor was a pinch-me moment, but to have two is an immense privilege. Thank you for making this book better, for shaping it into what it is today, and for taking care of both me and these stories. I am indebted to the entire team at Headline and Macmillan. Thank you for believing in me and for giving me the time and space to write. To Holly, Hannah and Lou – your support has been so appreciated. To Amy Cox for my gorgeous cover design – thank you for bringing my vision to life in ways beyond my imagination.

To my copy-editor Liz and my lawyer Meryl – thank you for your diligence and for the improvements you made. To Katie Packer – for making my dreams come true and championing *Pixel Flesh* since day one, and to Sarah Emsley, I am so grateful for you all.

To my team of support at Aevitas, I owe so much. To Gus Brown, Tom Lloyd-Williams, Checkie Hamilton and Vanessa Kerr – thank you for all that you do behind the scenes and for helping to make this journey so smooth. To Sara O'Keeffe who very kindly read my initial proposal and provided great feedback and support – thank you.

To my friends and first readers – thank you for listening to me talk endlessly about this book and the ideas within it, and thank you for reminding me that I am brave enough to finish it. You all mean more to me than you will ever know and I will never tire of your beautiful faces. To Jessie – your unwavering encouragement and radiant kindness was everything on the first draft. To Alex Peters – your endless patience, insight and brilliant brain were invaluable support. To Aimee – for being my rock and my eternal sunshine. To Aeron – for inspiring me and believing in me when I didn't think I could do it, for the food deliveries and the endless reading recommendations. Thank you for expanding my world, I am so proud to know you. To Bea – for always making me feel like a superstar and for being so ferociously my friend. I love you so much. To Shope, for your utter grace and wisdom. I feel so lucky to exist in your orbit. And to Freya – for being my lighthouse, my guiding light, I'm so grateful to have had you on this journey with me.

To the team at ICE Cambridge, but notably to Lucy Durneen. Thank you for creating a safe space for me, and thank you for letting me in. Your kindness, empathy and solidarity meant more to me than you could ever know. And to my classmates in

Creative Writing – thank you for making me a smarter person and a better writer. Particular thanks to Becky, Ro, Patrick and Ty – thank you for all of your feedback and for improving my work tenfold.

To the team at Villa Lena, and to the artists I was lucky to meet and share space with – Annika, Djenaba, Flora, Leonard, Catherine and Megumi – you will always hold a special place in my heart. I wrote some of my best work in the walls of the Fattoria, surrounded by your love and support. I cherish that time like nothing else.

To Sasha and Harmony – thank you for all of your support on research and for your help with the glossary. To Sophie, Rachel and Yasmin at Raven Beauty – for making me feel special and for believing in everything *Pixel Flesh* stands for. To Sharmadean Reid – for being my mentor and my beacon as I started out, I will always be grateful for what you saw in me, for nurturing and encouraging my talents and for teaching me so much.

To the judges of the RSL Giles St Aubyn Award – thank you for bolstering me and for supporting my research. The prize allowed me to reach more women and tell more stories, and for that I am so grateful.

To Roo, for being absolutely no help at all, but for making me smile and forcing me outside at least once a day.

And to the team at Refuge – thank you for all that you do, and for helping me to get back on track.

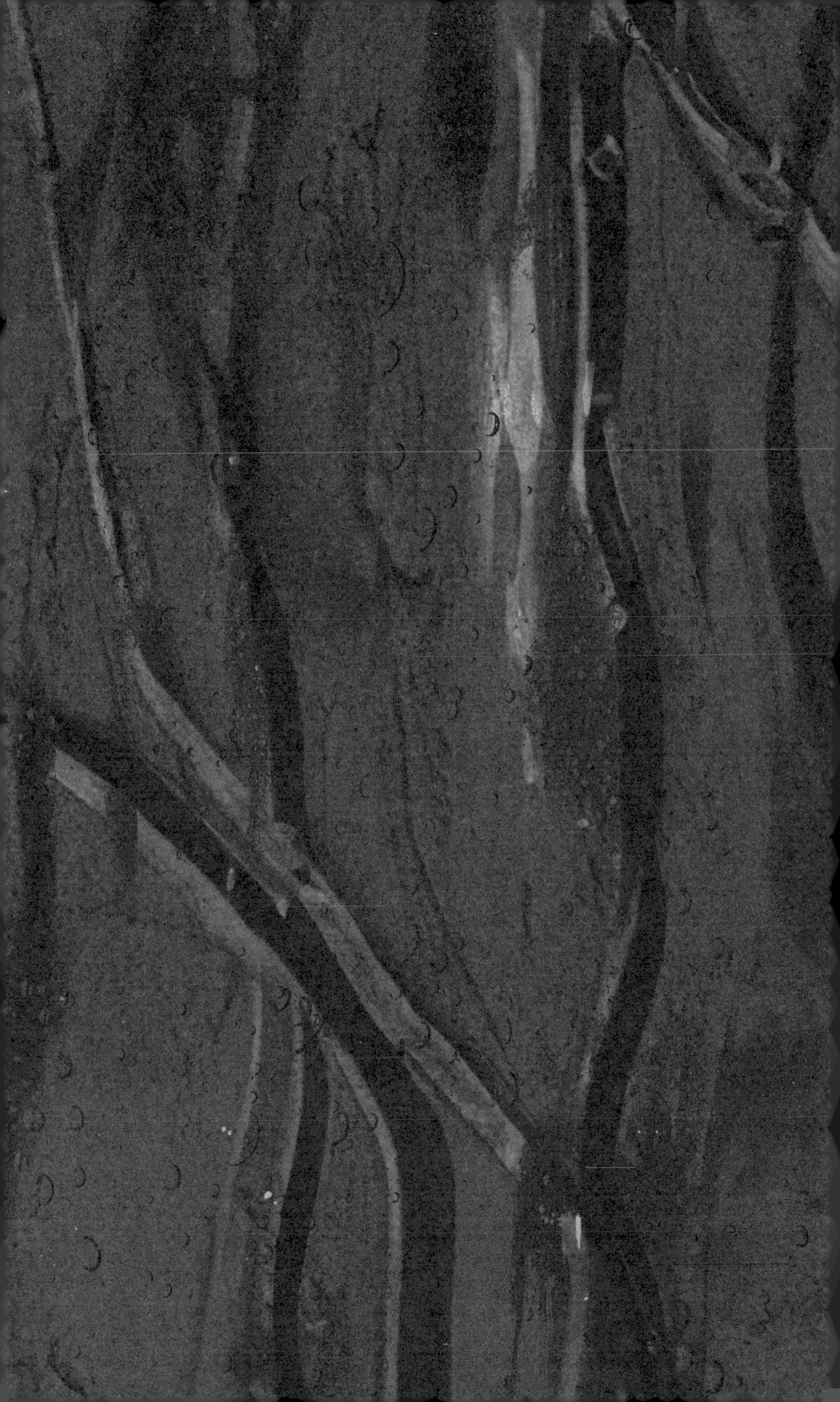